Understanding Geothermal Systems

by Jeff Persons, CM

RSES SUSTAINABILITY SERIES

ISBN-13: 978-1-61607-184-4
ISBN-10: 1-61607-184-2

© Copyright 2012 by the Refrigeration Service Engineers Society. All rights reserved.
First printing.

No part of this publication may be reproduced or distributed in any form or by any means, or stored in a data base or retrieval system, without prior written permission of the publisher. RSES disclaims liability for any personal injury, property, or other damages of any nature whatsoever, whether special, indirect, consequential, or compensatory, directly or indirectly resulting from the publication, use of, or reliance on this document. RSES also makes no guaranty or warranty as to the accuracy or completeness of any information published herein.

Introduction

GEOTHERMAL SYSTEMS FOR FIELD INSTALLERS AND TECHNICIANS

A comprehensive study and resource manual that serves as a "best practices" guide for the design, installation, and maintenance of geothermal systems, this book draws on the author's more than 30 years of hands-on geothermal field experience. The text covers geothermal systems and controls from their widespread introduction to the U.S. market in the early 1970s to the multistage ultra-high-efficiency systems of today. Study topics include both open-loop and closed-loop applications, subsurface geology, loop design, water chemistry, antifreeze solutions, system installation, and controls. Emphasis is placed on identifying common installation and service mistakes, and on learning from those mistakes.

This book gives business owners, sales staff, installers, and technicians a step up on the competition and imparts the knowledge necessary to maintain consumer confidence and appreciation. Geothermal systems represent one of the best means available for meeting the growing interest in renewable energy technology.

Table of Contents

CHAPTER ONE
Understanding Geothermal Systems.................................1

CHAPTER TWO
Geothermal Site Considerations..................................23

CHAPTER THREE
Open-Loop Systems...37

CHAPTER FOUR
Closed-Loop Systems...59

CHAPTER FIVE
Piping..83

CHAPTER SIX
Loop Fill Solutions...109

CHAPTER SEVEN
Controls...125

CHAPTER EIGHT
Putting It All Together......................................161

APPENDIX
Information Resources..183

◀ CHAPTER ONE ▶
Understanding Geothermal Systems

INTRODUCTION

Over the past 60 years, the HVACR industry has changed dramatically. The pre-1950s were dominated by *coal-fired systems*. Heat distribution often was managed by means of cast iron radiators, and air conditioning was something you experienced at a movie theater. As *oil heating systems* became more common in the 1950s, storing and stoking coal into a boiler or furnace gradually became a thing of the past. In those days, oil cost 12 to 15 cents a gallon and natural gas was considered a nuisance. In oil-producing areas, the night sky glowed with natural gas flares, lit to relieve the reservoir pressure by venting the "worthless" natural gas and allowing the "valuable" oil to be extracted. In hindsight, it is likely that 50 to 70% of our easily recoverable natural gas resources were vented simply so that the oil could be pumped out. By the late 1950s, as oil-to-gas conversions became more practical, *natural gas heating systems* gained in popularity. The "bigger is better" theory applied to equipment sizing at that time, and many of the early natural gas furnaces were lucky to have an annual efficiency of 45%. Central air conditioning was still a luxury in the 1960s, but little by little began to enter the mainstream.

Today, the evolution of the HVACR industry continues. Instead of furnaces, boilers, and air conditioners, we now refer to "indoor environmental control systems." The days of cheap oil and gas are over. Our global population has increased by at least three times in the past 60 years and shows no sign of slowing. As global demand escalates, the fossil-fuel resources on which we depend have grown increasingly scarce. The time has come to develop alternative ways of managing our environment. Renewable resources—such as solar, wind, and geothermal energy—offer the basic means to reduce our dependence on fossil fuels. While these three approaches allow for the direct production of electricity or hot water, a fourth renewable resource, one that combines the power of geothermal energy with the efficiency benefits of a heat pump unit, allows for the storage and retrieval of thermal energy by using the earth's thermal mass as a "thermal storage battery."

A *geothermal heat pump* simply "moves the Btus" of thermal energy needed for heating and cooling, rather than "creating new Btus," as a conventional fossil-fuel furnace does. As a result, the source energy needed to operate a geothermal system is significantly less than the source energy needed to provide fuel for a normal gas furnace or electricity for a conventional air conditioner. In fact, the net reduction in energy consumption is on the order of 70 to 80%. The heating conversion efficiency for the majority of top-model geothermal heat pumps exceeds 450 to 500%, which means that they have a *coefficient of performance* (COP) of 4.5 to 5.0. The air conditioning efficiency, or *energy efficiency ratio* (EER), for geothermal heat pumps normally ranges from 17 to more than 30 EER.

In addition to their incredible efficiency, residential geothermal systems frequently include an auxiliary heat exchanger, called a *desuperheater*, as a means to make or assist in the production of domestic hot water. According to U.S. Department of Energy estimates, hot water production by the average geothermal system typically provides 60% of an average home's domestic hot water, and does so at approximately one-third the cost of operating a conventional hot water heater.

BASIC PRINCIPLES

Geothermal heating and cooling is a simple and highly efficient energy storage and retrieval technology that uses the earth as a massive thermal storage battery. The transfer of heat between the earth and the conditioned space is made possible by a series of polyethylene pipe circuits that are either buried 5 ft below the earth's surface, submerged in a pond, or inserted into vertical heat-exchange wells. In some cases, when there is a plentiful supply of well water available and local codes allow, a geothermal system may operate as an "open-loop" system. In an open-loop application, well water provides the needed heat transfer and then is discharged to the surface, into a nearby pond or lake, or returned back to the aquifer via a second return well. Figure 1-1 shows some common types of geothermal installations.

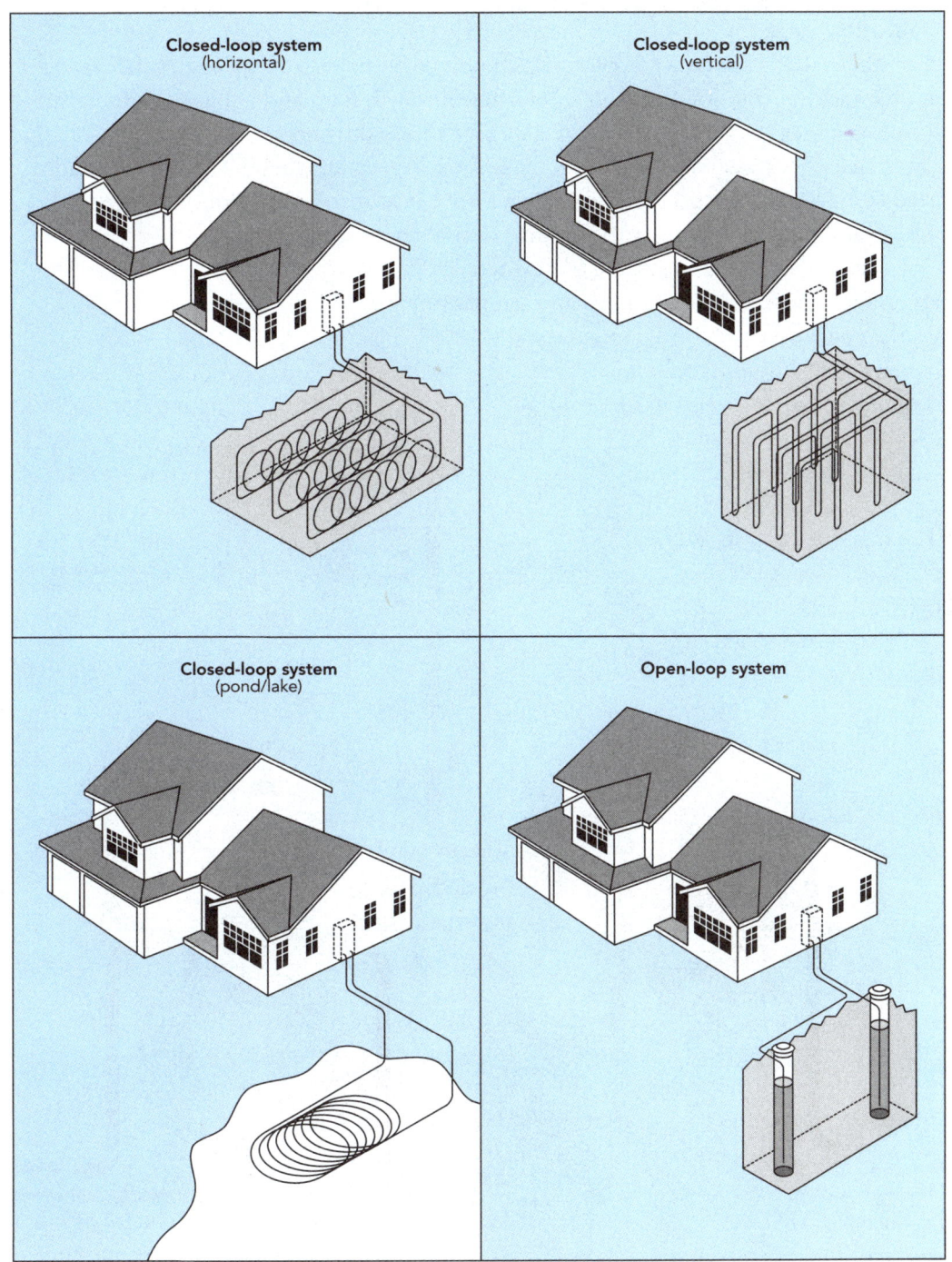

Figure 1-1. Common types of geothermal installations

Operation cycle

A geothermal system uses a very small amount of electrical energy to circulate water or an antifreeze solution between a polyethylene earth loop and a fluid-to-refrigerant heat exchanger. The heat exchanger is located inside the heat pump cabinet. Operation of the system is similar to that of a refrigerator, whereby an environmentally friendly refrigerant is used to extract heat from the antifreeze solution. As the liquid refrigerant absorbs heat from the antifreeze, it changes from a liquid to a vapor state (*heat of vaporization*), and passes to a compressor. The compressor then compresses the refrigerant, increasing its pressure and temperature to provide warm air (90 to 95°F) from a condenser coil for heating the home. As the hot refrigerant vapor cools and condenses (*heat of condensation*), it circulates back to a *thermostatic expansion valve* (TEV). The modulating orifice of the TEV regulates the volume of the condensed refrigerant as it changes from

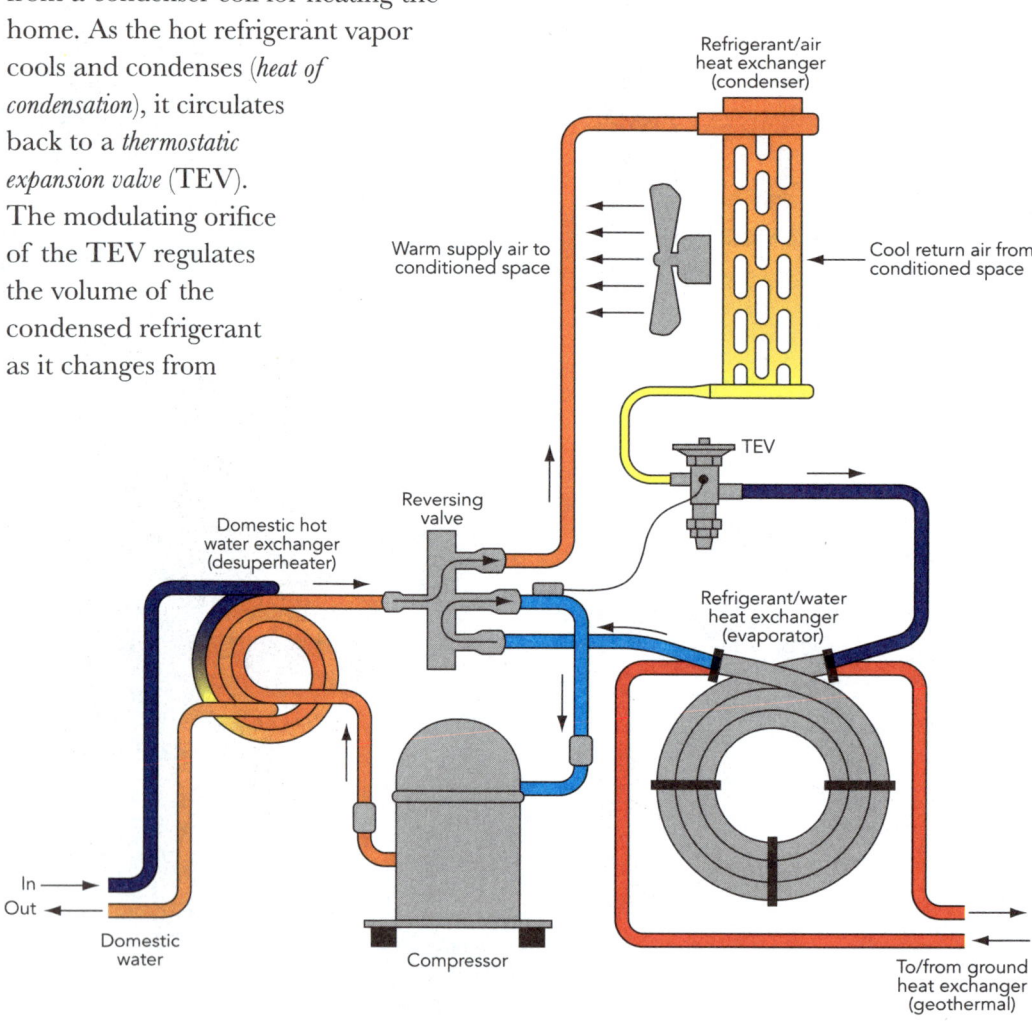

Figure 1-2. Geothermal heat pump operation (heating mode)

a high-pressure, high-temperature liquid state to a low-pressure, low-temperature saturated state. The refrigerant then enters the loop-side heat exchanger (evaporator), and the cycle is repeated. Figure 1-2 shows a geothermal heat pump in the heating mode. For air conditioning, a *reversing valve* (often referred to as a "four-way valve" or a "changeover valve") reverses the flow of refrigerant to cool the home and reject heat back to the antifreeze loop.

A bonus of the typical residential geothermal system is that it contains a second heat exchanger, specifically designed to heat domestic hot water. Water is circulated from the base of a hot water tank through the heat exchanger, where excess heat from the geothermal unit (superheated high-pressure refrigerant vapor from the compressor discharge) is transferred to the water. A geothermal system is capable of heating up to 60% of the domestic hot water used in an average home.

SYSTEM COMPONENTS

Compressors

Standard-efficiency compressors. Single-speed reciprocating compressors (see Figure 1-3) that use R-22 are still found in many older systems. R-22, which is an ozone-depleting HCFC refrigerant, was discontinued in new equipment manufactured after January 1, 2010, and was replaced primarily with the newer and more environmentally friendly R-410A. Typical heating efficiencies for a reciprocating compressor range from 300 to 350%, and cooling efficiencies range from 12 to 20 EER. In a geothermal application, the typical service life for a reciprocating compressor is 15 to 18 years. As Energy Star rating standards have become more stringent, standard-efficiency reciprocating compressors have largely given way to higher-efficiency scroll compressors as a means of qualifying geothermal systems for tax credit incentives.

Figure 1-3. Reciprocating compressor

Medium-efficiency compressors. Many of the geothermal systems built prior to January 1, 2010 have single-stage scroll compressors that use R-22. Those manufactured after this date operate with R-410A (see Figure 1-4). Typical heating efficiencies for a single-stage scroll compressor range from 350 to 400%, and cooling efficiencies range from 15 to 24 EER. Scroll compressors have fewer mechanical parts and are less prone to mechanical failures than reciprocating compressors. The typical service life for a scroll compressor employed in a geothermal application is 20 to 25 years.

High-efficiency compressors. Several different types of high-efficiency compressors are used in geothermal systems, including:

> *Compliant scroll compressors* use R-410A, an HFC refrigerant that can transfer more heat energy per pound (has a higher "specific heat") than R-22. This means that lower-horsepower compressors can be used to attain the same cooling capacity with a significant increase in system efficiency (due to reduced electrical loads). Typical heating efficiencies for R-410A scroll compressor systems range from 360 to 460% (COP 3.6 to 4.6), and cooling efficiencies range from 16 to 28 EER. The projected service life for a scroll compressor is 20 to 25 years.

Figure 1-4. Scroll compressor

> *Dual-capacity reciprocating compressors* also use R-410A. Typical heating efficiencies range from 370 to 530% (COP 3.7 to 5.3), and cooling efficiencies range from 15 to 36 EER. The projected service life for a dual-capacity reciprocating compressor is 12 to 18 years. *Note:* The two-stage reciprocating compressor has been largely replaced by the unloading scroll compressor (discussed in the following paragraph), and is likely to be found only in systems manufactured between 2000 and 2006.

> *Dual-capacity unloading scroll compressors* like the one shown in Figure 1-5 provide efficiencies

Figure 1-5. Dual-capacity scroll compressor

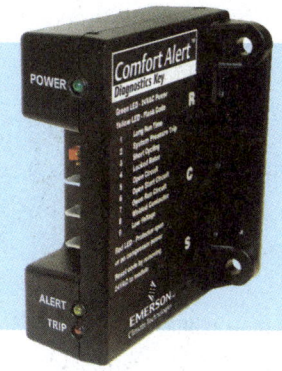

Many geothermal systems that use the Copeland Ultra Tech scroll compressor shown in Figure 1-5 also use the Comfort Alert (or CoreSense) compressor protection module. This module monitors the individual voltage and current conductors to the compressor, preventing compressor operation and providing a fault status indication with a diagnostic code if an imbalance is sensed on any of the conductors to the compressor.

that rival or exceed those of dual-capacity reciprocating compressors. Closed-loop efficiency ratings for selected geothermal models average 450 to 500% for heating and 27 to 30 EER for cooling. Unloading scroll compressors are highly reliable—like traditional scroll compressors, they have a minimum of mechanical parts. However, unlike earlier two-stage reciprocating compressors—which needed to stop, equalize refrigerant pressures, and then restart in order to change capacity ranges—unloading scroll technology allows for capacity changes while the compressor is in operation. This substantially reduces the number of system compressor ON/OFF cycles during intermediate weather periods, improving overall system efficiency and comfort.

Fan motors

Permanent split-capacitor motors. Permanent split-capacitor (PSC) motors, such as the one shown in Figure 1-6, have been an industry standard for many years. The PSC motor operates at a design maximum of 1,040 rpm. Most PSC motors are wired to operate on only one or two of three or four speed settings. This speed is typically "factory-set" and can be changed only by a qualified service technician.

Figure 1-6. Typical permanent split-capacitor (PSC) motor

The use of a run capacitor with a PSC motor results in higher starting torques and better motor efficiencies than were possible with older shaded-pole motors. Despite its ability to provide a high starting torque, the PSC motor suffers efficiency losses when operating at lower speeds. If set for continuous fan operation, a PSC motor typically will run at its highest speed (and power consumption) setting.

PSC fan motors are found in older geothermal systems and in a limited number of new systems. As Energy Star efficiency guidelines become more stringent, a growing number of geothermal system manufacturers will find it necessary to phase out PSC fan motors in favor of higher-efficiency variable-speed motors or permanent-magnet, brushless dc blower motors. Most PSC motors have factory-sealed sleeve bushings that do not require oiling. The typical service life of a PSC motor is in the range of 11 to 14 years.

Electronically commutated motors. The *electronically commutated motor* (ECM), examples of which can be seen in Figures 1-7 and 1-8 on the next page, was introduced in the late 1980s. An ECM is two components in one—a motor control and a three-phase motor with a permanent magnet rotor. The motor control is a microprocessor-based variable-frequency drive that converts single-phase ac power to dc power, and then converts dc power to three-phase power to operate the motor. This gives the ECM programmability, a wider range of operation, and the ability to automatically adjust speed, torque, or both—depending on its operating program—to provide the required airflow.

There are two types of indoor blower ECMs:
- the *constant-torque* or "standard" ECM
- the *constant-airflow* or "premium" ECM (often referred to as a "variable-speed" ECM).

The "standard" ECM is designed with five speed taps and the ability to maintain a constant *torque* as system parameters change. The "premium" ECM is designed with precise airflow and comfort selections, selected on the HVAC system control board, and the ability to maintain a constant *airflow* as system parameters change. Changes to system parameters may include airflow restrictions caused by undersized ductwork, closed or blocked registers or grilles, or dirt load on air-side components such as filters and heat exchangers. Both types of ECMs provide better airflow performance than PSC induction motors. The constant-airflow ECM will provide better performance than the constant-torque ECM when the *total external static pressure* (TESP) is higher than that recommended by the HVAC system manufacturer. It should be understood, however, that both types have their limits, and will use more energy (and potentially create more airflow noise) when the TESP is higher than recommended. Should the

Figure 1-7. Constant-torque ("standard") ECM

Figure 1-8. Constant-airflow ("premium") ECM

fan begin to exceed its design limits, the fan control can transmit a "fan fault" notice to a central status monitor to alert the owner that attention is needed.

Another advantage of ECMs is that they are more energy-efficient than PSC motors—about 20% more efficient at their rated speeds. Note that ECMs maintain their efficiency at *all* speeds, while PSC motors decrease in efficiency at lower speeds. Therefore, the efficiency difference between the two is greater when the ECM is not operated at maximum speed. This is especially notable in applications in which "continuous fan" settings are beneficial for maintaining indoor air quality. When a comparison is made between the low-speed fan setting for a 1-hp ECM (consuming only a little more power than a 100-W light bulb) and the typical high-speed constant fan setting for a similarly sized PSC fan motor (running at over 740 W), the savings become obvious.

ECMs have pre-lubricated factory-sealed ball bearings that provide a motor service life of 15 to 20 years. A quick-change control hub allows for easy replacement of the motor controller without the expense of replacing the entire motor assembly.

A growing consumer interest in clean air makes the energy-saving features of the ECM a first choice for many customers, especially since electronic air filters operate best with a "continuous fan" setting. Both types of ECMs are found in most Energy Star-rated geothermal equipment. *Standard high-efficiency systems* employ "standard" constant-torque ECM fan motors like the one shown in Figure 1-7. *Ultra high-efficiency systems* employ "premium" constant-airflow ECMs like the one shown in Figure 1-8. Proper installation setup and airflow measurements are necessary for both types to achieve proper performance, comfort, and system longevity.

Desuperheaters

The vast majority of residential geothermal systems include an energy-saving feature called "domestic hot water assist." A separate, isolated heat exchanger, referred to as a *desuperheater* (see Figure 1-9), transfers warmth from the superheated refrigerant compressor discharge line (compressor discharge vapor temperatures are typically above 130°F) to a domestic hot water tank. A small low-wattage circulator pump draws cold water from the bottom of the domestic hot water tank, passes it through the isolated heat exchanger, and returns it to the hot water tank. When the geothermal system is in the cooling mode, the desuperheater produces free hot water. In the winter, when the system is in the heating mode, the geothermal system provides both domestic hot water and heat for the structure. Most geothermal systems allow the hot water assist feature to operate whenever the system is on. It typically provides up to 60% of the average home's hot water needs. A few specialized geothermal systems are designed to provide 100% domestic hot water production.

Figure 1-9. Hot water desuperheater

Because the high-temperature refrigerant line that heats domestic water can easily exceed a temperature of 160°F, most hot water assist features include an automatic high-temperature limit to prevent recirculation of water once the return water temperature exceeds 120 to 130°F. While the hot water assist function typically can supply up to 60% of a normal home's hot water needs, its capacity is limited by the size of the geothermal system. The larger the system, the more hot water can be produced. Conversely, if a geothermal system is sized at less than 3 tons, the hot water assist function becomes less significant.

Some manufacturers recommend pulling the water from the top of the water heater. A copper tee is inserted in the cold water supply line. The water is pulled up via a dip tube and then returned to the bottom of the tank. This method prevents any sediment from being pulled from the bottom of the tank and entering the desuperheater. The desuperheater coaxial heat exchanger is piped in the compressor discharge line and is located between the compressor and the reversing valve. Potable water is pumped through the desuperheater at a low rate (ideally 0.4 gpm per ton), so that the desuperheater does not function as a condenser and take too much heat from the system. If the leaving water temperature becomes too high (above 130°F), the circulating pump is de-energized so that the unit does not supply dangerously hot water to the water heater. The desuperheater coax is a double-wall, vented heat exchanger to prevent the possibility of contaminating the water supply should a failure occur.

Figure 1-10. Domestic hot water circulation pump

Hot water circulation pumps

As has been noted, the capability to assist with the production of domestic hot water is a benefit of geothermal systems. This hot water is circulated by a small, fractional-horsepower pump (see Figure 1-10). Most geothermal systems now include the pump pre-installed with the desuperheater coil. These pumps are typically 230-V, $1/40$-hp, wet-rotor circulators. The pump is fused and controlled by a thermal limit sensor in the water line linked to a control relay that cycles the pump with the compressor. In this fashion, the pump operates whenever the compressor is on and the hot water tank is below the fixed-temperature sensor limit of 120 to 130°F.

Reversing valves

The *reversing valve*, shown in Figure 1-11, provides a simple means for changing the

Figure 1-11. Reversing valve

direction of refrigerant flow in a geothermal system, thereby switching modes from heating to cooling. A reversing valve is operated by an electric solenoid coil connected to a pilot valve. When the solenoid coil is energized, the pilot valve opens, allowing high-pressure refrigerant to move a sliding piston assembly inside the reversing valve to one side or the other, depending on whether the thermostat is calling for heating or cooling. The pilot valve solenoid may be energized during the heating cycle or during the cooling cycle, as specified by the equipment manufacturer.

Accumulators

The majority of unitary geothermal systems operate with balanced refrigerant charges. These systems typically are built without accumulators. For those geothermal systems that incorporate multiple heat exchangers or use a refrigerant lineset to connect to a remote coil, accumulators are commonplace. For such systems, liquid refrigerant may migrate to the suction line during an OFF cycle and then be drawn directly into the compressor on start-up. The *suction-line accumulator* (see Figure 1-12) serves as a buffer tank to capture this liquid refrigerant before it can enter the compressor. (Because the accumulator is located between the reversing valve and the compressor, the function of the suction line does not change during a conversion between heating and cooling.) Once liquid refrigerant is trapped inside the accumulator, an internal orifice meters a small amount of the liquid refrigerant and allows it to blend with refrigerant vapor as it passes to the compressor. The orifice also allows any trapped oil that has built up in the bottom of the accumulator to return to the compressor. The accumulator may hold a portion of the liquid refrigerant charge, or slowly evaporate and redistribute the refrigerant into the system.

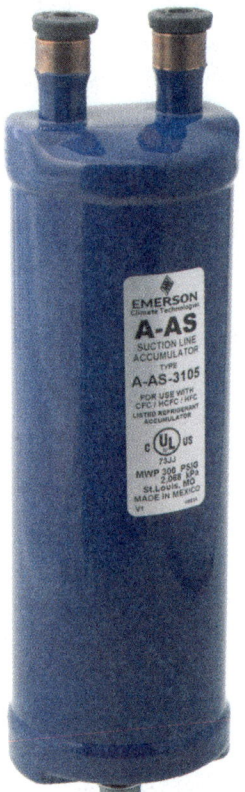

Figure 1-12. Suction-line accumulator

Expansion valves

In early geothermal systems, which ran predominantly on well water and had a constant supply fluid temperature, capillary tubes were used to regulate refrigerant flow between the condenser and evaporator coils. As geothermal systems evolved and began to include closed-loop applications, capillary tubes could no longer manage the wide range of system conditions efficiently. A few geothermal manufacturers began using separate thermal expansion valves—one for each coil—as is customary with high-efficiency air-source heat pumps. This method helped produce the desired efficiency, but had its own problems (described later in this section). An effort to simplify refrigerant control and overcome the need for separate thermostatic expansion valves (TEVs) led to the development of the *balanced-port thermostatic expansion valve*. A balanced-port TEV like the one shown in Figure 1-13 can operate effectively in a bi-flow refrigerant capacity, which means that a single metering device is able to function for both heating and cooling.

Figure 1-13. Balanced-port TEV

The balanced-port TEV is ideal for geothermal systems. Both condenser and evaporator coils are packaged in the same cabinet and share a common vapor line with the compressor, which means that the TEV's temperature-sensing bulb can always be mounted on the cold suction line to the compressor. This method of controlling refrigerant flow via a TEV sensing bulb mounted on a common suction line simplifies system operation and improves TEV reliability.

Older systems with separate TEVs and coils mounted in close proximity to the compressor may be subjected to excessive compressor discharge temperatures or pressures if the system is undercharged or operating at a very high head pressure. Should you encounter this situation and suspect problems with the TEV, check with the TEV and equipment manufacturers before replacing the TEV. Make certain that the operating conditions will not exceed the engineered allowances for either the *maximum operating pressure* (MOP) or the *maximum rated pressure* (MRP) of the replacement component.

Heat exchangers

The *heat exchanger* is critical to the heat transfer that takes place between the refrigerant and the source fluid (regardless of whether that source fluid is antifreeze in a closed

Figure 1-14. Coaxial heat exchanger

loop or well water in an open loop). Three types of heat exchangers are in common use in geothermal systems:

- coaxial
- coil-in-can
- brazed-plate.

Coaxial heat exchangers. *Coaxial heat exchangers* constitute the fluid-side heat transfer for the majority of manufactured geothermal systems. A coaxial heat exchanger is constructed from a spiral-fluted copper tube (fluid side) surrounded by a heavy-wall outer steel tube (refrigerant side). Together, the two tubes are hydraulically formed into a spiral configuration and brazed to keep the water portion and the refrigerant portion of the heat exchanger isolated from each other. Figure 1-14 shows a coaxial heat exchanger of the type commonly used in a geothermal heat pump.

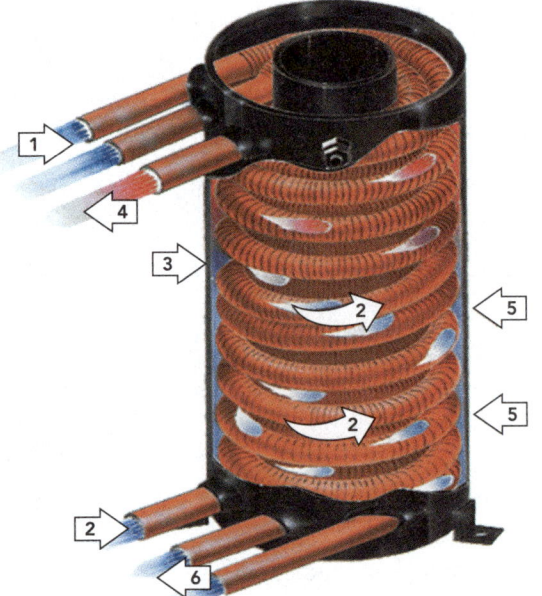

1. Water enters two upper water tubes.
2. Liquid refrigerant enters lower refrigerant tube and follows long spiral flow path.
3. Surface of copper tubing releases heat from water side. Refrigerant evaporates rapidly, resulting in very low pressure drop on refrigerant side.
4. Liquid refrigerant absorbs heat from water and begins to boil off, exiting heat exchanger as vapor.
5. Water tubes cross over at midpoint of heat exchanger (outside tube becomes inside tube and vice versa), resulting in two tubes of same length, with equal pressure drop and equal heat exchange.
6. Cooled water exits two lower water tubes.

Figure 1-15. Coil-in-can heat exchanger

Coil-in-can heat exchangers. Several manufacturers use a compact *coil-in-can heat exchanger* (see Figure 1-15) to provide excellent heat transfer in a small space. Typically, these heat exchangers are constructed from heavy-wall copper tube, which is internally and externally enhanced with fins and grooves to provide heat transfer for both fluid and refrigerant. Once coiled and formed, the copper tube is welded and brazed into a heavy steel container vessel. In some instances the vessel also serves as a suction-line accumulator or receiver for the system. This type of heat exchanger maintains its efficiency best when used with clean antifreeze solutions. If an enhanced-tube heat exchanger is used with a water supply subject to mineral fouling (as might be the case with some open-loop installations), service technicians should always suspect and run diagnostic checks for a fouled heat exchanger. If that proves to be the case, the heat exchanger may need to be cleaned before attempting to add refrigerant.

Brazed-plate heat exchangers.
Brazed-plate heat exchangers like the one shown in Figure 1-16 are found in many specialty hot water and hydronic geothermal systems. They also are used in some compact systems intended for locations with limited space, such as commercial office ceiling cassettes and small ducted zone systems. Brazed-plate heat exchangers are usually made from stainless steel. They are very compact with excellent heat exchange. Fluid and refrigerant passages within a brazed-plate heat exchanger run counterflow to each other. Clearance between plates may measure little more than 1 to 2 millimeters. Only the cleanest of

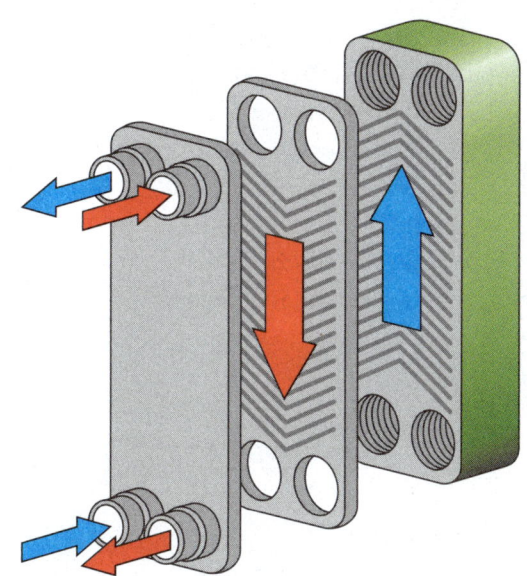

Figure 1-16. Brazed-plate heat exchanger

loop solutions must be used. No scale formers or sediment can be allowed to be present in the fluid. Installations that incorporate brazed-plate heat exchangers also must include "Y" strainers on the entering side of the heat exchanger to prevent the entry of any foreign material. Failure to protect these heat exchangers from scale or debris in a system will result in a system failure and costly downtime for back-flushing—or worse, the removal and replacement of the brazed-plate heat exchangers.

Geothermal flow centers

A *geothermal flow center* is a self-contained combination pump with a flush-and-purge valve assembly. The flow center dramatically simplifies installation labor, as well as the task of flushing and filling the geothermal loop. The flow center's three-way valves are located to allow for the isolation of the closed-loop piping for service to pumps and geothermal equipment.

Two types of flow centers are in common use. They may be classified as pressurized and non-pressurized. Both are pictured on the next page. A *pressurized* flow center (see Figure 1-17) may be left in the system when a system pressure test is conducted. A *non-pressurized* flow center (see Figure 1-18) is designed for atmospheric pressure only and must be valved out of the system when a pressure test is conducted. The reservoir tank, which makes up the main body of an atmospheric flow center, creates an automatic means to remove air and provide make-up solution to the geothermal loop.

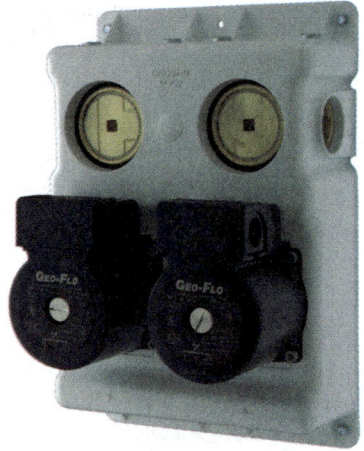

Figure 1-17. Pressurized flow center

A field service note: Atmospheric flow centers may be perceived by some as a means to flush and fill a geothermal loop. Contrary to this belief, the circulation pumps on conventional atmospheric flow centers do *not* provide sufficient flow to be effective at flushing air and debris from multicircuit geothermal loops. The piping harness for an atmospheric flow center must include the necessary valves to allow for "power flushing" of the geothermal loops using a portable flush cart designed for this purpose.

GEOTHERMAL VS. CONVENTIONAL SYSTEMS

A common question that people ask when discussing geothermal heat is "Will I be warm?" The simple answer is "Yes—and probably more comfortable than ever before." A traditional fossil-fuel heating system is normally "on" for a few minutes, blowing hot air, and then "off," waiting for the next thermostat cycle. A geothermal system operates with a lesser heat output than a fossil-fuel furnace, and typically provides a 20 to 25°F temperature rise between return and supply. Longer run cycles help to reduce thermal stratification and produce more uniform temperature conditions throughout a home.

Figure 1-18. Non-pressurized flow center

Generically, geothermal equipment performs the same basic functions as an air-source heat pump. The primary difference between the two is the substitution of a fluid-to-refrigerant heat exchanger and a loop pump in place of the traditional outdoor condensing coil and fan. The same troubleshooting skills employed by an experienced heat pump technician in measuring fluid flow, pressure drop, temperature change, etc., can be adapted to diagnosing the operation of a geothermal system.

There is no need to reverse operation and run a geothermal system in the air conditioning mode to defrost an outdoor coil. The demand for auxiliary electric heat to help maintain a comfortable temperature during a defrost cycle is eliminated, because there is no defrost cycle. The supply air temperature remains uniform throughout the heating cycle. Geothermal systems, unlike air-source heat pumps (which require a lineset and an outdoor condenser), are factory-sealed and charged with refrigerant. Because the refrigerant system is totally self-contained, there is no noisy outdoor condenser to annoy the neighbors or wake up the occupants every time the defrost cycle initiates.

The typical geothermal system is capable of providing most of the heat needed for maintaining comfort in almost any home. Those familiar with ASHRAE energy usage calculations can relate to the fact that, throughout most areas of the country, 50% of a home's design heat loss occurs during 97% of the winter operating hours, and the remaining 50% of the heat loss occurs during the 3% of run hours when the outdoor temperature is at its very coldest. A geothermal system takes advantage of this principle, providing economical, energy-efficient heat for the greatest portion of the required Btu output—and adding a minor amount of supplemental heat as electric resistance to maintain the desired temperature for those very few hours of operation (the 3%) when assistance is needed.

Geothermal systems use the same type of ducting found in conventional air conditioning systems. Typical ducting designs call for air volumes of 350 to 400 cfm per ton of capacity. As with conventional systems, a geothermal system will perform best if the home uses high side-wall return air intakes. High side-wall returns serve to pull warmer air off the ceiling areas and return it via the supply air vents, thereby reducing drafts caused by older floor-level return air intakes. For two-story homes, because warm air rises and the second floor is traditionally the most difficult to cool, every attempt should be made to draw the largest portion of the return air from the second floor.

Geothermal systems are ideal for zone controls. Two-stage compressors and ECM variable-speed fans can be adapted to a wide variety of zone control systems to provide close comfort control to multiple zones in larger homes. ECM fans are able to overcome most static pressure restrictions imposed by poor duct design and deliver the programmed air volume to zones that were previously under-supplied by older, constant-rpm fans.

As was noted earlier, domestic hot water is a by-product of compressor operation in geothermal systems. With conventional systems, the utility company must be paid twice—once for heating and air conditioning, and again for hot water. But hot water production with a desuperheater and circulation pump means that a geothermal system can make "free" domestic hot water even while operating in the air conditioning mode. In the heating mode, domestic water is heated as the system warms the home.

IMPORTANCE OF PROPER GEOTHERMAL LOOP DESIGN

The geothermal loop and its design are as important to a geothermal installation as is a clean condenser coil to a conventional air conditioning system. The efficient operation of a geothermal system relates directly to the design and installation of the geothermal loop's heat exchanger. Information found on the Internet or provided by equipment suppliers may specify a standard loop length per ton of system capacity. With geothermal loops, these "rules of thumb" need to be regarded with extreme caution.

Some of the factors that influence loop heat transfer and overall system performance include:
- system capacity
- system operation hours
- soil temperature and annual variation
- soil/rock composition
- soil moisture content
- water table
- thermal conductivity of the soil/bedrock
- thermal conductivity of the grout used in vertical heat exchange wells
- burial/drilled depth.

Individuals interested in gaining a rudimentary understanding of these factors and how they influence the design of a geothermal loop can acquire a working knowledge of geothermal systems in a four-day intensive training program for the accreditation of geothermal installers. The four-day course is presented by International Ground Source Heat Pump Association (**IGSHPA**). Attendees who pass the **IGSHPA** accreditation exam also receive certification from North American Technician Excellence (**NATE**).

When considering a geothermal loop, keep in mind that most rule-of-thumb guidelines presume ideal soil moisture and burial depth conditions. They also may be based on design minimum and maximum operating temperatures for the geothermal system. Should soil conditions be less than optimum, the rule-of-thumb loop will prove to be inadequate—causing the system to operate at below-freezing conditions for long periods of time in the winter, and likely run over temperature in the summer. Such real-world circumstances must be taken into account, since a geothermal system will not deliver the efficiency and savings for which it was intended when forced to operate at the extreme limits of its design.

A geothermal loop buried in dry, well-drained soil requires approximately three times as much loop pipe to attain the same heat exchange as wet, saturated soil. Undersized loops are likely to operate at subfreezing temperatures and draw frost to the loop pipe. As the frost lens forms against the pipe wall, it forces the soil away from the pipe. When the frost lens melts, the loop pipe is left in a void with no soil contact for heat transfer. Without the needed soil contact, the loop will overheat rapidly during the summer months. The effect on the geothermal system is similar to trying to run an air-source heat pump without a condenser fan.

Geothermal sales and installation crews need to be cognizant of soil and rock conditions for each installation location. Should conditions change, project allowances must be made to increase the loop lengths or adapt the loop design to ensure the needed heat transfer for an effective system. The following chapters provide many insights into the practical application of field knowledge needed for the design and installation of a successful geothermal system. ◆

ILLUSTRATION CREDITS
FIGURE 1-2: GEO-HEAT CENTER
FIGURE 1-3: BRISTOL COMPRESSORS
FIGURE 1-4: BRISTOL COMPRESSORS
FIGURE 1-5: COPELAND
PAGE 7 SIDEBAR: EMERSON CLIMATE TECHNOLOGIES
FIGURE 1-6: A.O. SMITH
FIGURE 1-7: GENTEQ
FIGURE 1-8: GENTEQ
FIGURE 1-9: ENERTECH GLOBAL, LLC
FIGURE 1-10: GRUNDFOS
FIGURE 1-11: EMERSON CLIMATE TECHNOLOGIES
FIGURE 1-12: EMERSON CLIMATE TECHNOLOGIES
FIGURE 1-13: EMERSON CLIMATE TECHNOLOGIES
FIGURE 1-14: PACKLESS INDUSTRIES
FIGURE 1-15: AQUA SYSTEMS INC.
FIGURE 1-16: API HEAT TRANSFER INC.
FIGURE 1-17: GEO-FLO PRODUCTS CORPORATION
FIGURE 1-18: B&D MANUFACTURING, INC.

◀CHAPTER TWO▶
Geothermal Site Considerations

INTRODUCTION

There is no such thing as a "simple quote" when considering a site for a geothermal installation. Contractors who quote air-source heat pumps may be accustomed to carrying a spreadsheet with pre-assigned prices for each size system. In most cases, it is relatively easy to find a location for the outdoor condenser for an air-source heat pump. This saves time and makes for a speedy quote—often the contractor can concentrate on closing the sale in the same visit. When quoting for a geothermal system, a suitable area for the geothermal loop needs to be established. A geothermal installation depends on obtaining good thermal contact with the earth, and consideration must be given to the space it occupies. It is rare for a geothermal sale to be closed on the initial site visit. Substantial site investigation is essential prior to the sales call. The focus here is to learn as much as possible about the project site *before* the first visit. Each site has its own characteristics and requirements.

First and foremost is an investigation of property records. Most county auditor websites have search tools that allow for retrieval of public domain property information using the address, owner's name, or parcel numbers. This information is useful for providing the location and dimensions of the property and surface structures, as well as the square footage of structures and easements that might compromise the area available for loop installation. Most auditor websites now also allow for satellite imagery showing additional surface features, such as driveways, sidewalks, trees, and landscaping. The ability to locate and incorporate these factors into a system design prior to giving

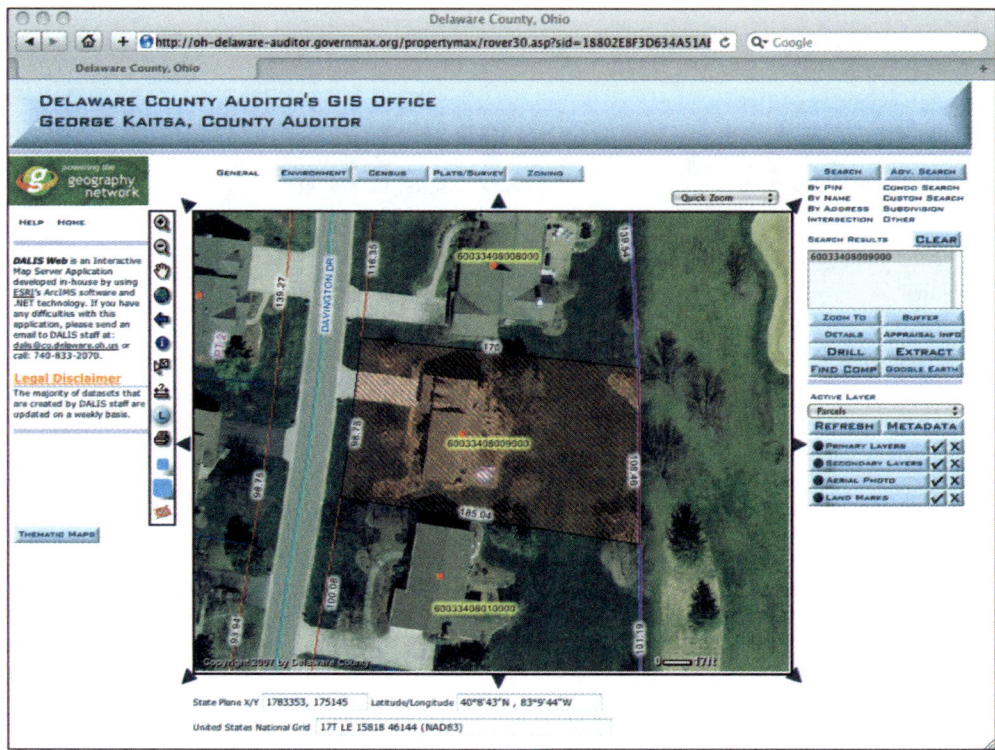

Figure 2-1. Aerial view

the potential customer a quote speeds up the entire process. If there is no satellite information on the local auditor's site, access to mapping search engines such as Google Maps/Earth or MapQuest can provide aerial views. The screen shot shown in Figure 2-1 provides an excellent example of the many features that may be available on a local auditor's website. Note that the shaded area shows lot line dimensions, surface landscaping, and a utility easement at the street. The city engineering office has development maps for locating water, sewer, gas, and electric lines. Information-specific sections of an auditor's website provide dimensions and square footage for each area of the home—and, in many cases, a curbside photo that reveals construction details (see Figure 2-2).

SITE CONSIDERATIONS

In addition to the helpful information provided by an auditor website review, the project site also must be investigated with consideration to the following items:

- topography
- vegetation/landscaping
- subsurface geology
- utility locations
- easements
- surface water features (streams, ponds, drainage).

Topography

It is a good idea to review images from online sources and superimpose topographic coverage when available. Widely spaced topographic contour lines indicate flat or gently sloping ground, which should be relatively easy for staging excavation and drilling operations. Contour lines that are closer together indicate areas with steeper slopes, which may present access problems for drilling rigs and excavation equipment. Look at the sample screen shot shown in Figure 2-3 on the next page, for example. The closely spaced contour lines superimposed on the middle portion of the satellite image reveal drainage patterns and steep ravines that would hinder the installation of a geothermal loop.

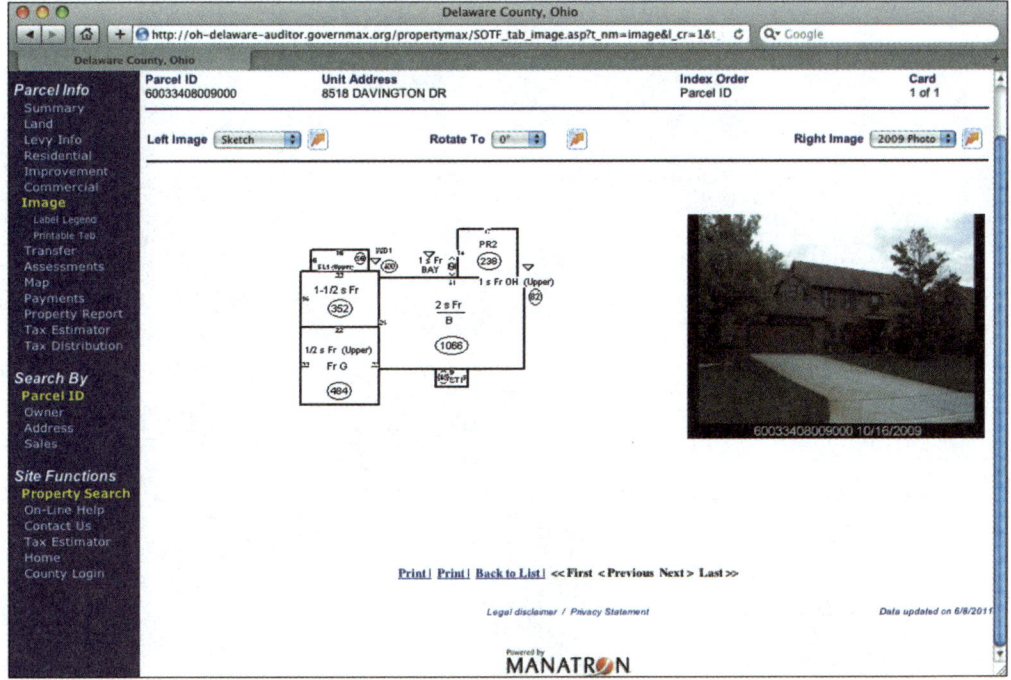

Figure 2-2. Floor plan sketch and curbside photo

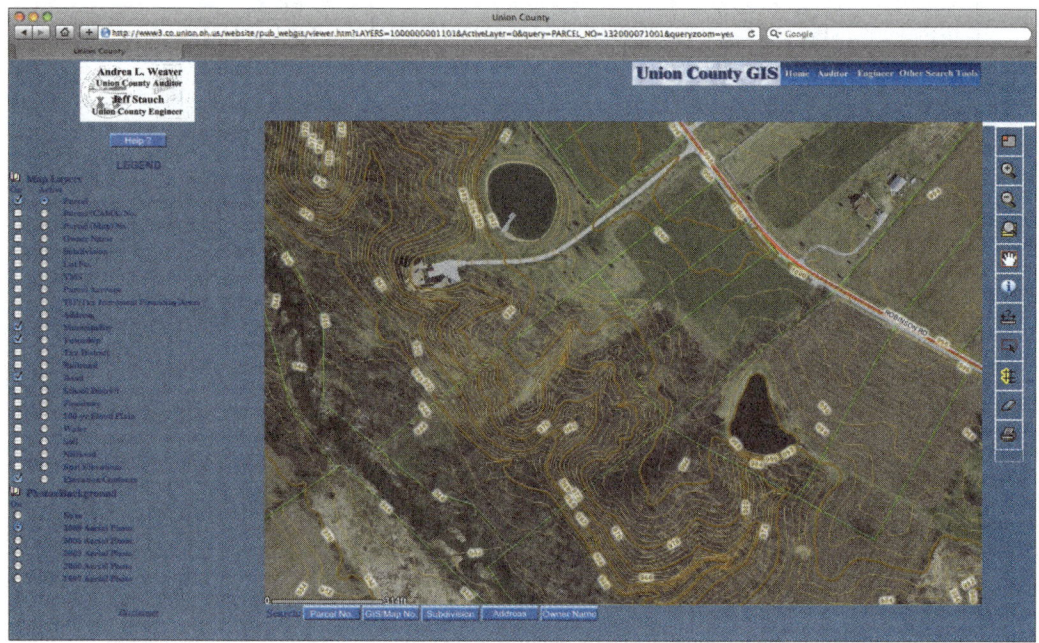

Figure 2-3. Topographic satellite view

Figure 2-4. Extended horizontal loop installed in saturated soil area

Vegetation/landscaping

Satellite images reveal surface vegetation and landscaping. Advance knowledge of the available "open area" helps in determining the type of loop best-suited to the property. When working with open trenches, always try to keep trenches outside of the "umbrella" of large trees. Excavation below the foliage umbrella risks damage to the root system and loss of the branches served by the severed roots. If a property is heavily wooded, it is better to anticipate using vertically drilled loops—or, if subsurface conditions permit, a loop installed by horizontal directional drilling methods.

When on-site, observe and identify the major species of surface vegetation. Vegetation can be a good indicator of the soil type and its moisture content. Trees such as cottonwood and willow prefer wet, saturated soils. Hardwood trees such as beech, oak, hickory, and maple prefer drier soils. Juniper can be an indicator that limestone bedrock is close to the surface.

Moisture content has a major effect on the thermal conductivity of the soil. Typically, the higher the moisture content, the better the thermal conductivity will be. High thermal conductivity leads to higher overall efficiency for a given length of earth loop. Figure 2-4 shows an example of saturated soil conditions found at a project site where old-growth cottonwood trees predominate.

Subsurface geology

Subsurface geology can be a major factor in loop design and cost. Investigate the site conditions prior to the first site visit. Nearly every state has a Department of Natural Resources and a geological survey. Communicate with your local survey office to obtain maps and information on subsurface conditions for the area you serve. Drilling records for water wells and geotechnical work that may have been done at your project site constitute a principal source of subsurface information. Many states require the registration of drilling logs for all wells. These wells may be for private water systems, irrigation, oil, gas, or injection purposes. In many cases they can be accessed online. If a project is commercial, it is likely that a geotechnical/foundation engineer has already made a series of test borings to determine the density and moisture content of soils from the surface to as deep as 35 ft. These records should be available from the building owner or architect, and can reveal conditions found within normal horizontal loop burial depths. Figure 2-5 on the next page shows an example of a full-featured water well log and drilling report of the kind that can be found online. It provides information on the thickness of the glacial clay overburden, depth to bedrock, rock type, water table, water availability, and pump test data for a residential water well.

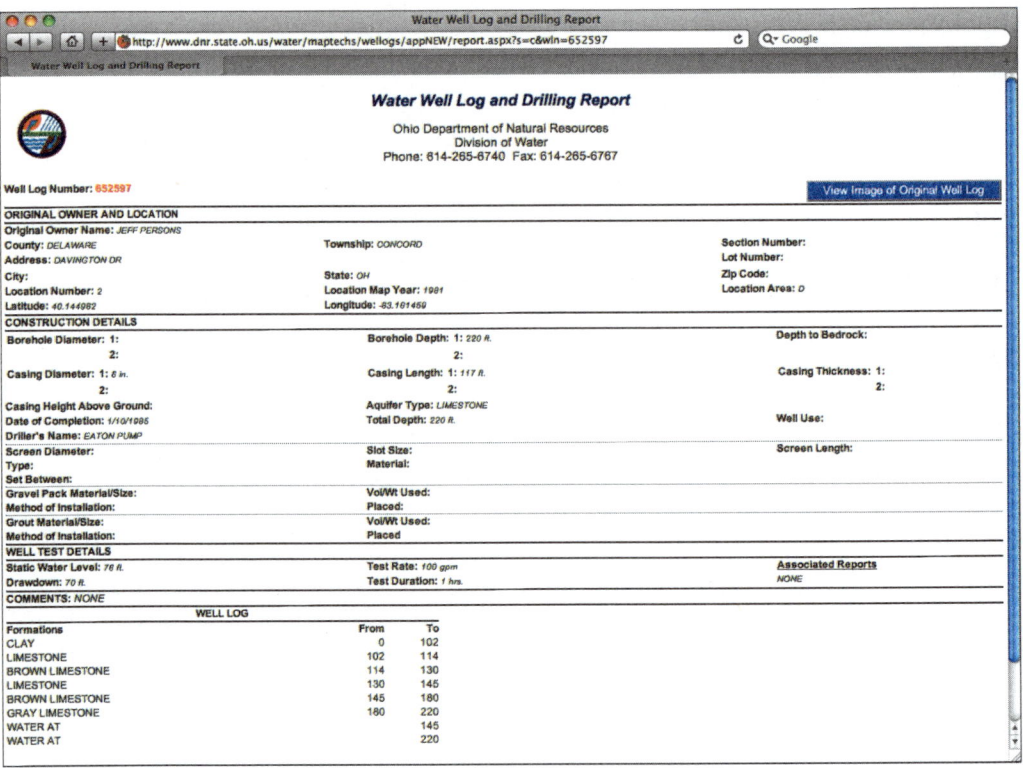

Figure 2-5. Drilling log for residential water well

Subsurface conditions can have a significant effect on the cost of installing a loop. For example, a farming area characterized by well-drained soil may be underlain by a permeable sand and gravel deposit. If this sand and gravel layer is above the local water table, it is likely to be dry in all seasons. Dry sand is a very poor conductor of heat, and as a result requires up to three times as much loop footage as wet saturated soil. If the loop in this scenario is sized and installed based on saturated soil conditions, it will lose heat transfer quickly during the peak seasons and render the geothermal system inoperative at a time when its operation is most needed. Advance knowledge of the soil type from drilling records would have alerted the installing contractor that the project had to be quoted with a larger horizontal loop, or designed to use vertical loops (which make contact with more stable saturated soil or bedrock conditions).

Note: For a complete listing of state and provincial geological surveys, consult the Appendix at the back of this book.

There are many drilling methods that may be utilized for installing vertical loops. Each has its own application and associated cost.
- *Auger drilling* typically is used for soft-sediment, shallow-depth vertical installations. A variation of auger drilling is the *bucket auger*, which may be used to install helix-coiled vertical exchangers in caisson wells.
- *Wash drilling* or *waterjet drilling* is used for sand, silt, and clay formations.
- *Directional drilling* is employed for unconsolidated sand, silt, and clay formations. Directional drilling has been adapted to include small-footprint drilling equipment that is also capable of inclined and vertical drilling. This equipment is particularly suitable for smaller city lots, where full-size drill rigs may have limited access.
- *Rotary percussion drilling* (rock drill) works well for bedrock formations that are close to the surface. The small size of a rotary percussion drill makes it especially adaptable to track-mounted equipment (such as a skid steer) and allows for drilling in limited-access locations.
- *Air rotary drilling* and *mud rotary drilling* utilize drag bits or roller cones in unconsolidated and soft rock formations.
- *Downhole air-hammer rotary drilling* may be employed for hard rock conditions.
- *Sonic drilling* is well-suited for unconsolidated sand and gravel and highly fractured rock conditions.

Figure 2-6 shows examples of the last three of these means of installing vertical loops.

Figure 2-6. Vertical loop installation methods
L–R: air rotary drilling (soft rock), downhole air-hammer rotary drilling (hard rock), sonic drilling (unconsolidated sand and gravel and highly fractured rock)

At the time of this printing, vertical loop drilling costs appear to range (roughly) from as low as $5 per foot to as much as $30 per foot. In some instances, where sources of subsurface contamination and hazardous materials may be encountered, the cost may go even higher. In general, vertical loops are least costly when installed in uniform unconsolidated clay soil, weathered bedrock, or sedimentary sandstone and shale formations. The installed cost can increase if loose sand and gravel formations are encountered. Loose sand and gravel formations may need to be cased off with PVC or steel well casing to prevent a "washout" (the formation of a subsurface cavity). Once the "loose area" is stabilized, drilling may proceed. After the vertical heat exchanger is inserted, the casing is recovered for use on the next well. Each step in the process adds more to the total installation cost.

If the rock type is classified as a hard rock formation, the preferred drilling method typically calls for the use of either mud rotary "tri-cone" drilling equipment or downhole air-hammer rotary drilling equipment. These drill rigs are very heavy and often require special road permits for transport. As with all heavy machinery, the larger and more powerful the rigs are, the more fuel they consume—and naturally, the cost of drilling increases with the cost of the fuel needed to operate the equipment.

When extensive sand and gravel or heavily fractured rock formations are encountered, drilling methods may require the use of sonic drilling rigs. Sonic drills operate by means of sonic vibrations, which serve to liquefy and displace the surrounding strata as the drill stem moves into the earth. Once the design depth is achieved, loop lines are inserted inside the sonic casing and the casing is vibrated back out of the ground to allow for grouting and sealing of the well bore. Sonic drilling methods typically demand a higher price, due to the expense of the drilling equipment and the need to replace drilling rods and fittings that fatigue from the sonic forces they transmit to the formation.

Utility locations

The best source for identifying on-site utilities is your local utility protection service, which will locate and mark underground utilities at no charge. These services are intended to prevent accidental damage to public utility lines and are commonly managed by the local gas, electric, phone, and cable companies. Contractors must check with their local utility location services to obtain information on the process for calling in a "locate request." In many areas, the requirement to "call before you dig" is a state law. Most services mandate how many days prior to commencing work a "locate request" must be called in. They may also limit the period of time for which a request remains in effect. If construction delays exceed the effective marking date, an additional request must be made before work may continue.

Failure to notify the locating service prior to an excavation places the excavating contractor and those subcontracting to the excavator at fault and responsible for any damages. The importance of using this service is exemplified by a recent incident in which a subcontractor cut an unmarked major fiber-optic trunk line, causing over $250,000 in repair costs to the utility and untold inconvenience to a major university.

Simple observations made from aerial photos and on-site surveys also can reveal the presence of utilities that may impact installation operations. Fire hydrants probably will be installed along the main water line. Water shut-off valves identify where the line exists at the street, and its entrance to the home may be used to trace the anticipated burial path when the line cannot be accurately marked. All gas lines should be identified with marker wire and located by the utility protection service. Electric phone and cable lines are either overhead and visible, or underground and need to be located and marked by the utility protection service. If site work entails moving heavy equipment below overhead utility lines, these lines need to be identified with marker collars or disconnected and taken down during the work process.

The photo below shows an 8-in. unmarked sanitary line encountered by a directional boring machine at a depth of 10 ft. Repair materials were provided by the city sanitation department, which failed to locate and mark the buried line (a city official chose to presume that no excavation would endanger the sanitary line). The contractor's cost, however, included a full day of lost time for a six-man crew plus additional production delays at a very busy time.

Sanitary sewer lines typically have a manhole cover every 100 to 300 ft. Manhole covers identify the main line. By lifting a cap, you can verify the depth and direction of the mains. However, locating the main does not necessarily identify the service from the home to the main. Sewer lines often are *not* marked by the utility protection service— be sure to state directly to the locating service that sewer lines may be implicated by excavation activity. Failure to identify a sanitary sewer line can be costly (see sidebar).

In addition to public utility lines, there may be buried lines that are considered the owner's property, and these will not be identified by the public utility locator service. If the project site has in-ground sprinklers, lighting, an electronic dog fence, outdoor cooking appliances, or outbuildings that have electricity, water, or sewer (this includes septic tanks, aeration tanks, and leaching fields), then there are more lines that may need to be identified. In some instances, geothermal contractors simply write in a clause stating that they are not responsible for damage or repair to unidentified underground utilities. This clause is always prudent, but there's a significant amount of lost time when an avoidable line is cut and requires repair.

Locating unmarked utility lines. Enlist the assistance of the property owner to help identify the location of known underground lines. A good investment for geothermal contractors is an underground cable locator. A cable locator and signal transmitter can assist in identifying a wide variety of underground lines and tracing wires from a home to the water well or to an outbuilding. Downspout lines can be traced by using an electrician's wire tape to snake the drain line. With the snake in the drain, connect the signal generator to the snake line and then trace out the line with the receiver tool.

Satellite photos can be useful in identifying previous drain lines and trenches. There is a good deal of truth to the old saying, "The grass is always greener over the septic tank." Drain lines and leaching field lines often show up in aerial photos. If the first photo you open does not reveal their location, try using the dated image feature that lets you go back in the Google archives to look at photos taken at earlier dates. Typically, a photo from late summer or winter, when yards are dry, will reveal the location of the leaching field. Look at the screen shot shown in Figure 2-7, for example. This 2002 aerial photo was taken in winter and clearly shows the location of sanitary laterals in the leaching field. The sump pump, downspout, and sanitary perimeter drains parallel the north property line and run to a drainage ditch at the street.

Identifying underground utilities will help avoid unfortunate surprises and the potential cost of repairs once a project starts. Accidentally intruding a geothermal loop into a leaching field can create major problems for the sanitation system and invoke the wrath of the local county health inspector. Some county health departments are working on legislation to ensure that geothermal loop designs are included with construction documents and do not infringe on areas designated for primary or secondary sanitary fields. Soil drainage and permeability, as they apply to the sanitary system, will take priority over geothermal loop fields. Knowledge of these developments is essential to the design of a geothermal loop that complies with future sanitary code standards.

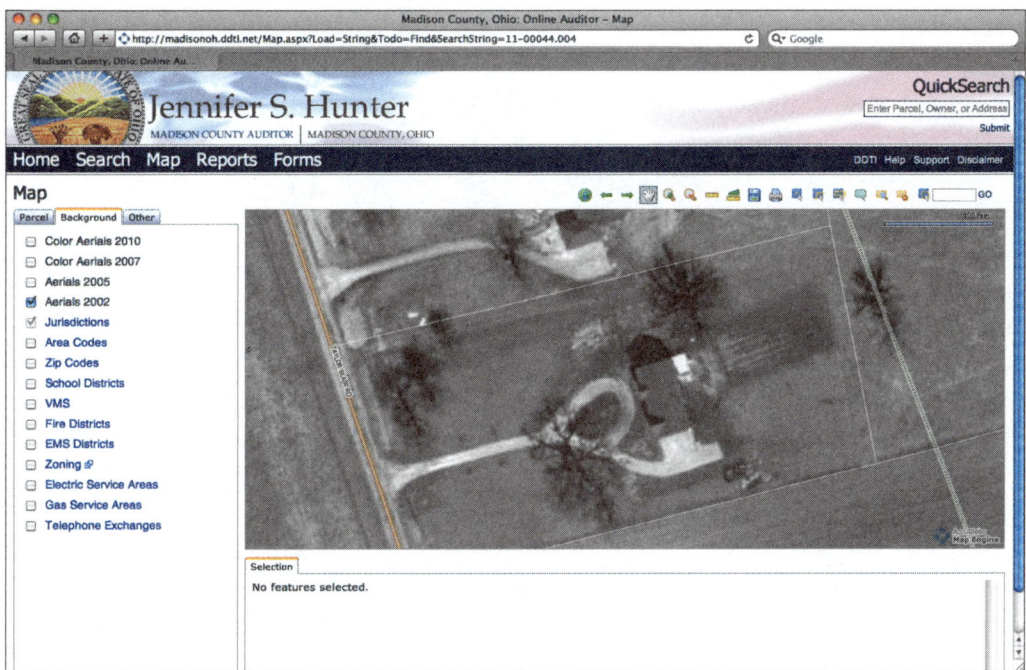

Figure 2-7. Aerial view in winter

Easements

Utility and drainage easements are sections of a property that are set aside for the specific purpose of running underground or overhead utilities. The primary easement for most properties is at the street, where water, sewer, gas, and electric lines typically are located. In some instances there also may be an easement at the back property line or along a side lot line. Easements allow for utility right-of-way and must be accessible by utility crews at all times. Any infringement on an easement by a geothermal loop is subject to damage by utility crews and possible legal action by local authorities.

In many jurisdictions, there are regulations similar to those for easements that apply for sanitary and construction reasons. Health codes in Ohio, for example, require that water wells be kept a minimum of 50 ft away from a sanitary field and septic tank. Likewise, a minimum distance of 50 ft must be maintained between a water well and a horizontal or vertical geothermal loop. Ohio codes also require that a water well be no closer than 10 ft to a building foundation. The same 10-ft minimum distance restriction applies to geothermal wells and manifolds. If a geothermal vertical loop is to be drilled within the foundation area of a building, prior code approval is advised.

Regulations for clearances between water wells, geothermal wells, loops, septic tanks, and leaching fields can vary among states and health departments. It is the responsibility of the installing contractor to be familiar with and comply with local codes when designing a geothermal installation.

Surface water features

Water and drainage features are important for both "open-loop" and "pond-loop" geothermal installations. Open-loop installations use well water for their heat transfer and typically discharge the spent well water to surface drainage, such as a lake, stream, or pond. In some instances, especially when heavily fractured rock is available, a return well may be used to recharge the spent water back to the aquifer. Return wells that do not access fractured formations often experience mineral fouling conditions and overflow. For this reason, the majority of open-loop installations typically discharge spent water to a local surface water feature.

Lakes and ponds make excellent sources for geothermal heat exchange. In order for a pond to be an effective heat exchange medium for a single-family residence, it should be within 300 ft of the residence and have a minimum size of a half-acre with a minimum depth of 8 ft.

Why is the size of the pond important? Consider the heat of rejection created by a 4- to 6-ton geothermal system in relation to the evaporative cooling afforded by the exposed water surface of the pond. If the area of the pond is a half-acre or larger, surface cooling from evaporation will help control the water temperature, preventing overheating by the geothermal loops. In the winter, water has its maximum density at 38.6°F. The lowest water temperatures occur when the pond has an exposed surface with no ice and strong cold winds accelerate the evaporative cooling of surface water. Once the pond surface is covered with ice, the evaporative heat loss is eliminated and the temperature in the deep area of the pond rises back toward 38°F. Providing heat exchange in a pond typically requires only half as much geothermal pipe in contact with the water as might be needed if the pipe was to be buried in damp, heavy soil.

If ponds smaller than a half-acre are used, you can expect temperatures to run higher and lower than might be normal for a larger pond. These temperatures may affect aquatic life and increase algal growth. To compensate for the smaller size, it may be necessary to use pond water treatment and aeration fountains for thermal and algae control. Commercial pond installations require larger and deeper ponds. Such systems can be cooling-dominant and will benefit from the use of fountains, which should be sized to aerate the water at a flow rate equivalent to the gpm used within the building.

The ideal pond installation has a controlled drainage area, either spring-fed or with clean inflow, and no heavy silt load. Ponds that receive silt-laden water or water high in agricultural nutrients are not good candidates, since they may require frequent dredging. Figure 2-8 shows a 4-ton loop being floated into a clean, well-maintained pond. When filled with antifreeze, the loop coils with their concrete block weights will settle to the bottom of the pond and will provide heating, cooling, and hot water for a family of four. ◆

Figure 2-8. Installing a pond loop

ILLUSTRATION CREDITS
FIGURE 2-4: JEFF PERSONS
FIGURE 2-6: JEFF PERSONS
PAGE 31 SIDEBAR: JEFF PERSONS
FIGURE 2-8: JEFF PERSONS

◄CHAPTER THREE►
Open-Loop Systems

INTRODUCTION

From as early as the 1940s until the late 1970s, water-source heat pumps were designed for use with either city water or well water. Typically, they were intended to operate with boiler and cooling tower water supplies. Water temperatures generally ranged between 60 and 80°F. On occasion, well water systems also made use of modulating water flow controls. Modulating controls like the one shown in Figure 3-1 on the next page allowed the boiler/tower systems to take advantage of lower well water temperatures by increasing the flow for the heating mode and then decreasing the flow for the air conditioning mode. (Early geothermal systems often used two valves—one controlled by head pressure for the AC cycle and a second controlled by suction pressure for heating.) Many service technicians who maintained these systems developed a sixth sense for water quality and how it could affect operation of these early "water-cooled" AC and heat pump systems.

The first oil embargo in the early 1970s spurred a renewal of interest in water-source (geothermal) heat pumps. Within a few short years, thousands of open-loop (well water) systems were sold and installed by individuals who had little or no experience with water quality. As might be expected, a significant number of these "open" systems encountered difficulty with the quality of their water supplies. The purpose of this chapter is to impart the knowledge derived from many years of experience working with water chemistry, geology, water wells, and water systems, particularly as these subjects relate to geothermal heat pumps. The material provided in this chapter is vital to the successful installation and service of open-loop geothermal systems.

ANALYZING A PROPOSED OPEN-LOOP SYSTEM

Code regulations/environmental considerations

Before embarking on an open-loop application, take the time to do an objective analysis of the code-related and environmental issues that may affect its implementation. The following checklist provides insights into the major issues that may influence your decision. This list is by no means definitive. There will always be changes in local codes and regulations that may have an impact on whether you decide to implement an open system or not. If you are planning an open system, first consult with local water and health officials to determine if there are any conditions, restrictions, or permits required that are *not* included in the following list:

Figure 3-1. Pressure-actuated water-regulating valve

- Are there local, city, county, or state restrictions on the use of well water? Some areas have restricted or protected water rights and forbid the extraction of ground water.
- Is there an adequate water supply for maintaining operation of the geothermal system and meeting the home or commercial demands at the same time? The water requirement for a geothermal system depends on the manufacturer's design and on the local water temperature. Typical well water temperatures (see Figure 3-2) follow closely and average 2 to 3°F higher than the mean annual air temperature. The necessary water flow rate for an open-loop system may range from as little as 1.5 gpm/ton for water supplies above 55°F to as much as 3 gpm/ton for water supplies as low as 40°F. Operation in the heating mode with a water supply below 40°F typically requires closed-loop methods.
- How will the "spent" water be discharged? Water usage during periods of extremely hot or cold weather can easily range from 7,000 to 14,000 gallons per day for an average size home. Does the property have access to a lake, pond, or natural drainage? If not, is a second well, used as a return well, an option?
- Is there a second use for the water? Irrigation, livestock, waterscaping, snowmaking for ski resorts, processed water supply for municipalities, and industrial processes are all possible second uses.

- Is high-volume water extraction likely to have an adverse impact on the well water supply for adjacent properties? If so, who is responsible and what are the options?
- Does the customer have a positive attitude toward the use of well water as a heating and cooling source?

Water chemistry considerations

Next, you will need to investigate some important issues relating to water chemistry:
- The untreated water supply should be potable. The use of treated water from a water softener is cost-prohibitive.
- The "raw" (untreated) cold water should not have an objectionable rotten-egg odor, caused by the presence of hydrogen sulfide. (If the cold water has no odor but the hot water does, see the next item in this list.) Hydrogen sulfide is an aggressive gas that will corrode heat exchangers, copper piping, and valves. Cupro-nickel heat exchangers offer extra resistance against hydrogen sulfide, but providing the same level of protection for the remainder of an installation is difficult.

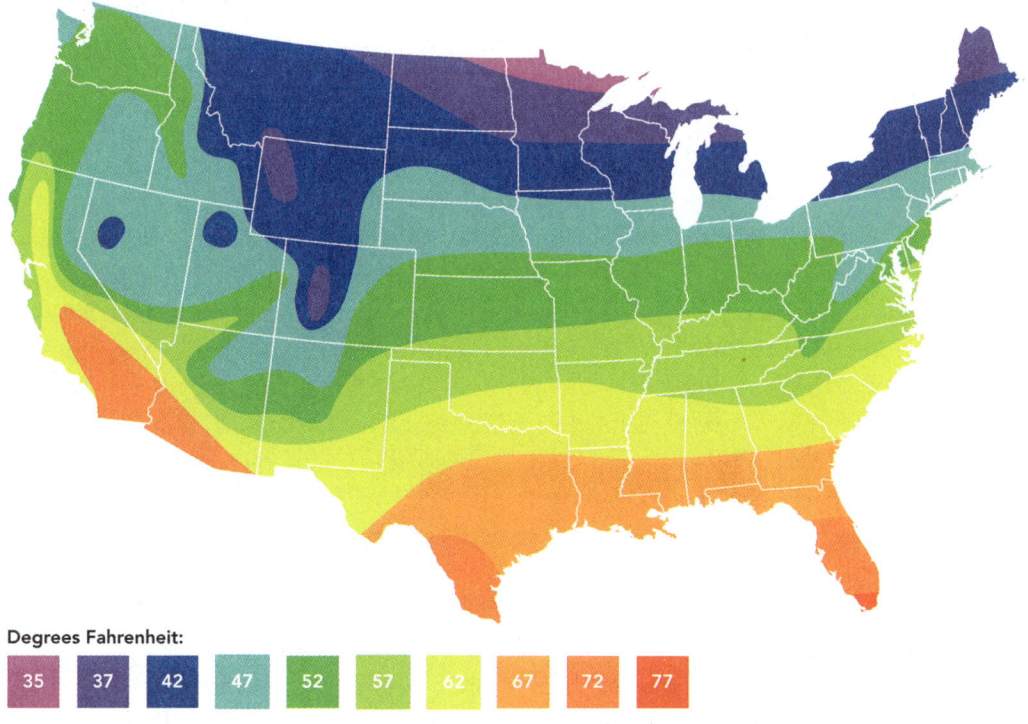

Figure 3-2. Groundwater temperature map

- Hot water in a soft water system can cause rapid corrosion of the magnesium anode in a hot water tank. One byproduct of this corrosion process is a sulfur odor on the hot-water side of the piping system. While the odor is offensive, it does not indicate a sulfur problem with the source water. In most instances, removal of the magnesium rod or its replacement with an aluminum rod will solve the bad odor issue.
- Hydrogen sulfide is an oxygen scavenger—that is, it will oxidize and precipitate as a black scale when exposed to oxygen. The discharge of water high in hydrogen sulfide into surface ponds is known to deplete oxygen, creating fish kills. To reduce the hazard to aquatic life, water with free hydrogen sulfide must first be aerated to provide a positive oxygen balance prior to its discharge.
- Mineral scale deposits such as iron sulfide and magnesium sulfide have a black crusty or carbon-black appearance. The black precipitate is difficult to clear from heat exchangers and piping systems. It is best to avoid water supplies with iron sulfide and magnesium sulfide problems.
- Chloride, as sodium chloride salt, should be within potable limits. High chlorides, as might be experienced in coastal areas or locations with saline aquifers, can lead to the deterioration of copper heat exchangers. In such cases, marine-grade cupro-nickel heat exchangers must be used. Chlorides in excess of 300 ppm are considered corrosive to most metals.
- "Hard" water (caused by the presence of calcium carbonate) is often blamed as a scale former. In truth, hardness is less a factor in the creation of scale deposits if the water supply has sufficient dissolved carbon dioxide to keep the hardness minerals in solution. The amount of carbon dioxide in solution depends on the origin of the water supply, as well as its temperature and pressure. Most well water supplies contain dissolved carbon dioxide. However, just as with a carbonated beverage, any change in temperature and/or pressure allows the carbon dioxide to come out of solution. When this happens, the equilibrium holding the remaining hardness minerals in solution is upset and scale deposits begin to form.
- The greatest offender in creating problems for open-loop systems is elemental iron. When present, elemental iron causes iron stains on plumbing fixtures and landscaping. Most water supplies have some iron content. As long as iron remains in solution, it is not a problem. However, if oxygen contact with the water supply begins the oxidizing process, iron can become a major maintenance expense. Oxygen is likely to mix with the water in wells supplied from shallow aquifers or from fractured-rock systems that have rapid recharge from the surface. The process of iron precipitation can get started before the water reaches the well pump. Such water supplies are plagued with heavy iron accumulations that choke pump

impellers and plug piping and water strainers. They should be avoided as sources for supplying geothermal systems.

- Like elemental iron, iron bacteria, when present, can cause the incrustation of pump impellers and piping and the clogging of water filters. Iron bacteria create a slimy mass, which is easily identifiable in toilet flush tanks. The bacteria are naturally occurring and do not present a health hazard. However, cleaning deposits from a geothermal system's heat exchangers and all of the associated well piping, from pump to discharge area, can represent a major maintenance expense. The presence of iron bacteria can be identified by checking toilet flush tanks for slimy red deposits and by observing a water sample in a clear container for several days. If the water sample develops an orange sediment that clumps together at the bottom of the container, bacterial iron is present and it is best to avoid its use with an open-loop system.

- *pH* is a measure of the acidity or alkalinity of the water supply. The pH scale ranges from 0 to 14. Values below 7 are acidic and corrosive, those above 7 are alkaline and scale-forming. Water supplies with a pH below 6.5 are known to be corrosive. Well water—or city water, for that matter—derived from mountain snowmelt or from fractured metamorphic or igneous aquifers can be high in carbon dioxide and low in hardness minerals. Such water is known to be particularly corrosive. Just as sugar dissolves much faster in hot water than in ice water, the corrosiveness of a "soft" water supply (one that is low in total dissolved solids) doubles with every 10°F rise in temperature. Copper hot water piping, desuperheaters for domestic hot water production, and brass valves are at particular risk with low-hardness, low-pH water supplies. In such situations, domestic hot water piping is best managed with CPVC or PEX pipe. Hot water distribution systems and desuperheater piping between geothermal units and a water heater are best managed on a "home run" basis, without any metallic connections hidden inside walls or ceilings. Because of the highly corrosive effect of soft and low-pH water supplies, it is prudent to provide a floor drain for the equipment location. Experience also suggests the benefit of a water moisture alarm or home security sensor for the floor area around the installation to alert the customer if there is a plumbing failure.

WATER VOLUME

In Chapter Two, local water well drilling logs were used as a means of learning about subsurface drilling conditions. These same records provide useful information for determining the availability of an adequate volume of water for an open-loop installation. For locations where a supply well needs to be drilled, the information

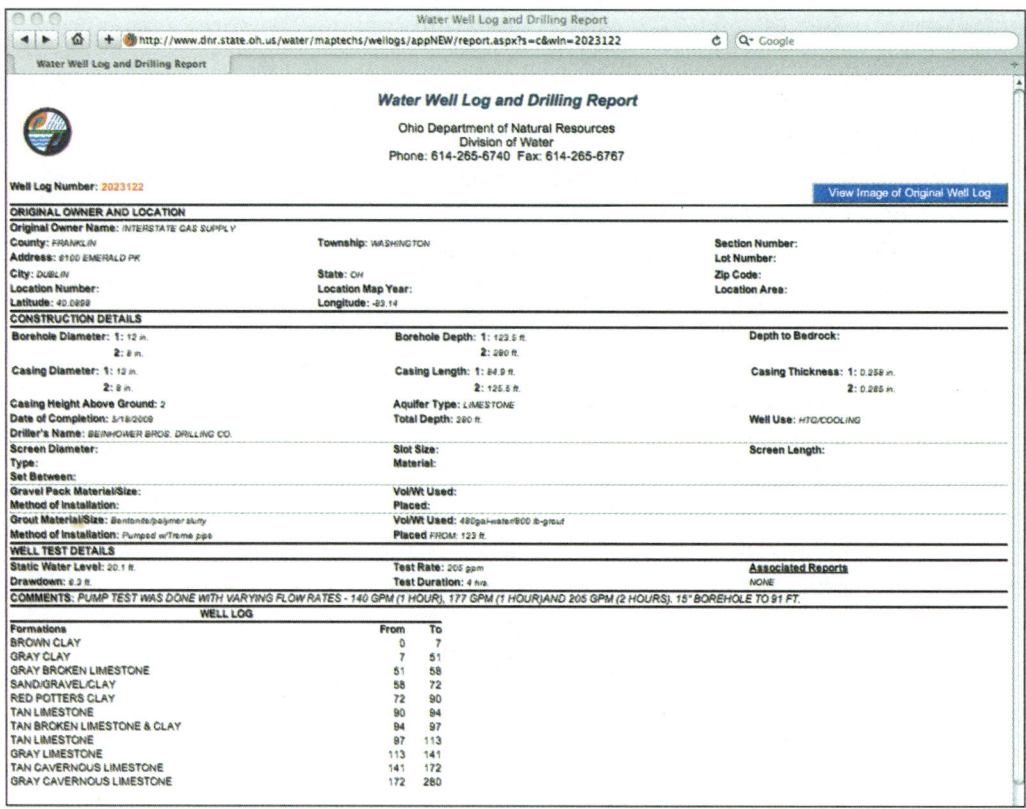

Figure 3-3. Water well drilling log

provided from local well logs and from well contractors with experience in the area can provide insights into the likely "productivity" of a well. Experience teaches contractors to verify the water quality and volume before installing a geothermal system. It's also wise to have a backup plan if the well does not produce as anticipated. Take a look at Figure 3-3 above, which shows an example of a typical well log. The log includes the total well depth, the static water level, a pump testing rate, and a drawdown or change in water level with the test pump in operation.

> As you examine the well log shown in Figure 3-3 above, note that the drilling contractor in this case carefully recorded changes in subsurface geology, rock type, color, and drilling conditions. The well was drilled to 280 ft, a static water level was recorded at 20.1 ft, and the well was test-pumped at 205 gpm with a drawdown of 6.3 ft. As a water supply well, this is an excellent well for a commercial application.

Water well and pumping volume considerations

Pumping power. Pumping power can play a major role in the overall efficiency of a project. The power needed for a specific installation depends on the total dynamic feet of head (TDH) against which the pump must operate. The total resistance that the pump must overcome consists of:

- static head—the vertical distance, in feet, that the water must be lifted from the pumping water level in the well to the elevation of the expansion tank or pump pressure control
- friction head—the pressure drop, in feet, caused by friction as the water moves through piping, fittings, and system components
- pressure head—the service pressure provided by the pump to the building, expressed as equivalent feet of head by multiplying the operating pressure in psi times 2.31 ft/lb.

Expressed mathematically:

TDH = static head + friction head + (pressure head × 2.31)

Power requirements increase in direct proportion to the TDH. This relationship can be advantageous to system efficiency when the water pumping level is near the surface and minimal energy is needed to move the well water. For efficient design purposes, it is best to limit open systems to pumping water levels that are within 100 ft of the surface. In such applications, a properly sized well pump that operates within the "peak" of its efficiency curve typically will consume from 44 to 54 watts per hour (W/hr) per gpm of pump capacity. As an example, assume that an application for a 3-ton geothermal open system has the following criteria:

Water flow rate = 6 gpm
Water pumping level = 100 ft
Water supply pressure = (60 psi × 2.31 ft/psi) = 138 ft of head
Piping pressure drop = 12 ft of head
TDH = 250 ft of head
Pumping power at 250 ft TDH = 54 watts per gpm of pump capacity (from pump manufacturer's data)

The pumping power should average 324 W/hr for the 6-gpm flow (54 W/gpm × 6 gpm). If the same 3-ton system were to operate in a closed-loop application, a traditional

230-V high-head loop pump circulating at a design flow of 9 gpm would consume up to 385 W/hr. In this example, you can see that the open-loop well water system, with its reduced pumping power requirement and constant loop temperature, has a definite efficiency advantage over the closed-loop installation. If, however, the pumping level increases to 200 ft below the surface, the application requires an increase in pump horsepower and the power usage increases to an average of 80 W/hr per gpm, or 480 W/hr for the 6-gpm flow.

The principle illustrated in this example holds true for almost all applications that have properly sized well pumps and clean water supplies. The situation changes dramatically when a pump becomes "bound up" with iron deposits and loses its pumping efficiency. Heavy iron or scale deposits within the pump impeller stack can cause the pump to lose capacity and run continuously at a reduced pressure. In severe situations, the pump may become so fouled with mineral deposits that it is unable to attain its shutoff pressure and remains in continuous operation until discovered and replaced. When this condition persists, it is likely that the geothermal system will have a history of high energy bills and safety lockouts due to inadequate water flow. In such situations, the best solution is a conversion to a closed-loop installation.

Drawdown. As illustrated in Figure 3-4, *drawdown* is the change in water elevation between the static water level (when the pump is not operating) and the pumping water level (when the pump is operating). The water table near the well drops when the pump extracts water from the well. In three dimensions, the effect of this decline in the water level looks like an upside-down cone, and is called the "cone of depression."

When it comes to drawdown for an open-loop installation, less is better. A water well with minimal drawdown (typically less than 30 ft for wells with a deep pump setting, or less than one-third the distance between the static water level and the pump setting for a shallow well) has the ability to provide a water volume far greater than the rate at which the well is pumped. Water wells with minimal drawdown are more dependable in the long term. These wells are characterized by subsurface conditions that encounter open fracture systems or highly permeable sand and gravel deposits.

Conversely, tight formations have very pronounced drawdowns (typically in excess of 30 ft for wells with a deep pump setting, or more than one-third the distance between the static water level and the pump setting for a shallow well). Tight formations are subject to mineral encrustations due to the release of dissolved carbon dioxide as the well water transitions from a higher pressure to a lower pressure upon entering the well.

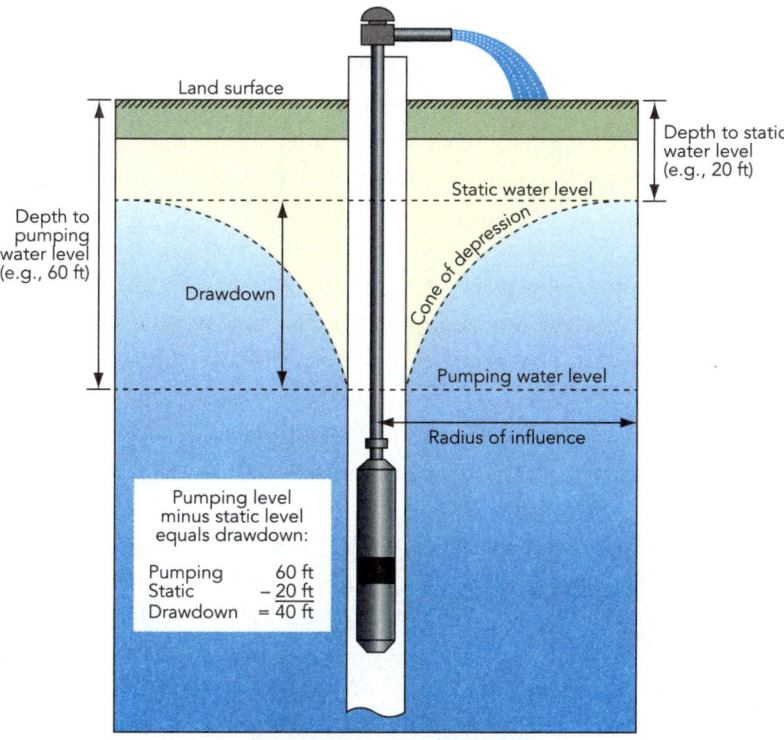

Figure 3-4. Drawdown

Loss of carbon dioxide upsets the chemical equilibrium of the water, resulting in the precipitation of minerals and the eventual plugging of the formation around the well.

In the case of a bedrock well, where the water table may lie within rock strata below the base of the well casing, the cycling of the well pump causes the water level to rise and fall each time the pump operates. This creates a condition described as "formation breathing," as the rock surface alternately inhales air and oxygen when the water level drops and then exhales when the pump cycles off and the water level rises. Oxygen is introduced into the formation as it "breathes." When elemental iron is present, the iron oxidizes and precipitates, clogging the pores within the rock strata and effectively sealing the well. Oxygen mixing with water entering the well from within the drawdown area causes iron precipitation within the well pump body and plumbing system, leading to increased maintenance for the well and geothermal equipment. The ideal situation for a bedrock well is a static water level and a pumping water level high enough to remain within the cased well depth, thereby eliminating the "breathing" problem and protecting the formation from oxygen exposure. A good guideline for an acceptable drawdown is to use caution whenever the drawdown exceeds the lesser of 30 ft or one-third the distance between the static water level and the pump depth setting. For an accurate measure of well drawdown and how a well responds during periods of extended pumping, it is advisable to perform a pump test.

Pump testing

The success of a good open-loop installation ultimately depends on a successful pump test. For a new water well, the pump test can be performed at the time the well is drilled and will not need to be repeated. However, if the well has been in use for several years, it is best to perform a follow-up pump test to document pump capacity and current water level conditions. A pump test can be performed independently, or subcontracted to the contractor who services the pump and well system.

Figure 3-5. Pump test apparatus

An ideal pump test may run for up to 72 hours to simulate a long period of continuous operation. The water flow rate should be fixed to deliver a volume that allows for operation of the proposed geothermal equipment plus domestic loads. When the flow is adjusted properly, the pump should remain in constant operation without cycling. (A pump that cycles off and on during a pump test will render water level data useless). All water discharged for the pump test should pass through an in-line water filter. The filter is necessary to identify the presence of oxidized iron, sand, and sediment that may have an adverse impact on an open-loop installation (see Figure 3-5).

Pump tests typically are recorded on a graph, with the horizontal axis indicating elapsed time and the vertical axis indicating the water level. This places the initial portion of the graph within the first 100 minutes, when the change in water level is most pronounced (see Figure 3-6). The water level in the supply well should be measured before the test and at 5-minute intervals for the first half-hour of operation. Water level measurements may extend to an hour or longer for the first few hours and, if possible, twice daily thereafter until the test is terminated. The test may terminate once the drop in water level remains constant for at least three hours, or after 72 hours if the level continues to drop slowly. If the well pump catches air and loses flow, the test fails and must be terminated immediately. The ideal test will achieve equilibrium within one to three hours, proving that the pumping rate can be sustained for extended periods of time without depleting the water supply. For installations in which the pumping water level continues to recede and fails to stabilize over a 72-hour period, it is best to consider a closed-loop design. Once a pump test is terminated, the water well should recover to its original static water level within a period of time comparable to that in which the well attained equilibrium while pumping.

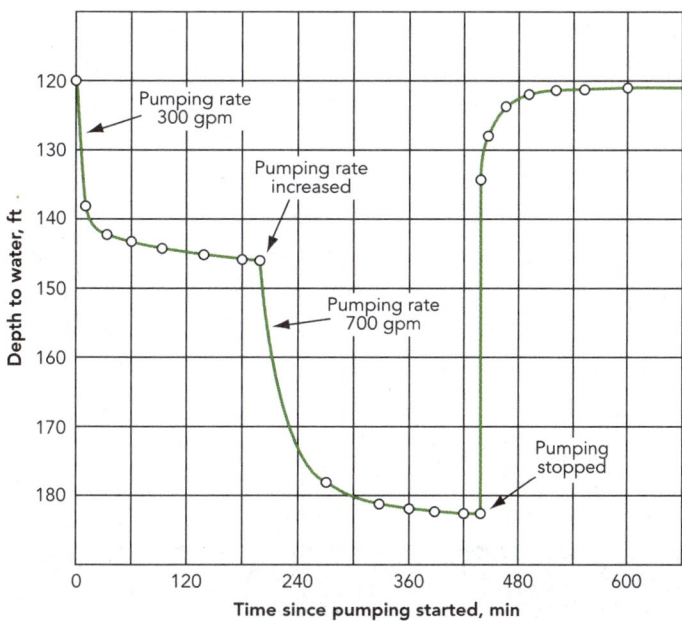

Figure 3-6. Drawdown pump test of high-capacity well (conducted at 300 and 700 gpm)

WATER DISCHARGE

The customary method of discharging water from an open-loop system is to pipe the outflow water to a surface feature. Lakes, streams, ponds, and drainage ditches are common discharge points. Some people may be disturbed by the thought of "wasting" the water. There are, however, many environmentally sound open-loop installations in which the discharge water is returned to the aquifer as "recharge." Prime examples of this capability abound in downtown Louisville, Kentucky, where the Gault House

Hotel and the Louisville Waterfront Office Building complex operate with 4,700 tons of geothermal equipment. The buildings are supplied from four water wells drilled into the river gravel deposits. Water discharge is returned via storm sewers to the river, where it again replenishes the sand and gravel aquifer from which it came.

Louisville is not alone in this endeavor, of course—there are homes and businesses all across the country that overlie massive deposits of sand and gravel and have easy access to shallow groundwater. Rural areas may use the spent well water to replenish ponds for livestock. Golf courses and ski resorts use their wells for heating and cooling lodges and clubhouses. After exchanging the "free Btus" from the water, the discharge is directed to a water hazard or secondary use for irrigation or snow-making. City water departments that depend on well water take advantage of its thermal potential for heating and cooling offices, fire stations, and maintenance facilities before sending it on to become treated water for distribution. Direct discharge to the surface becomes an issue only when the extraction rate from a well exceeds the recharge to the aquifer and water levels begin to decline—which would be evidenced by a continually receding water level during a pump test.

Alternatives to surface discharge

Infiltration tile. Field tile may be used as an infiltration field, with discharge water managed in the same way as it is in a sanitary infiltration (leaching field). These systems require close attention to detail and an incredibly high infiltration rate to succeed. Sanitary system designs are based on household sanitary discharge. Domestic loads may be as little as 40 to 60 gallons per person per day. A geothermal system, by contrast, may handle 7,000 to 14,000 gallons per day. Obviously, these water volumes are dramatically different. To be effective, an infiltration field must be installed in well-drained, sandy soil. If the project site allows for rainwater to infiltrate from surface depressions within an hour after a heavy rainfall, it is likely that soil permeability will be high enough to manage discharge from a geothermal system.

Typical field tile used for infiltration is packaged in flexible polyethylene coils with a sock filter wrapped around the exterior to prevent clogging with fine soil and discourage roots. Infiltration lines should be kept outside the home and should not penetrate the foundation wall. They are installed in much the same way as solid PVC drain lines, with an upturned riser pipe at the exterior foundation wall similar to that provided for a spouting drain. Infiltration lines should be in solid pipe for at least the first 20 ft leading away from the foundation to help prevent movement of the discharge water back toward the foundation and foundation drains. They should be set below the frost line and slope away from the source to encourage water to move away from the home and infiltrate along the length of the line. When possible, the lines should be tested with the same volume of water used by the geothermal system prior to covering the trenches. Visual observation of the water infiltration rate serves to validate operation of the infiltration trench and allows for extension of the line if conditions prove inadequate. Infiltration lines may need to operate when soil conditions are totally saturated, as might be the case during a spring snowmelt. To accommodate periods of total saturation, the infiltration line should have a surface discharge point at its far end or terminus to allow for release of excess water without causing a backup toward the home.

Return wells. In some cases, a return well may prove a viable means of recharging the spent geothermal water back to an aquifer. Return wells can be successful when the geologic formation consists of fractured or cavernous rock. A tight formation that has a significant drawdown as a supply well is likely to fail when used as a return well. Several factors need to be considered in planning for a return well:

➤ The fluid dynamics of a water supply well make it much easier to withdraw water from an aquifer than to force the water back into the same formation from which it came. Simply stated, most wells can "make" twice as much water as they can "take." When a well pump operates, water flows by gravity and barometric pressure along the hydraulic gradient toward the supply well. The flow toward the supply well originates many tens of feet from the well and increases in velocity as it nears the well bore. A useful comparison might be the way air "exhales" from a balloon. Now think of a return well as trying to inflate the balloon: The water must be forced under pressure against the minimal surface area of the well bore. A return well typically requires at least twice as much hydraulic pressure to force water back *into* a formation as it takes to withdraw or pump water *out of* the supply well. Figure 3-7 on the next page shows the relationship between an operating supply and return well. From the illustration, it is easy to see how a return well with a shallow water table will have a tendency to overflow.

➤ Water viscosity affects the ability of a return well to accept water. Warm water from the summer air conditioning cycle has a lower viscosity and is easier to recharge than is cold effluent from the winter heating cycle.

➤ Mineralization from carbonate minerals can reduce return well function. Water discharged to a return well normally is discharged at a lower pressure than that provided from the supply well. The reduction in water pressure from supply well to discharge well releases dissolved carbon dioxide from the water. The chemical equilibrium is upset and the water acquires a scale-forming tendency.

- Iron fouling is another significant factor in return well maintenance. Discharge water often is exposed to oxygen upon entering the return well. Oxygen contact can be avoided if a dip tube is used to extend the discharge water line to an elevation below the water level in the return well.
- An extended dip tube may eliminate the oxygen contact issue, but the dip tube itself can create additional problems. In an airtight system, a dip tube can create a siphon effect on discharge water lines that extends all the way back to the system water flow control valves. Negative pressure creates an extreme cavitation sound at flow restrictors and a pronounced water hammer effect as control valves close. The negative pressure created if the water table is more than 28 ft below the

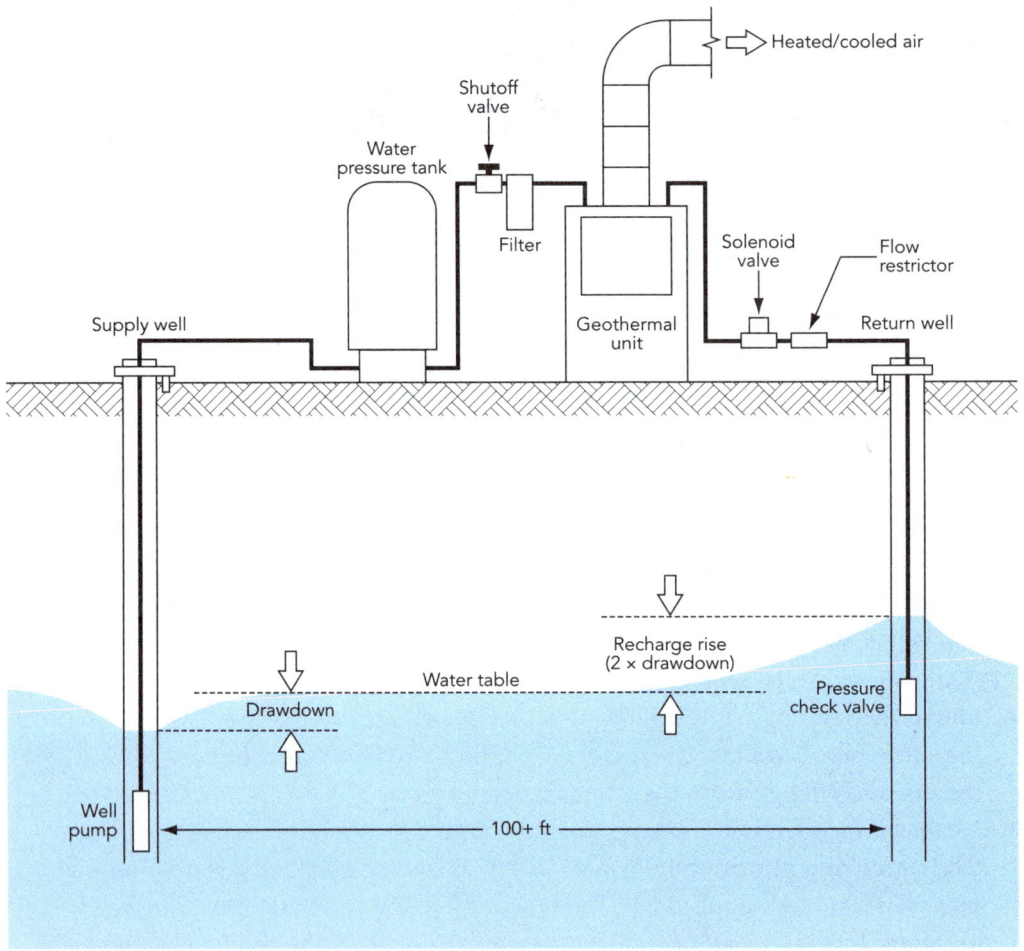

Figure 3-7. Open-loop system with return well

equipment elevation will exceed the vapor pressure of the water, causing the water to vaporize (boil off) at room temperature! The chemical reaction when this occurs is no different from scaling up a steam humidifier, and just as rapid.

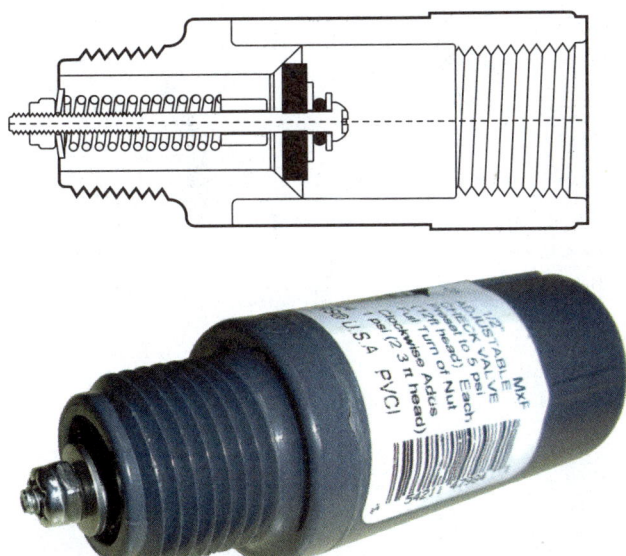

Figure 3-8. Adjustable spring check valve

➤ One solution to the siphon effect created by a dip tube is to install an adjustable pressure check valve or pinch valve at the bottom of the dip tube. For projects with a discharge water level within 30 ft of the equipment elevation, adjustable pressure check valves may be a practical solution. Adjustable pressure check valves like the one shown in Figure 3-8 are typically PVC and are adjustable up to ±15 psi (34 ft of head pressure). They must be preset and tested at the surface prior to mounting at the base of the dip tube and installation in the return well.

➤ Hydraulic pinch valves are industrial products designed to be used as shutoff devices for fluids carrying debris and solids. Some pinch valve manufacturers make valves that essentially act as adjustable pressure relief valves. As shown in Figure 3-9 on the next page, a pinch valve consists of an encased rubber tube that can be compressed (pinched) by air or hydraulic pressure to open, close, or restrict fluid flow. Pinch valve operation is managed by a pressure cell and $1/4$-in. pressure line to the surface, where the pressure can be adjusted to provide positive back pressure for the return line while the system is at rest and yet allow passage of fluid during operation. Due to the commercial nature of pinch valves, they typically are used with larger-diameter wells and commercial projects.

➤ Many factors are involved in selecting the location of a return well. It is best to consult with a ground water professional familiar with the hydraulics of local aquifers. Typically, low-tonnage residential applications should maintain at least 150 ft between supply and return wells. In this respect, the greater the separation is, the less likely it is that there will be thermal "communication" between supply and return wells that could interfere with system operation. Commercial installations generally require substantially greater distances between supply and return, with calculations based on the thickness of the penetrated aquifer, aquifer permeability, the hydraulic gradient, and the thermal mass of the area of influence between supply and return wells and how it relates to the volume and temperature of water discharged on an annual basis.

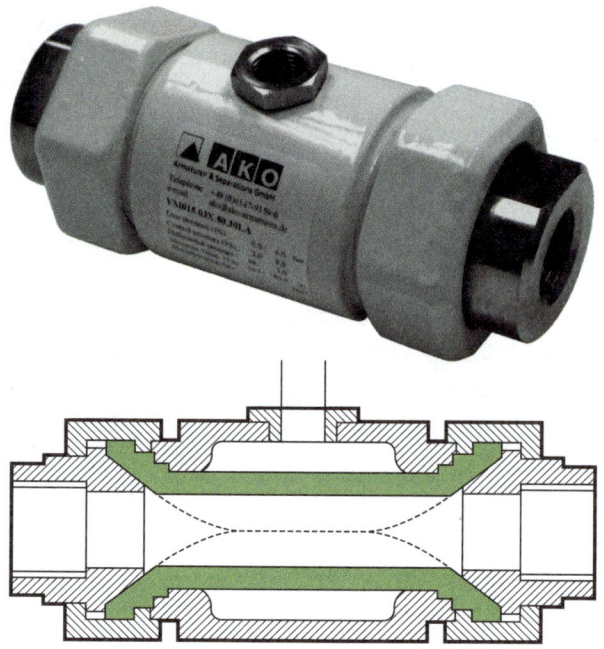

Figure 3-9. Pinch valve

SUGGESTIONS FOR A SUCCESSFUL INSTALLATION

Open-loop systems can be highly reliable when the proper precautions are taken with their selection and installation. A review of these guidelines for avoiding and dealing with problems follows:

> - Use caution when well water must be supplied from a pumping water level in excess of 100 ft. With increased pumping head, pumping horsepower must increase and total system efficiency is reduced. The pumping watt penalty in documented open-loop installations with pumping levels in excess of 300 ft can reduce the efficiency of a ground-source heat pump from a customary COP of 4.5 to a value of less than 2. In such situations, the designer must make a close examination into cost-effectiveness and potential savings to justify the installation.
> - Avoid water supplies that are subject to excessive drawdown when the pump runs. A good rule of thumb is to limit drawdown to 30 ft for deeper wells, or one-third

the distance between the static water level and the pump setting for shallow wells, whichever is less. The pressure differential across the near-well formation created by a greater drawdown in water level promotes the precipitation of minerals and the eventual clogging of the formation. Well maintenance to clean and restore water flow is more likely to be required in wells that experience dramatic drawdown during pump operation.

- Avoid raw water supplies that show evidence of heavy iron precipitation. Heavy elemental iron accumulation on water filters indicates that the water supply has been subject to exposure either to oxygen or to iron bacteria prior to its entry to the well. Heavy iron precipitate will reduce system and pumping efficiency, creating maintenance issues that are likely to negate any savings provided by the geothermal system.
- Maintain water under pressure from the water supply to the discharge side of the geothermal system at all times. Place flow restrictors and water solenoid valves on the discharge side of the geothermal system to maintain the heat exchangers under full pressure whenever the system is not in operation.
- Avoid the use of ferrous metals (galvanized and black iron fittings) when working with raw water. Ferrous metals are low in the galvanic series and are the first to be corroded.
- Use PVC for interior water piping to avoid pipe corrosion issues.
- Oversize water supply and return pipe to reduce pressure drop and flow velocity. Reduced flow velocity minimizes the water hammer effect as a valve closes. Increased pipe size provides a safety factor if a water supply is likely to cause fouling or incrustation.
- Interior water discharge lines that run to surface drainage must be maintained with a trap prior to their discharge point to prevent air and oxygen from entering the discharge line and initiating mineral deposits.
- Exterior water discharge lines for surface discharge should be oversized, typically 3- or 4-in. PVC solid pipe with a cleanout riser outside the foundation wall. Glue-joint PVC pipe provides a sturdy material immune to penetration by landscaping roots and foundation vegetation. Solid glue-joint pipe directs the water away from the foundation to prevent backflow and excess load on foundation drains.
- Discharge 3- or 4-in. pipe is best laid with a $1/4$-in. per foot grade to the final outlet point. If discharging to a surface area, the pipe does not need to be buried below the frost line, as long as the pipe has a grade and drains itself without trapping water within the frost depth.
- Discharge to a pond should be above the highest water level to prevent the possible formation of ice in the discharge line.

- ▶ If discharging to a field tile for infiltration into the ground, the discharge line should be below frost depth.
- ▶ Installations should incorporate boiler drains and ball valve shutoff valves at the geothermal equipment (see Figure 3-10). Boiler drains facilitate the use of compressed air to blow out heat exchangers and discharge piping. Air purging of the heat exchanger and water lines will dislodge most of the iron deposits created by the vast majority of problem water supplies. If air purging of the heat exchanger is followed up with a thermal shock process (freezing the heat exchanger while purged with compressed air), the frost developed within the iron-coated heat exchanger piping will be loosened by the frost action and can be flushed from the system when the water is turned back on. This process rarely needs to be repeated more than twice to clear a fouled heat exchanger completely and restore system capacity. The compressed air and thermal shock process is less hazardous and time-consuming than traditional acid flush procedures for cleaning heat exchangers and piping.
- ▶ All open-loop installations should incorporate inline strainers with 30-mesh screens to stop small grit and debris from interfering with solenoid valve operation (see

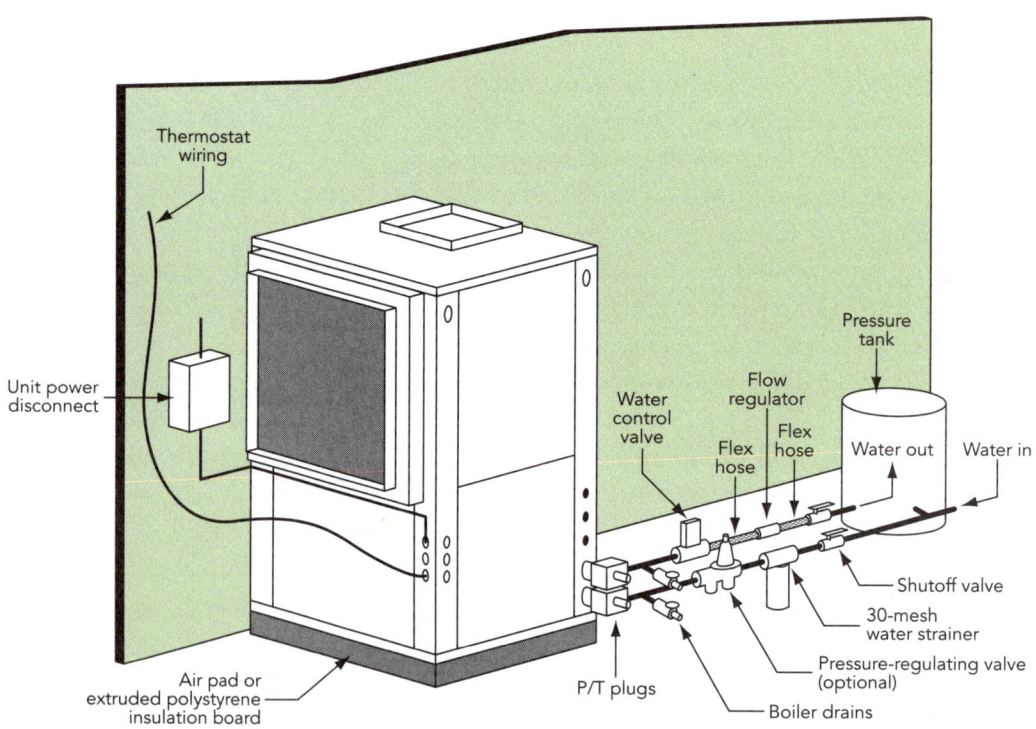

Figure 3-10. Typical open-loop/well application

the spin-down sediment filter shown in Figure 3-11). Inline strainers sold at home improvement stores typically have fine, 100- or 120-mesh screens that are too tight and will plug rapidly with the lightest sediment. Avoid the use of fine-mesh screens when installing a geothermal system.

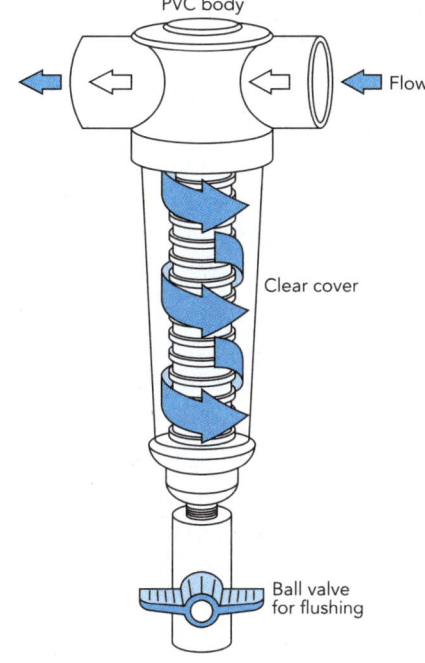

Figure 3-11. Spin-down sediment filter

➤ Well pumps should be sized to allow for operation of the geothermal system plus normal house loads at the same time. A pump should be sized to operate within the peak area of its efficiency curve.

➤ Water pressure tanks used with geothermal systems should be of the bladder type, which isolate the pre-charged tank air from the well water provided by the pump. Avoiding air contact helps maintain dissolved iron in solution, thus reducing the potential for oxidation.

➤ Water pressure tanks should be sized to prevent pump short-cycling. An ideal pump and tank installation will limit the pump to six cycles per hour or less. More frequent pump cycles can lead to premature failure of the pump wiring, motor, and starting components.

➤ One way to size an expansion tank is to specify a tank with a water delivery capacity that is twice the gpm volume of the pump. Be careful not to confuse delivery capacity with tank volume. For example, a bladder-type water tank typically contains two-thirds compressed air and one-third water. With this in mind, the design maximum delivery capacity for an 80-gallon tank is in the range of 24 to 26 gallons, which is adequate for a pump that operates at 12 gpm.

➤ Follow the manufacturer's recommendations for the open-loop water temperature and flow rate for the system at your project location. Most geothermal systems require an open-loop flow of 1.5 gpm for water temperatures above 50°F. This flow rate must increase for the heating mode to as much as 3 gpm per ton at an entering water temperature of 40°F. Equipment that must operate with water temperatures below 40°F is better used in a closed-loop system design with antifreeze to prevent ice formation within the heat exchanger.

SUMMARY

An open-loop geothermal system is one of the most cost-effective means of utilizing a ground-source heat pump (GSHP). The constant temperature provided by well water produces uniform capacity and consistent high efficiency for both heating and cooling. Unlike closed-loop GSHPs, whose performance varies with loop temperature, open-loop systems are able to maintain full design capacity and efficiency under the most extreme conditions, in both summer and winter. In northern climates, the winter loop temperature of a closed-loop GSHP often falls below the freezing point, causing frost to accumulate under and around the insulated coaxial heat exchangers. As the frost melts, the resultant residual moisture contributes to rusting and pit corrosion of the steel-jacketed heat exchangers, leading to their eventual failure. Open-loop geothermal systems operate at substantially higher temperatures and are not subject to the same degree of condensation and frost accumulation as their closed-loop cousins. The reduced potential for condensation, coupled with a "dry" open-loop heat exchanger, dramatically lessen the potential for a corrosion failure. From this author's experience, coaxial heat exchangers in open-loop systems appear to outlast their closed-loop counterparts by as much as ten years, with many open systems surviving for 30 years or longer.

Open-loop systems have a definite advantage over closed-loop systems in both installed cost and efficiency, especially when the water supply is clean, plentiful, and easily returned back to its source or to surface features. In many instances, a single high-capacity water well may be sufficient to provide the needed thermal energy for several hundred tons of geothermal equipment. The potential savings realized by using an open-loop system for a commercial installation can easily reduce the project cost by 40 to 50% over that of a closed-loop system. Commercial open-loop systems have found wide appeal for applications in which ground water or industrial process water is in plentiful supply. One need only look to a number of large-scale projects that utilize this advantage—many are located along riverfront properties in cities like Pittsburgh, PA, Seattle, WA, Louisville, KY, and Dayton, OH. Others are found in a multitude of sites across the country where shallow groundwater is in abundant supply.

For situations in which the water supply may come from a swimming pool or is brackish or acidic—as might be the case for installations in coastal areas or for district heating and cooling systems that operate with water from abandoned mines—heat exchangers constructed from cupronickel, stainless steel, or titanium offer alternatives for managing aggressive waters but still allow for direct use of the supply water.

When the water supply has a tendency to cause scaling or fouling of piping and heat exchangers, large commercial systems can utilize well or process water in a hybrid open-loop/closed-loop fashion. Isolating the raw water from the building loop with a plate-frame heat exchanger creates a treated "closed loop" for the geothermal units and an "open loop" on the raw-water side of the system. In such instances, the use of two or more plate-frame heat exchangers allows a heat exchanger to be isolated for cleaning and maintenance without shutting down the entire system.

Generally speaking, when provided with a plentiful, clean, non-fouling source of water, the open-loop method provides the most economical and efficient way to install a GSHP. However, the integrity of an open-loop installation and its operation can be ensured only when the installing contractor has a thorough understanding of the water source, its quality, the water delivery system, and all related controls. A complete grasp of the total system on the part of the installing contractor has a direct impact on the service, maintenance, and reliability of any open-loop system.

ILLUSTRATION CREDITS
FIGURE 3-1: JOHNSON CONTROLS
FIGURE 3-2: ENO SCIENTIFIC
FIGURE 3-4: OHIO DEPARTMENT OF NATURAL RESOURCES
FIGURE 3-5: JEFF PERSONS
FIGURE 3-8: SPEARS MANUFACTURING CO.
FIGURE 3-9: ALB. KLEIN OHIO LLC
FIGURE 3-10: CLIMATEMASTER
FIGURE 3-11: CAMPBELL MANUFACTURING, INC.

◀CHAPTER FOUR▶
Closed-Loop Systems

INTRODUCTION

Closed-loop geothermal installations are seen as a reliable way to achieve geothermal efficiencies for systems that are installed in areas where well water is not available, of poor quality or insufficient quantity, or unable to be used because of code requirements or ecological reasons. A wide variety of piping materials and methods have been used over the past 30-plus years. Current technology focuses on the use of high-density polyethylene pipe, typically specified as standard dimension ratio 11 (SDR11) and rated for 160 psi with an ASTM minimum cell classification of PE345464C per ASTM D-3350. Polyethylene pipe is joined by a fusion welding process that heats the pipe to temperatures as high as 500°F. The junctions made by this process are stronger than the pipe material and ensure a leak-free connection when proper procedures are followed. After flushing, closed-loop systems are filled with water in warm climates or an antifreeze solution in cold climates. With a clean solution, a closed-loop geothermal system should function for the lifetime of the equipment without the need to clean a heat exchanger or replace the system fluid. Reduced maintenance is one of the chief reasons for selecting a closed-loop system (as opposed to an open-loop system, which has a greater likelihood not only of requiring maintenance, but also of consuming a fresh water resource).

A variant of closed-loop technology uses the complete burial of copper refrigerant lines within the earth. This is known as the *direct expansion* (DX) geothermal method. Several manufacturers specialize in the production of DX systems. The refrigerant management methods utilized by these manufacturers and the manner in which the copper-tube loops are designed and installed are "system specific." For that reason, DX geothermal systems will not be covered in this text. While many of the basic principles still apply, the design and installation of a DX geothermal loop is best managed under the direction of the manufacturer.

Contrary to information promoted on the Internet—or, for that matter, in system sales courses—the design of closed-loop installations is *not* a "one size fits all" proposition. Contractors are strongly urged to take IGSHPA's geothermal Accredited Installer Workshop course to acquire a more thorough working knowledge of soil and rock heat transfer and how the thermal conductivity of various soils and rock types can affect the design of geothermal loops. Technicians who successfully complete the IGSHPA exam receive both IGSHPA accreditation and NATE certification. Professional accreditation is a valuable credential to carry and is widely required for participation in many residential, commercial, and public works projects.

Loop sizing (that is, determining the required length of individual loop circuits) is a function managed by loop design software and the input information provided by the installing contractor. Such software simplifies what was once the equivalent of 40 hours worth of manual calculations. Loop design software takes into account the local degree-hour weather data, the heat loss and heat gain of the structure, soil temperature conditions at the proper burial depth, the soil or rock type and its water content, the type of loop to be installed, and the design loop maximum and minimum temperature.

With respect to design parameters, the best-performing loops are those that are buried in wet, saturated soil and designed with a minimum temperature of 30°F or warmer and a maximum temperature of 90°F or cooler. Contractors are advised to exercise caution when using "default" settings, which may set minimum and maximum temperatures at 27°F and 100°F, respectively. These settings will result in a loop design that calls for the minimum length needed. If the thermal conductivity of the soil or rock is less than optimum, the system may run over or under temperature and "fault out" on its safety controls. No contractor needs an "albatross" application that creates a bad reputation. For example, the seemingly simple assumption that a loop will be in wet, saturated soil 24/7 will lead to problems if the soil proves to be dry and well-drained (a situation that would require nearly three times the effective heat exchange length). In such a scenario, a system installed with the minimum length loop would be destined for failure in its first or second season of operation.

The following types of closed-loop designs are commonly profiled in manufacturers' software:
- vertical loops
- horizontal directional-bore loops
- horizontal trench loops
- lake and pond loops.

VERTICAL LOOPS

Single-bore loops

Single-bore loops typically use 1¼-in. or 2-in. high-density polyethylene (HDPE) pipe. Single-bore loops are characteristic of applications in which the surface area for drilling is limited and the geologic formation allows for the drilling of a single well. Single wells that use 1¼-in. heat exchangers are usually less than 600 ft in total depth and may accommodate ±3 tons of heat exchange capacity. Figure 4-1 shows a single-bore vertical loop.

There are several steps involved in testing and installing a vertical heat exchanger. As the well-drilling process reaches its design depth, the loop pipe (equipped with a return "U"-bend fitting, as shown in Figure 4-2 on the next page) is filled with clean water and pressure-tested. The hydrostatic test serves two purposes. Its primary purpose is to verify the integrity of the vertical heat exchanger prior to insertion into the well. The second purpose is to add weight to the pipe, creating a neutral buoyancy and facilitating its insertion to the total well depth.

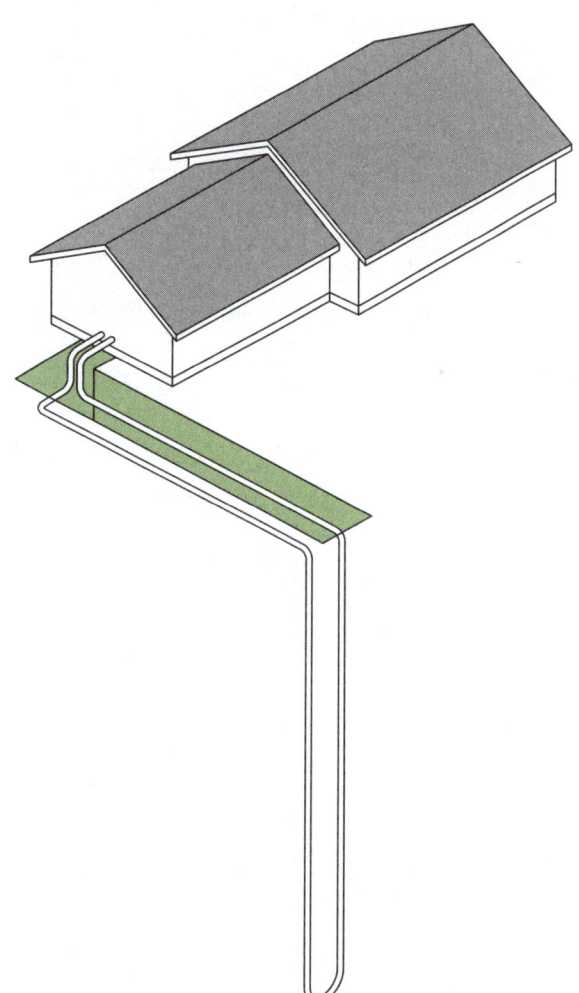

Figure 4-1. Single-bore vertical loop

CLOSED-LOOP SYSTEMS **61**

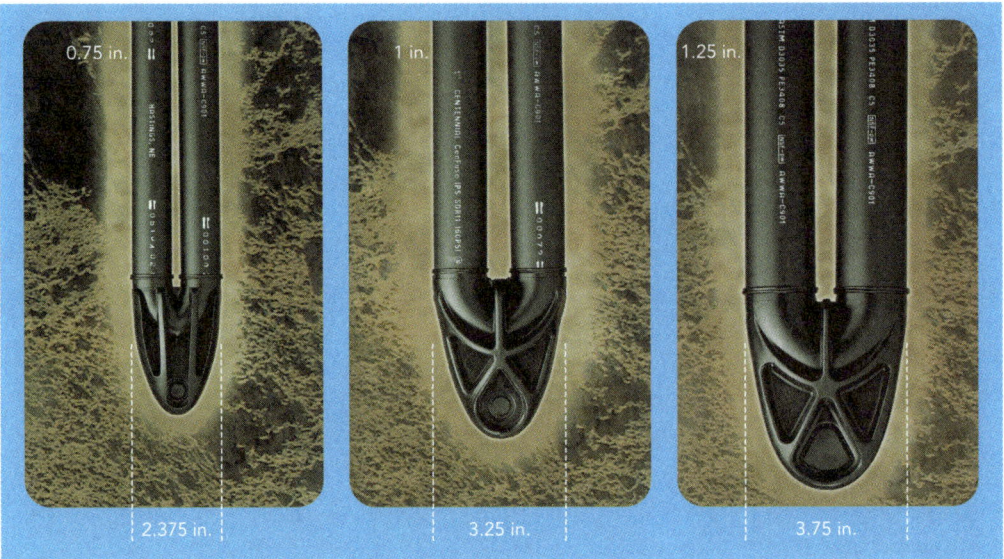

Figure 4-2. Typical "U"-bend fittings

Prior to insertion, a 10-ft section of $1/2$-in. rebar is taped to the lead section to hold the loop lines vertical as they are lowered into the borehole. Finally, just before insertion, a third pipe (called a "tremie pipe") is loosely strapped to the assembly. The tremie pipe serves to deliver a bentonite clay grout, which fills the well from the bottom to the top and displaces any water and drilling fluid contained within the well bore. As the bentonite grout is pumped into the well, the tremie pipe is withdrawn for use in the next well. The grout forms a heat-conducting sanitary seal that promotes heat transfer between the loop lines and the formation. As a sanitary seal, the grout also prevents cross-communication between aquifers of differing quality and contamination from surface sources.

The best heat transfer for a vertical geothermal well is achieved when a borehole penetrates a formation with a high standing water table. Formations that are dry or in which contact with the local water table is minimal may require the use of a "thermally enhanced" bentonite grout. Conventional bentonite grout, when placed in a dry borehole, is subject to drying as the loop warms in the air conditioning mode. As the grout dries and dehydrates, it develops shrinkage cracks and may lose much of its initial thermal transfer with the surrounding formation. In these instances, the use of a thermally enhanced grout (which may contain up to 75% silica sand) will reduce the potential for shrinkage and help maintain thermal contact with the formation.

Sometimes two vertical heat exchangers are inserted in the same well bore. The double heat exchanger assemblies are prefabricated and shipped to the project site as coiled bundles. You might think that this technique would double the heat transfer potential of a single well bore, but the physics of radial heat transfer dictate that the process actually results in a steady-state heat transfer improvement of between 11 and 20%. Steady-state heat transfer is ultimately limited by the thermal conductivity of the surrounding formation, not necessarily by the number of tubes in the well bore. The use of double "U"-tube heat exchangers can be an advantage in situations where drilling costs are high or the surface area for drilling is limited.

Multiple-bore series loops

Multiple-bore series loops were standard practice for geothermal loops installed in the early 1980s. Typically, the geothermal wells used vertical heat exchangers fabricated from HDPE pipe ranging in size from $1^{1}/_{4}$ in. to as large as 2 in. These early systems were designed so that each vertical well was connected in series with the next well. When using series-connected wells, the installer needed to pay close attention to piping pressure drop and pump sizing to assure adequate circulation for the geothermal equipment. Calculating pressure drop for the series loop was as easy as adding up the straight lengths of pipe and the equivalent lengths for the elbows, and then selecting a pump to manage the pressure drop and flow rate for the geothermal equipment. The hard part came when it was time to flush and fill a series loop. Air trapped in the surface-level connector lines needed to be forced down each of the series verticals before it could circulate back to the flush cart. The pumping head for flushing quickly became the additive value of the "P"-trap depth created by each vertical well in the series. For flushing and purging, pumps with pressure capabilities in excess of 120 psi often were needed to clear the air from these multiple-well vertical loops. Once purged, these series systems worked very well. However, the larger vertical loop sizes—as great as 2 in. in diameter—meant that these systems had a substantially higher installed cost (due to the larger-diameter wells, the additional grout needed to accommodate the wells, larger and more costly pipe, and up to four times as much antifreeze as is needed for parallel vertical loop designs that function with smaller-dimension HDPE pipe).

To minimize loop cost, most installers prefer to work with the smaller-diameter well bores and pipe sizes made possible with parallel vertical loop designs. There are, however, times in which a parallel loop design might be modified to incorporate one or more series-connected wells. This situation occurs when an adverse drilling condition prevents a well bore from attaining the specified depth. In such cases, the well field may need to be redesigned to add additional wells or create one or more series-connected wells whose combined loop length equals the specified length of the initial well. Adapting to a series circuit does not detract from the heat exchange capability of the loop design—it simply divides the heat exchange between two or more wells to meet the installed length requirement.

For economic reasons (trenching, fusion fittings and labor), it is generally accepted that a depth of 50 ft is the practical minimum for vertical wells. Figure 4-3 below shows a multiple-bore vertical loop piped in a series configuration.

Multiple-bore parallel loops

Multiple-bore parallel loops constitute the vast majority of vertical loop installations. Well depths may vary by application and required heat transfer. Well depths for most applications range between 150 and 300 ft. The classic design for most multiple-bore parallel loop installations calls for a single "U"-tube heat exchanger in each well. This design is the result of several factors intended to maximize heat transfer while reducing cost. For residential projects, the geothermal pipe used for each vertical loop is typically either ¾-in or 1-in. polyethylene pipe, specified as SDR11 and rated for 160 psi. The smaller pipe has several advantages over the 1¼-in. pipe used for series loops:

➤ Smaller vertical loop lines allow for insertion in a smaller-diameter well.
➤ Reduced-diameter wells generally are easier and faster to drill.

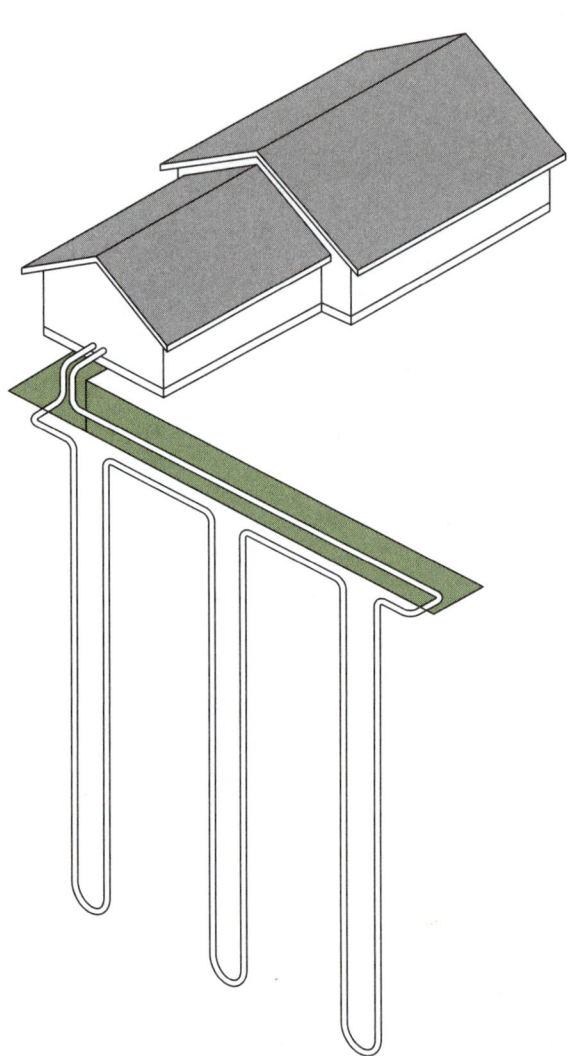

Figure 4-3. Multiple-bore vertical loop

- ➤ Reduction in well volume reduces grout material cost.
- ➤ Reduction in pipe size reduces fluid volume and antifreeze cost.
- ➤ Smaller pipes reduce piping material cost.
- ➤ Reduced wall thickness of the smaller loop pipe allows for improved heat transfer per square foot of pipe wall surface in contact with the well grout.

Figure 4-4 shows a multiple-bore vertical installation with the loops connected in a parallel configuration. Manifolds for parallel loops use a *reverse-return* design to equalize the flow between the supply line and the return line for each individual loop. As illustrated in Figure 4-5 on the next page, the first circuit on the supply manifold becomes the last circuit on the return manifold. Each successive circuit follows the same sequence. In this manner, the pressure drop for the manifold piping is equalized for all circuits and each circuit receives the same fluid flow regardless of the circulation volume.

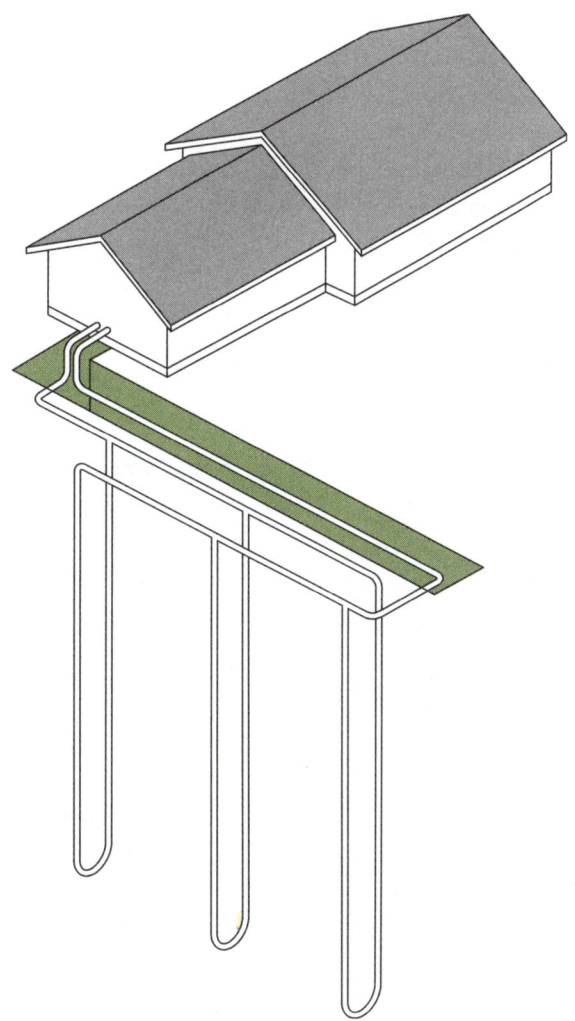

Figure 4-4. Multiple-bore vertical loop with reverse return

HORIZONTAL DIRECTIONAL-BORE LOOPS

Horizontal directional boring equipment was developed for the utility industry to facilitate the installation of underground utility lines without disruption to the surface.

The same technology has rapidly gained a foothold as a cost-effective means of installing geothermal loop lines. Figure 4-6 shows directional boring equipment in use. Of course, no single drilling method is well-suited for all conditions.

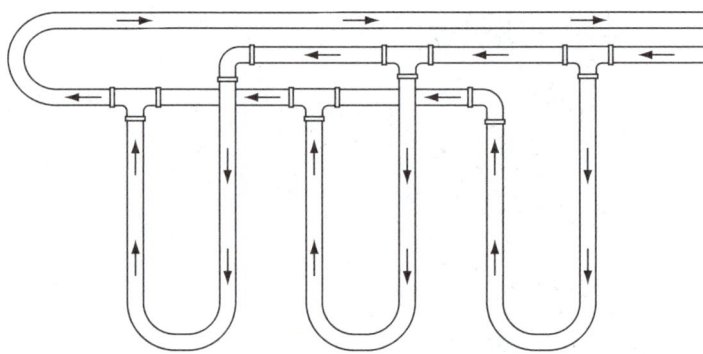

Figure 4-5. Reverse-return piping

Directional boring requires moist clay or silty clay soil for successful geothermal applications. If sand, areas of gravel and cobbles, hardpan, or bedrock are encountered, the drilling process can be compromised and alternative looping methods may be necessary. Drilling fluids used for directional boring must be designed to help break the ionic bonds in the clay soils that they penetrate. Once the ionic bonds are broken, the clay becomes less cohesive. This allows for easier drilling and the settlement of the clay soil around the loop lines improves. Bentonite grout used in horizontal

Figure 4-6. Directional boring for geothermal loop

Figure 4-7. Beveled boring bit

directional boring is the same as that used in vertical loop installations. While the lines are technically grouted in as they are pulled back, the integrity of the grout is highly dependent on soil moisture for its thermal conductivity. A dry grout, like a clay soil, will have a tendency to shrink and lose thermal contact with the loop lines.

Directional boring methods generally involve drilling a series of horizontal bores from a common manifold location. A typical target boring depth is 10 ft, with a length determined by the dimensions of the property. Depending on soil conditions, boring lengths may range from 160 to 300 ft per ton.

To help guide the boring tools, the drill head has a beveled face (see Figure 4-7) and a positional transmitter that reports to a surface receiver. The receiver operator tracks the movement of the drill bit as it progresses and signals the machine operator to stop rotation if an obstacle is encountered. Once the beveled drill bit has been positioned in a new direction, hydraulic pressure is used to push the bit without rotation. The bevel on the bit essentially "steers" or guides the bit in the direction of the bevel, allowing the drilling process to change elevation or move to the left or right of an obstacle.

Figure 4-8. Pulling back loop lines

As drilling progresses to the design length, the bit is directed from its 10-ft depth back up to the surface. At the surface, a pulling shackle and cable harness are attached between the free end of the sealed geothermal loop lines and the boring bit. Each loop line with its "U" bend is then pulled back to the manifold area at the boring machine (see Figure 4-8), as Bentonite grout is pumped through the drill stem to lubricate and seal the bore. When this process is practical, horizontal directional boring can allow geothermal loops to be installed under paved driveways, parking lots, landscaping, utilities, and outbuildings with shallow foundations.

HORIZONTAL TRENCH LOOPS

Single-pipe, single-trench loops

Single-pipe, single-trench loops, commonly referred to as "race track" loops, use a single loop line in one big circuit (see Figure 4-9). Single-pipe loops normally are constructed from 1¼-in. or 1½-in. SDR11 polyethylene pipe. The loop pipe is placed in a narrow trench, typically 4 to 6 in. wide, created by a chain trencher. Pipe burial depth depends on the loop design and on the capability of the trenching equipment. Common burial depth ranges from 4 to 6 ft. Prior to placing the geothermal loop line, installers inspect the trenches and remove any rocks that may compromise the piping. Once the loop line is positioned in the bottom of the trench, clean backfill is bladed into the trench. Whenever possible, trench loops should allow for the addition of water to enhance the settling process. Adding water by garden hose during the backfill process accelerates settlement and improves initial system efficiency. Positioning the loop to take advantage of natural drainage by trenching across a drainage slope or swale can also help enhance surface water infiltration to saturate and improve heat transfer.

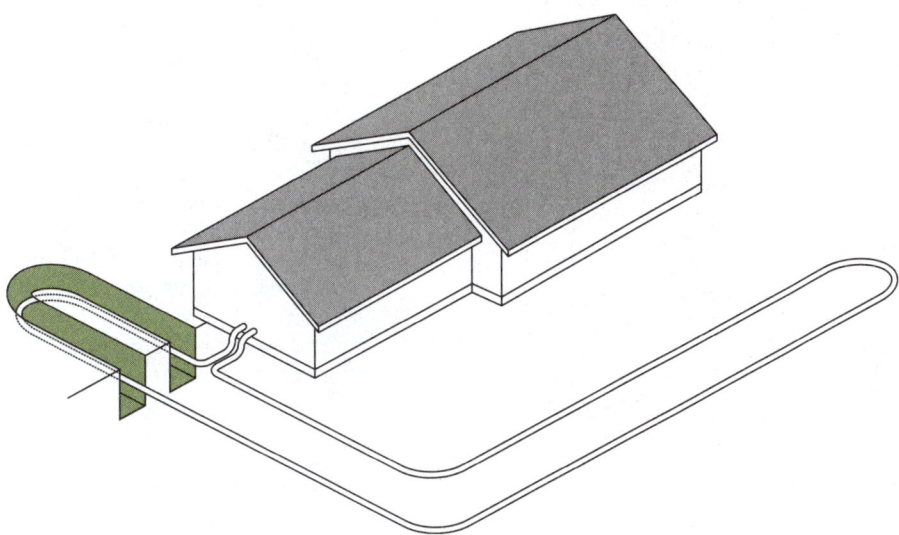

Figure 4-9. Single-pipe horizontal loop

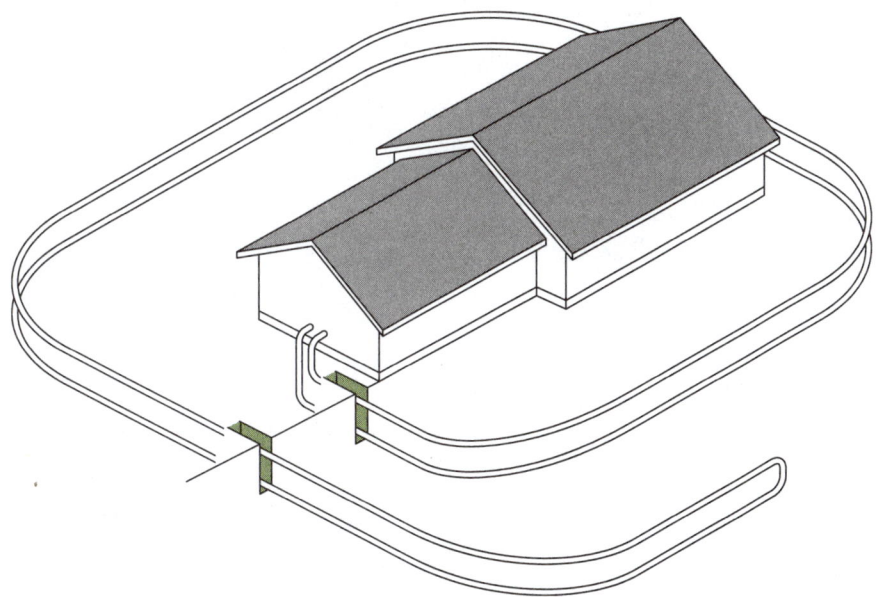

Figure 4-10. Double-pipe horizontal loop

Multiple-pipe, single-trench loops

Double-pipe, single-trench loops. *Double-pipe, single-trench loops* are a variation of the "race track" loop. Instead of making a large "out and back" loop in a single long trench, the double-pipe loop folds over on itself and follows the same trench back to the starting point (see Figure 4-10 on the previous page). Double-pipe loops can be configured with one pipe above the other, or side by side in a wider trench. Burial depths for vertically positioned double-pipe loops are typically at 6 ft (bottom pipe) and 4 ft (top pipe), or at 5 ft and 3 ft. Again, the depth depends on the loop design and on the capability of the trenching equipment. Double-pipe loops require less trench but use slightly more pipe. Due to the thermal interference that can occur between the two lines sharing the same trench, it is important to identify each line, with the shallow line as the "outgoing" line and the deeper line as the "return"

> Narrow, multiple-pipe, single-trench installations that require workers to enter the trench in order to position and secure loop lines are by far the most dangerous in which to work. The danger of a cave-in is a constant and life-threatening hazard. OSHA regulations limit trench depth to 5 ft when soil conditions are stable. These same regulations require that the sides be "laid back" when conditions indicate an unstable soil. Any excavation in excess of 5 ft must have the side walls laid back or provide a movable trench box to maintain worker safety.

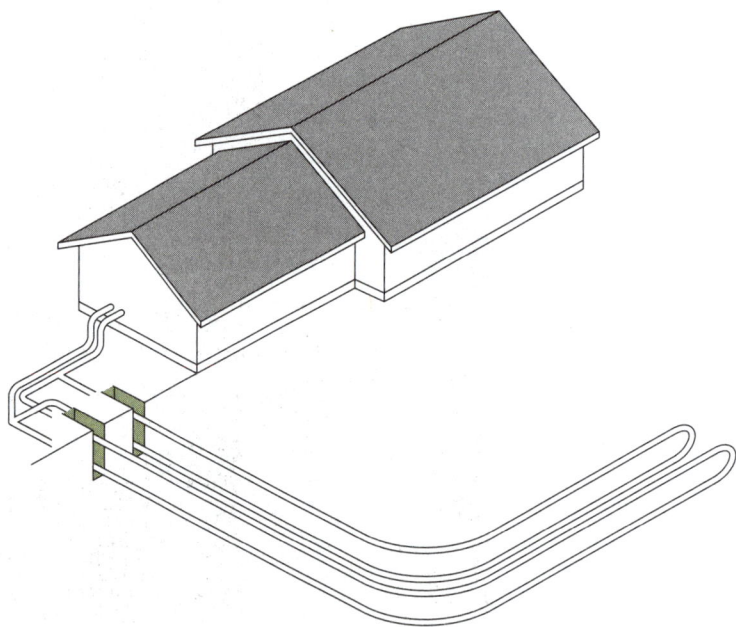

Figure 4-11. Double-pipe horizontal loop (parallel configuration)

line. This promotes counterflow heat exchange for better efficiency. Failure to provide counterflow fluid circulation in a vertically positioned double-pipe loop will result in poor thermal performance.

Double-pipe parallel loops. *Double-pipe parallel loops* rely on reverse-return manifolds (see Figure 4-11). Material costs and antifreeze volume are reduced by using smaller-diameter ¾-in. or 1-in. polyethylene pipe for the loop circuits. Residential systems of up to 6 tons typically connect ¾-in. or 1-in. loop circuits to 1¼-in. or larger manifold lines. Manifold line sizes depend on the system flow rate, pressure drop, and distance from manifold to equipment. Trenching and backfill methods are the same as for single-pipe and double-pipe horizontal trench loops. Loop circuit length is dependent on soil and operating conditions and may range from 400 to 1,000 ft per ton of system capacity.

Figure 4-12 illustrates safe practice for the installation of a double-pipe parallel loop. The damp, silty, sandy, weathered bedrock soil at this project site has poor trench wall stability. In such locations, trench wall cave-in is a constant threat. The loop line is laid out on the surface so that both lines can be positioned in the trench as the excavator progresses. Field technicians work safely from the surface. If a trench wall should

Figure 4-12. Installing loop lines safely

cave in, the loop lines are already in place and there is no need to clean out the cave-in area or adapt the loop to go over or around the cave-in.

Four-pipe and six-pipe parallel loops. *Four-pipe and six-pipe parallel loops* are a variation of the double-pipe parallel loop described above. The four-pipe and six-pipe loop designs (see Figures 4-13 and 4-14) find application on projects in which space for trenching is limited and excavations can be made with a backhoe.

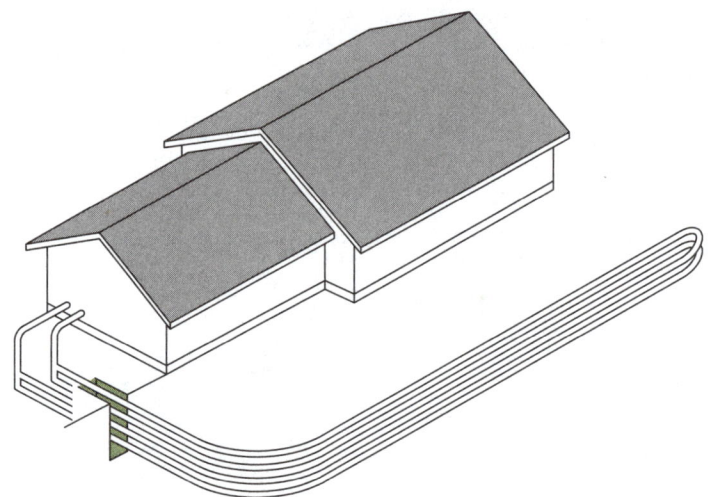

Figure 4-13. Four-pipe horizontal loop (parallel configuration)

The typical four-pipe or six-pipe trench is 2 ft wide and 5 ft (or more) deep. Individual loop lines are laid along the bottom of the trench. Landscape staples are used to hold the lines in position. When the outgoing lines reach the design trench length, expanded-radius bends loop the return lines up against the sides of the trench, where additional landscape staples are used to hold the lines in place.

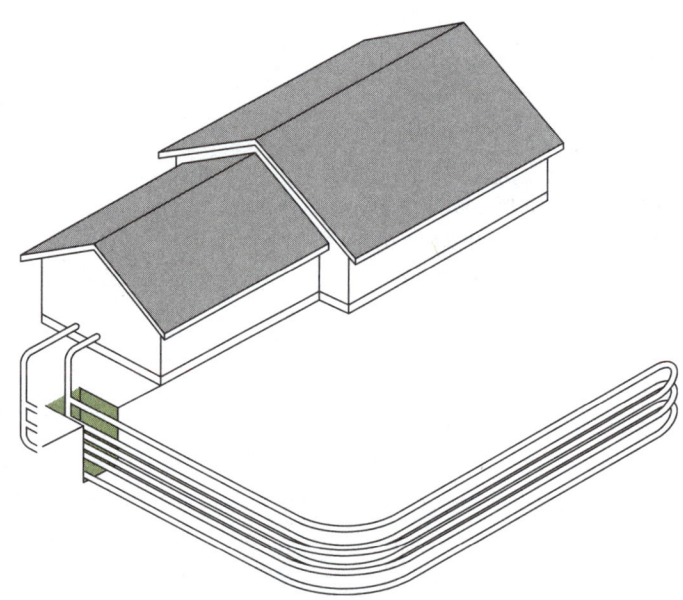

Figure 4-14. Six-pipe horizontal loop (parallel configuration)

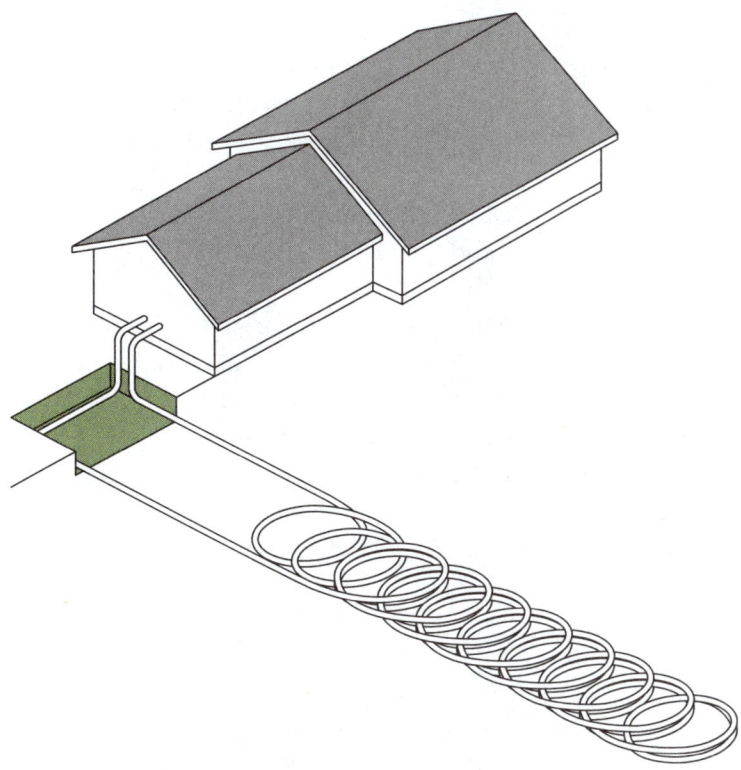

Figure 4-15. Compact slinky loop

Once all lines are in position, backfill minus any rock and coarse debris is bladed into the trench as cover for the lines. Watering to saturate the trench helps speed the settling process.

Slinky loops. *Slinky loops* are a more recent advancement in horizontal loop design. The "compact slinky" is formed by overlapping multiple loops of polyethylene pipe, each about 3 ft in diameter (see Figure 4-15). The amount of overlap between adjacent coils is called the "pitch." Slinky loops may be assembled in the field prior to laying them in the trench, or fabricated off-site during "downtime" between projects. Several factors have led to the popularity of slinky loops among installers:

➤ The needed heat transfer can be attained in a shorter and wider trench.
➤ For a given soil type, a compact slinky with an overlapping pitch can be adapted to a trench that is one-third the length of a standard double-pipe loop.
➤ An "extended slinky" with 18 to 20 in. of separation between the loops requires a trench that is about two-thirds the length of a comparable double-pipe loop.

> Worker hazard from wall movement is reduced. The wide trench required for a slinky loop allows workers to step away from a slumping trench wall.
> The use of a large backhoe or trackhoe makes excavation for a slinky trench faster and provides the ability to remove large rocks and boulders that may interfere with the horizontal loops.
> Slinky loop installation time can be minimized by prefabricating the loops, which can be rolled up for transport and then rolled out in the excavated trench.

While slinky loops offer many advantages, including speed of installation and greater worker safety in the trench, they require the same careful consideration of soil type, moisture content, and loop length as do traditional loops. A compact slinky placed in dry soil will quickly exceed the dry soil's heat transfer capability, causing the loop to run over or under temperature. Dry soil conditions typically require up to 1,000 ft of loop pipe per ton of system capacity. Additional loop pipe and an extended slinky loop design provide assurance that the loop will perform as intended, even in dry soil. Figure 4-16 shows an extended slinky loop of the kind needed to accommodate the desired heat transfer under dry soil conditions.

LAKE AND POND LOOPS

Lake and pond loops provide an economical alternative to horizontal and vertical loops. Three basic types of pond loops are in common use. They are: coiled pipe loops, slinky mat loops, and lake plate heat exchanger loops. The heat transfer provided by direct water contact and the resulting convection currents (created by the thermal difference between the loop exchanger and the

Figure 4-16. Extended slinky loop

pond water) allow for a 50% reduction in loop pipe compared to a horizontal earth loop.

To allow for adequate heat exchange in a pond without significant impact on water temperature, single-system residential installations typically require a pond of at least a half acre, with a minimum heat exchanger location depth of 8 ft. The ideal pond will be within 300 ft of the home and have a controlled drainage area to prevent the influx of silt-laden runoff water. When available, ponds with a depth greater than 8 ft will maintain a more consistent water temperature. The densest water accumulates in the deepest area. Water has a maximum density at 38.9°F and will stratify in the deep areas of a pond in winter, providing excellent heat transfer for a pond loop.

Pond temperatures are most stable when there is a surface covering of ice and snow. Ice serves to limit evaporative cooling of the pond water. Evaporative heat loss accounts for approximately 80% of the thermal loss from a pond. When high winds and sub-freezing temperatures prevail, the wind chill effect can reduce the temperature of a shallow or moderately deep pond to 34°F. Once a layer of ice forms, the evaporative loss stops and the pond temperature quickly stabilizes.

Snow on top of the ice simply serves as an insulating blanket from even colder surface temperatures. The performance of a pond loop can be expected to improve

Figure 4-17. Reverse-return header on 4-ton pond loop

as a pond makes this transition from an open body of supercooled water to a frozen pond with snow cover.

When designing for a pond loop, try to avoid ponds that have continuously operating fountains or air bubblers in the winter. While these features provide beneficial aeration in the summer, the area of open water that they create serves to increase the evaporative cooling of the pond water during the winter months, wasting valuable heat that might otherwise be available for use by the geothermal system.

Software tables for sizing pond loops to geothermal equipment typically default to a pond temperature of 39°F and a standard polyethylene heat exchanger pipe length of 300 ft per ton. Heat exchangers are built up with spacers between each layer of pipe on the 300-ft roll. Each coil is connected to a header sized according to system requirements (see the reverse-return manifold in Figure 4-17 on the previous page). As applied tonnage increases, so will the header size. Polyethylene pond loops require

Figure 4-18. Tying on ballast blocks

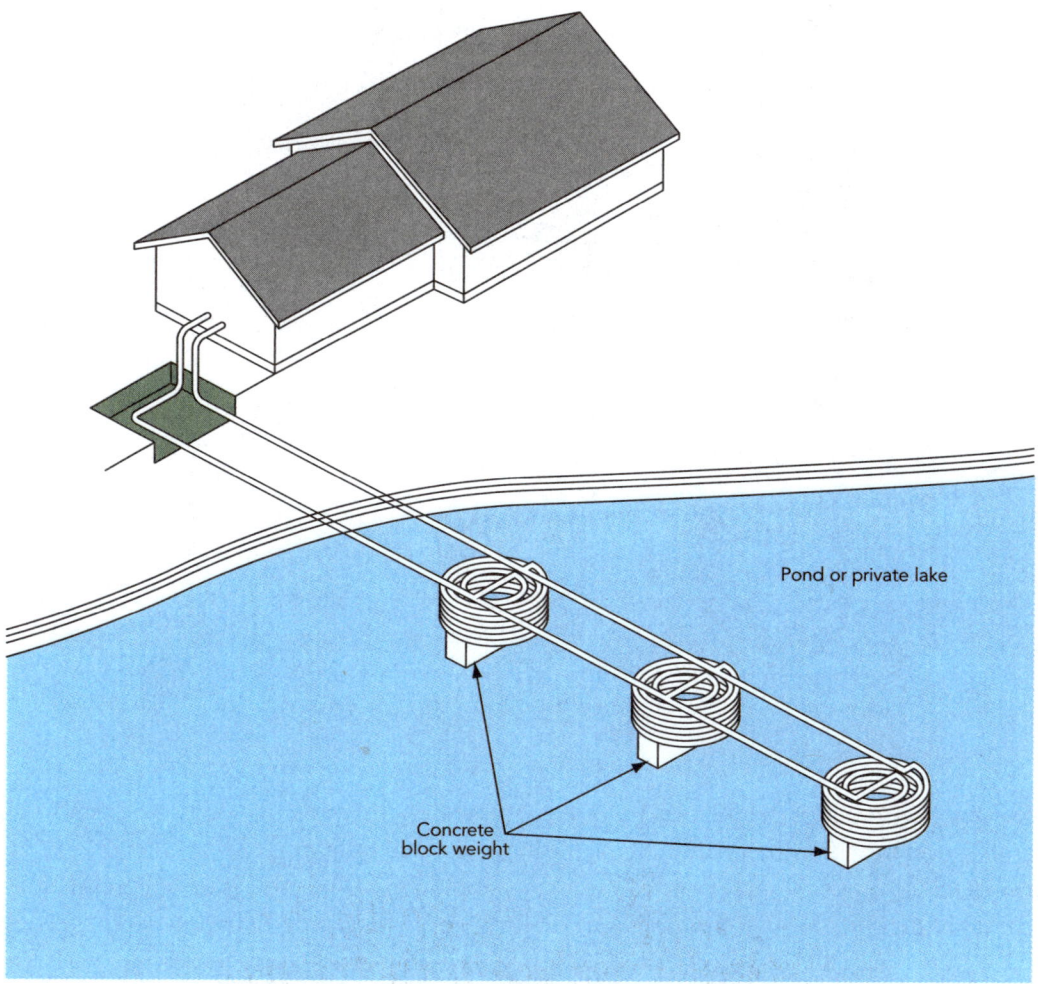

Figure 4-19. Submerged pond loop

ballast weights to reduce their natural buoyancy. Concrete blocks make excellent ballast weights. They also serve as a means of support for holding the coils up off the bottom of the pond. Pond loops are much easier to install if the concrete blocks are strap-tied to the underside of each coil as the coils are about to be floated into the pond (see Figure 4-18). Once floating in the pond, the assembly is positioned over the deep area. As the loops are flushed, they lose their buoyancy and settle to the bottom. The concrete blocks now serve as footings to keep the coils from resting on the pond bottom, thus allowing for convective water circulation around the coils. Figure 4-19 shows a typical pond loop using coiled pipe.

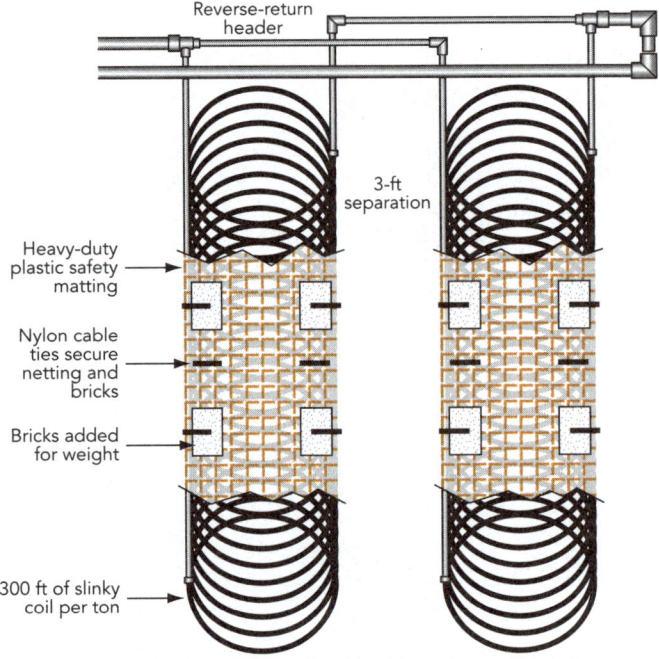

Figure 4-20. Slinky mat pond loop

Some contractors prefer to construct pond loops using *slinky mats* (see Figure 4-20). For the slinky mat pond loop, each loop is tied off to a rigid frame of PVC or scrap metal pipe. As the mat heat exchangers are floated into the pond, additional weight is added to reduce buoyancy. When the mat is flushed, it loses buoyancy and settles to the bottom.

Another type of heat exchanger used in pond loops is the *lake plate heat exchanger* (see Figure 4-21). Lake plate heat exchangers have widespread application in residential, commercial, and industrial installations. They function very well for rejecting heat from commercial geothermal applications in which the air conditioning function is dominant, and where pond landscaping fountains serve the same purpose as a low-maintenance cooling tower. The geothermal fluid circulated within the plates is totally isolated from the pond water and, unlike cooling tower water, the pond loop fluid requires no additional treatment to maintain its quality.

Commercially, lake plate heat exchangers allow for large cooling loads to dissipate their energy in relatively small ponds. When used for heating applications, lake plate heat exchangers should be oversized by at least 25% to assist in operation during those times when a small pond may drop to 34°F before the formation of an ice cover. Experience has shown that all pond loop heat exchangers (and more noticeably lake plate heat exchangers) can begin to ice up if building start-up loads or heating demands are extreme during periods of very low pond temperatures. If a pond loop heat exchanger does begin to ice up, the process can be reversed by one or more of the following methods:

- Reduce the load by turning down the thermostat. (This is normally the best solution.)
- Switch the system to the emergency heat mode for at least a full day to give the loop time to defrost.
- Force a defrost function by setting the thermostat for air conditioning and lowering the temperature sufficiently to stage the geothermal system on. Heat rejected to the pond loop by air conditioning will serve to melt and shed most ice—usually within 15 to 30 minutes for lake plate exchangers and within an hour or two for heavily iced coiled pipe heat exchangers.

SUMMARY

In review, the most important factors affecting the design and installation of closed-loop heat exchangers are low soil moisture conditions and abnormally cold or warm pond temperatures. All too often, loops that are sized by quick "rule-of-thumb" methods will prove to be undersized when anticipated conditions change. Installers

Figure 4-21. Lake plate heat exchanger

are advised to anticipate dry soil conditions and position loops to follow the contour of drainage areas to take advantage of natural soil moisture when it is available.

When working with pond loops, avoid depths of less than 8 ft. Shallow water is subject to sunlight-induced algae growth as well as to rapid changes in temperature, both of which can limit the effective heat exchange of a pond loop. In the case of pond loops, deeper is better. Deep water is less subject to algae growth, and water temperature is more stable.

The more thorough you are in the design and planning stage, the more successful the finished installation will be. Remember—a satisfied customer is always a great source for referrals! ◆

ILLUSTRATION CREDITS
FIGURE 4-1: WATERFURNACE
FIGURE 4-2: CENTENNIAL PLASTICS
FIGURE 4-3: WATERFURNACE
FIGURE 4-4: WATERFURNACE
FIGURE 4-5: WATERFURNACE
FIGURE 4-6: JEFF PERSONS
FIGURE 4-7: JEFF PERSONS
FIGURE 4-8: JEFF PERSONS
FIGURE 4-9: WATERFURNACE
FIGURE 4-10: WATERFURNACE
FIGURE 4-11: WATERFURNACE
FIGURE 4-12: JEFF PERSONS
FIGURE 4-13: WATERFURNACE
FIGURE 4-14: WATERFURNACE
FIGURE 4-15: WATERFURNACE
FIGURE 4-16: JEFF PERSONS
FIGURE 4-17: JEFF PERSONS
FIGURE 4-18: JEFF PERSONS
FIGURE 4-19: WATERFURNACE
FIGURE 4-20: CLIMATEMASTER
FIGURE 4-21: AWEB SUPPLY

◀CHAPTER FIVE▶
Piping

A BRIEF HISTORY OF GEOTHERMAL PIPING

Selecting the proper loop piping material can make the difference between a successful installation and a maintenance liability. Early experimental geothermal piping and loop designs employed a wide variety of material choices. Many lessons relating to the selection of piping material were learned. Two characteristics of potential piping materials proved particularly important: the *coefficient of thermal expansion* (that is, the change in dimension per degree of temperature change), and *thermal conductivity*.

Table 5-1 on the next page lists the coefficient of thermal expansion and the corresponding anticipated change in length of common piping materials per 100 ft of pipe for a 75°F temperature difference (which might be anticipated between the maximum high and low temperatures of a typical closed-loop geothermal installation). Table 5-2, also on the next page, lists the thermal conductivity of some common geothermal system piping materials. Close inspection of Table 5-2 shows that the thermal conductivity of high-density polyethylene pipe makes it the best choice for heat transfer when using a flexible, corrosion-resistant plastic piping product with a long life expectancy.

Learning from past mistakes

In many cases, the most expensive portion of a geothermal installation is the loop. Over the years, countless installers have experimented with a multitude of materials and looping methods in the hope of finding a "magical" low-cost means of installing

Material	Coefficent of expansion, in./(in. × °F)*	Change in length**
Steel	0.0000073	0.65
Cupronickel	0.0000090	0.81
Copper	0.0000093	0.837
304 stainless steel	0.0000096	0.86
Brass	0.0000104	0.938
PVC	0.0000280	2.52
CPVC	0.0000370	3.33
Polypropylene	0.0000503	4.25
Nylon Type 11	0.0000556	5.004
Polyethylene HD	0.0000600	5.40
Polybutylene (PB)	0.0000720	6.48
Polyethylene LD	0.0001110	9.99

* change in length ÷ (original length × change in temperature)
** in. per 100 ft of pipe per 75°F ΔT

Table 5-1. Coefficient of expansion for piping materials common to geothermal installations

the loop. In this regard, it is beneficial to be familiar with those methods that work and those that don't, and to understand why *Closed-Loop/Geothermal Heat Pump Systems: Design and Installation Standards*, published by IGSHPA, has come to be accepted as the standard reference work for the materials and installation methods to which the industry presently conforms.

Many of the mistakes experienced with early systems had to do with thermal contraction of piping materials. As the fluid temperature

Material	Thermal conductivity, Btu/(hr × ft × °F)
Steel	31.2
Cupronickel	17.0
Copper	223.0
304 stainless steel	9.24
Brass	64.0
PVC	0.109
CPVC	0.079
Polypropylene	0.057
Nylon Type 11	0.141
Polyethylene HD	0.225
Polybutylene (PB)	0.080
Polyethylene LD	0.190

Table 5-2. Thermal conductivity of common geothermal piping materials

dropped in the heating season, piping materials contracted, placing tension on the pipe and connectors and causing separation at glued joints and band clamp fittings. Early geothermal loop "pioneers" quickly discovered that thermal contraction was causing failures in PVC pipes with glued joints. For similar reasons, barbed nylon and plastic pin connectors held by stainless steel band clamps (commonly used for joining polyethylene pipe) could not withstand the tension forces created by thermal contraction over several hundred feet of pipe. Large natural gas distribution and transmission companies installed hundreds of feet of polyethylene gas lines with standard compression fittings serving as junctions. But polyethylene gas lines buried in the heat of summer, when the pipe underwent its maximum thermal expansion, suddenly began to contract and pull apart at the junctions as the soil approached freezing temperatures.

The solution to these failures was to develop fusion welding techniques that created a junction far stronger than the piping material itself. Fusion welding of polyethylene pipe was quickly adopted by the geothermal industry as a means of ensuring the integrity of underground loops.

Thermal conductivity also led to an evolutionary process in the selection of the in-ground piping material. Early efforts followed the logic that a pipe with high thermal conductivity was needed. Some installers attempted to use copper tubing for the earth loops. Copper has excellent thermal conductivity, but its heat transfer was found to be no greater than the conductivity of the soil surrounding the tube. If the soil happened to be dry, heat transfer into the soil was extremely limited and the quantity of copper tubing needed to attain proper heat transfer was not economically feasible.

In addition to the expense of the copper, the copper tube systems needed saturated soil conditions to utilize their heat transfer ability most efficiently. Elaborate soaking systems were designed to maintain soil moisture and saturated conditions around the earth loops. If the customer happened to be on a municipal water supply, the cost of water added up quickly, diminishing the savings provided by the geothermal system. With added moisture came acid soils, ammonia from decomposing topsoil, and freeze-thaw cycles from winter operation that all contributed to corrosion and failure of the copper tubing. To counteract the corrosion issues, copper systems typically are designed with a manufacturer-specified backfill material to "bed in" the copper lines for uniform heat transfer. For additional protection, cathodic methods using sacrificial anodes and passive electric currents can help to diminish the potential for corrosion, but add a whole new dimension to the installation process.

Copper loop systems dominate in the direct exchange (DX) geothermal market. DX systems circulate refrigerant directly through the cooper earth loops to attain optimal heat exchange. Because thermal conductivity between the copper tube and the surrounding soil is critical to the efficiency of DX systems, their installation and design is closely managed by the manufacturers and distributors that market these systems.

The economic compromise between reliable joining methods and effective heat transfer was to select a material that was inexpensive and had a coefficient of heat transfer that was similar to that of the surrounding soil. Initial efforts focused on two products—copper tube size (CTS) polybutylene pipe rated at 160 psi, and a thin-wall polyethylene product rated at 75 psi. While these two products have the advantage of low cost and better heat transfer, their shortfall is in their crush resistance when exposed to freezing soil conditions. Failures typically occur when weather conditions are at their absolute worst. Loop pipe placed around a tight corner in a trench or return bend can be further tensioned as the pipe contracts, forming a kink and restricting flow. Cobbles and sharp stones carelessly left in contact with low-density pipe create a pressure point. Any geothermal line can be compromised by a cobble or sharp stone lying directly against the pipe—if the system is subjected to subfreezing loop temperatures, frost will progress more rapidly through the stone than through the soil. As frost builds around the stone, the pressure of its crystallization (ice expands) can force the rock against the less resistant pipe, crushing the pipe and causing an eventual failure (see Figure 5-1).

This is the same action that causes large rocks to rise to the surface of a farm field during a cold winter. Each freeze-thaw cycle repeats the process, raising the rock a little closer to the surface. In at least one instance, a major housing development was built that used low-pressure, thin-wall polyethylene pipe for vertical heat exchangers drilled into granite bedrock. Due to the high cost of drilling, the system specifications called for a winter loop design temperature that was below 32°F. As winter progressed, the antifreeze temperature dropped below freezing. With the lines confined by solid granite, the pressure created by the formation of ice within the vertical bores caused the pipes to collapse. The geothermal system became inoperative and total replacement of the loops was required.

A second cause of early system failures resulted from the use of plastic pin connectors and stainless steel band clamps. Thermal contraction of the piping places band-clamped connectors in tension, causing separation and loss of fluid. Nylon elbow-band clamp connectors used at the top of vertical heat exchangers were particularly

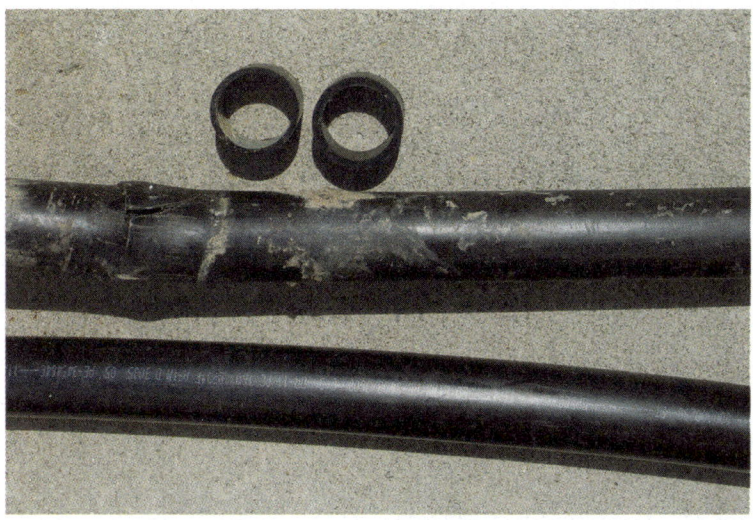

Figure 5-1. Failure of thin-wall polyethylene line

A sharp stone caused the side wall collapse and failure of the low-density polyethylene line shown in Figure 5-1. Failure occurred as several hundred feet of single-trench line contracted and pulled tight to a 90° bend near the foundation penetration. Polyethylene sample cuts resting above the failed section of pipe (rated at 65 psi) show that the wall thickness of the thin-wall SDR26, 65-psi pipe on the left is about half the thickness of the SDR11, 160-psi pipe on the right.

Figure 5-2. Tension failure cracks on inside radius of two nylon insert elbows

subject to this form of failure. The elbow connectors were distorted by contraction from both directions, just as a "wishbone" might be pulled apart. Failures of this nature are identified as cracks on the inside radius of the elbow, as shown in Figure 5-2. (The elbow on the right shows staining from long-term seepage loss of glycol antifreeze around the exterior of the fitting).

PIPING **87**

Despite some of the early problems, both polybutylene and low-density polyethylene geothermal loops work well. Many are still in operation. Where failures have occurred, they are generally due to the thinness of the pipe wall and its higher susceptibility to crushing damage from sharp stones and frost heave. Additional issues with the supply and manufacturing cost of polybutylene, combined with a desire for a more durable and crush-resistant material, led the geothermal industry toward the use of HDPE pipe—in particular, SDR11 HDPE pipe, which has a pressure rating of 160 psi and better resistance to crushing.

Any compromise resulting from the thicker pipe wall and slightly lower thermal conductivity of the SDR11 HDPE pipe is compensated for by the total linear footage of pipe used per ton of system capacity. The same principle holds true when project specifications call for the use of polyethylene pipe that has a higher pressure rating and wall thickness—it just takes a little more loop in order to provide the same performance.

ACCEPTABLE PRACTICES FOR EXTERIOR LOOP PIPING

The current industry specification for polyethylene pipe calls for the use of SDR11 pipe with an ASTM minimum cell classification of PE345464C per ASTM D-3350 and a pressure rating of 160 psi. In some instances, a commercial specification for high-rise buildings or for deep (300 to 500-ft) vertical loops may require a higher pressure rating to accommodate the combined hydrostatic pressure of the building plus the depth of the loop. In such cases, the commercial specification will call for SDR9 HDPE with a pressure rating of 200 psi. This precaution is taken to reduce pressure stress on the pipe caused by the combined hydrostatic pressure exerted by the hydraulic head created by the building piping plus the depth of the well.

While smaller residential projects are not likely to encounter issues with well depth and pipe pressure ratings, an understanding of the relationship between the two can be beneficial, especially for installations in which limited space for drilling requires an exceptionally deep well. Early geothermal contractors learned this lesson the hard way while experimenting with thin-wall, 65-psi SDR26 PE pipe. Thin-wall pipe had the advantage of better heat transfer, but suffered from a reduced resistance to crushing from heavy stone, frost heave, thermal contraction, and differential soil settlement. The thin-wall pipe also had problems with heat and pressure deformation when used for deep-well/dry-hole vertical applications in which the hydrostatic pressure exceeded the working pressure rating of the piping material.

Let's take a look at an example of a "worst-case" situation. If a building piping system has a static pressure of 20 psi at ground level and the geothermal wells are drilled to a depth of 300 ft in a dry formation, the theoretical pressure exerted on the polyethylene pipe at the bottom of the wells is:

$$20 \text{ psi} + \frac{300 \text{ ft}}{2.31 \text{ ft/psi}} = 20 \text{ psi} + 129.9 \text{ psi} = 149.9 \text{ psi}$$

In this example, if the loops were to use a low-density pipe rated at 65 psi, the operating pressure would be more than twice the rated pressure and failure would be eminent. A pipe specification for SDR11 PE with a pressure rating of 160 psi would be acceptable, but working near its limit. The SDR11 pipe likely would show marked changes in loop pressure as the fluid temperature warmed in the summer, causing the pipe to expand, and then cooled in the winter, causing the pipe to contract. For this example, a specification for SDR9 PE with a pressure rating of 200 psi would provide a higher level of confidence, more stable summer-to-winter fluid pressures, and a safety factor characteristic of commercial applications.

Question: Do all deep-well applications require the use of HDPE pipe rated for higher pressures?
Answer: No, for situations in which a static water level exists for a vertical well bore, the hydraulic head pressure exerted on the outside of the pipe by the surrounding water serves to counteract the pipe's internal hydrostatic pressure in such a way that the calculated pressure differential across the pipe wall at depth is the sum of the total head pressure within the pipe minus the hydrostatic head produced by the surrounding water table.

Consider an application with the same characteristics as in the example above (a building with a 20-psi system pressure and a 300-ft geothermal well). If the water level in the well bore is 100 ft below the surface of the earth, the portion of the well below water level (200 ft) would have a confining pressure of 86.6 psi (200 ft ÷ 2.31 ft/psi). The maximum pressure differential across the pipe, therefore, would be calculated as 149.9 psi − 86.6 psi = 63.3 psi. For this example, SDR11 PE pipe with a pressure rating of 160 psi would be an excellent choice.

In addition to the IGSHPA HDPE pipe specification, similar specifications exist for PEXa polyethylene pipe. PEXa pipe used for geothermal loops must conform to ASTM Specifications F-876 and F-877 or DIN 16892 and 16893. Piping with these specifications has a dimension ratio of 9 and a pressure rating of 160 psi. Connections are to be made by electrofusion, by metal cold-compression sleeve fittings, or by cold-expansion fittings with metal compression sleeves. Figure 5-3 shows an example of double-loop PEXa piping of the type used for vertical heat exchangers. A fully detailed specification for PEXa piping and connections may be found in the IGSHPA standards manual referenced earlier in this chapter.

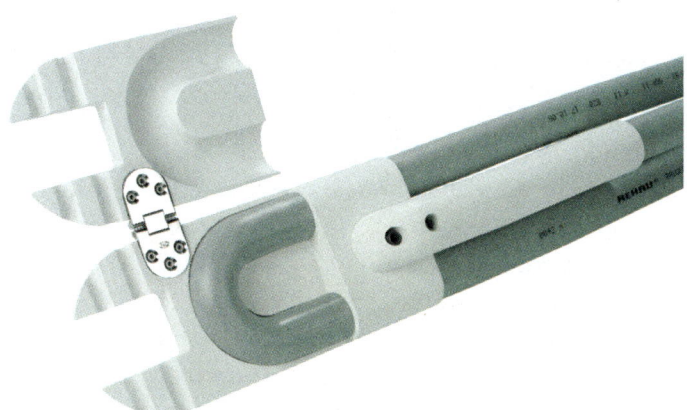

Figure 5-3. Double-loop PEXa vertical heat exchanger piping

INTERIOR PIPING

Closed-loop interior piping

Interior piping can be managed with a wide variety of materials. Local and state codes ultimately determine acceptable piping materials, particularly in commercial applications. Experience has shown that, when permitted, the criteria for closed-loop interior piping are best met by fusion-welded HDPE pipe installed as a continuation of the exterior loop. This avoids mechanical fittings, which are a major source of leaks caused by differential expansion and contraction. For interior piping, the HDPE pipe is purchased in 20-ft straight lengths. Careful planning and the use of fusion-welded fittings ensure the integrity of the interior piping. The use of $^1/_2$-in. closed-cell pipe insulation on all interior geothermal lines is highly recommended as a means of preventing the formation of condensation and frost, especially when a system must operate for extended periods of time to meet cold weather heat demands.

When HDPE pipe is suspended across floor joists, hangers should be sized to wrap around or suspend the insulated pipe. Hangers should be installed on every other joist or, when lines run parallel with framing, they should be spaced at intervals of 32 to 36 in. HDPE pipe is flexible and tends to expand and contract with thermal changes—consequently, pipe hangers should be installed to suspend the pipe freely rather than holding it rigidly against a surface were pump sounds or expansion and contraction noises may transfer into the framing.

HDPE interior piping should maintain the same size as the entering loop right up to the flow center. The recommended location for mounting the flow center is on the side or back surface of the geothermal system cabinet. Connections between the flow center and the geothermal unit typically are made with 1-in. ID high-pressure hose and band clamp adapter fittings or brass "O"-ring fittings. The rubber hose serves several purposes. First and foremost is the ability to make connections by sweeping the hose gently between the heat pump and the flow center fittings, rather than by using multiple rigid elbows (as would be necessary if the system were totally "hard-piped"). A second reason for the rubber hose connection is to prevent compressor harmonics from "telegraphing" back through the loop lines and into the framing in the home. (While the use of stainless-steel band clamps is discouraged for exterior work, their use is perfectly acceptable in situations where the clamps are accessible, as they are with connections to interior equipment and pumps.)

Figure 5-4. System installation showing closed-loop interior piping and connections

Figure 5-4 shows a clean system installation with the flow center mounted on the side of the system cabinet. Insulated loop lines hang from 2-in. "J" hooks. Insulated 1-in. radiator hose rated at 150 psi connects from the base of the flow center to system connections. Domestic hot water is piped in ¹/₂-in. PEX pipe to isolate the equipment from the hot water piping in the home.

Service notes

For matters of convenience, some contractors favor the use of PVC for closed-loop interior piping. As a precautionary note, PVC pipe is *not* recommended for closed-loop systems. PVC is subject to plastic deformation when exposed to high operating temperatures, and embrittlement at low temperatures. Current geothermal equipment designs are capable of elevating leaving fluid temperatures to as high as 120 or 130°F before safety controls turn off the compressor. At these temperatures, PVC pipe becomes soft and flexible, whereas HDPE pipe with threaded brass or "O"-ring connectors can accommodate these conditions without failure or leaks. Unlike HDPE adapters, threaded PVC fittings will swell with high temperatures and then shrink as loop temperatures fall in the winter. This dimensional change can be sufficient to create major leaks at threaded connections. If not discovered, a loop is likely to lose sufficient fluid to air-lock circulation pumps and create a system lockout fault. Repairs to a leaking threaded adapter require the replacement of the fitting and the use of a PVC union and isolation ball valve to allow for future adjustments (should the same high-temperature event repeat itself). High-temperature events responsible for the deformation of PVC piping materials are due to:

- the loss of heat transfer as a loop dries out in hot weather
- the failure of a loop pump
- a restriction in fluid flow
- pump cavitation resulting from the loss of fluid pressure.

Working with HDPE pipe

There are four primary methods for joining HDPE pipe and fittings:

- mechanical
- socket fusion
- butt fusion
- electrofusion.

Mechanical connections are characterized by brass insert connectors, adapters, and stainless-steel band clamps. Mechanical connectors should be limited to those connections that will always be accessible for service, such as connections at system flow centers and with equipment located inside the home or building. Mechanical connectors should *not* be used as the primary means of making underground connections and splices.

Socket fusion is by far the most common joining method for HDPE pipe in sizes of 1¼ in. or less. Current industry guidelines for preparing HDPE pipe for socket fusion are as follows:

1. First, the HDPE pipe is cut square with a ratchet cutter (see Figure 5-5).
2. If the pipe size is 1 in. or larger, a chamfering tool is used to cut a beveled edge on the pipe. (With larger-diameter HDPE pipe, a beveled edge makes positioning the fusion fittings much easier.)
3. Once cut to dimension and prepared, the pipe and fittings are cleaned with a clean, dry cotton cloth.
4. A holding clamp called a "cold ring clamp" is fastened on the straight section of pipe. A depth gauge is used to position the clamp at the proper distance from the end to be fused. The cold ring clamp controls the diameter of the HDPE pipe and prevents distortion. It also provides a stopping point for proper insertion depth of the pipe into the heating tool when the pipe and the fitting are pressed together.
5. Socket fusion is a method that utilizes a specialized heating tool and dies coated with a non-stick material. The dies, designed to accept the pipe being joined, are heated to 500°F. Both the tool and the dies are checked, either with a temp stick designed to melt at the design temperature or, more easily, with an infrared non-contact thermometer/gun (see Figure 5-6). The die temperature must be checked

Figure 5-5. Ratchet cutter is used to make clean 90° cut

Figure 5-6. After pipe is chamfered and cleaned, fusion tool is checked with infrared temperature gun

before every fusion to ensure that the tool is operating properly. (Low temperature can result in a cold fusion joint and a future system leak).

6. Once the tool attains its design temperature, the pipe and fittings are forced onto their respective dies and held in place for a length of time dependent on the size and dimension ratio of the material being joined (see Figure 5-7).
7. When the "heat time" countdown is complete, the pieces are pulled away from the hot dies and forced together. (Hot polyethylene remains workable for 15 to 20 seconds, which allows for the careful alignment of fitting and pipe before they are forced together. It is important to work quickly—but not *too* quickly, since a carelessly positioned fitting may require an entire section to be cut out and replaced.)

Figure 5-7. Fusion weld between ¾-in. pond loop coil and manifold tee

8. Once joined, the pieces are held in position for the amount of time specified by the manufacturer in order to allow the molecular structures of the **HDPE** pipe and coupling to fuse.
9. After a cool-down period, the cold ring is removed. Before applying any stress to the pipe or fusion fitting, observe the "at rest" time prescribed by the manufacturer.
10. Between uses, the non-stick surfaces of the hot fusion tool should be cleaned with a clean, dry cotton cloth (synthetic cloth will melt and should never be used). Keeping fusion tools clean prevents carbon buildup on the die faces and makes the tool easier to use.

Butt fusion is a technique used primarily on larger-diameter HDPE pipe. While socket fusion is possible on pipe sizes up to 2 in., the force needed to make a successful fusion weld increases with pipe size. As pipe size approaches $1\frac{1}{2}$ in., the required force becomes prohibitive. For this reason, most contractors use the butt fusion method on **HDPE** pipe that is $1\frac{1}{4}$ in. and larger. Butt fusion requires a greater investment in equipment than socket fusion, but the reward comes in reduced fitting and labor cost per connection.

To make connections by butt fusion:
1. The pipe ends to be joined are positioned and clamped in the pipe carriage assembly (see Figure 5-8). The "free" end of the pipe or fitting must be clamped in the movable side of the carriage. (The success of the weld depends on the temperature and force applied to the hot fusion faces. The movable side of the equipment must be able to float freely as the operator draws the sections together. Any resistance or pipe drag that counteracts this force can interfere with the process).
2. Once clamped in the carriage, the pipe faces are forced against a rotating surfacing tool that simultaneously shaves a smooth face on each portion to be joined.
3. The surfacing tool is removed from the carriage and the faces are drawn together to check for misalignment. If any misalignment is detected, the pipes are reclamped to correct the problem. The faces are resurfaced a second time until the pipes align with no sign of a gap or irregularity around the pipe faces.
4. When proper alignment has been achieved, the faces are separated. The heating iron is placed in the carriage and the faces are drawn up to contact the iron. The heating iron temperature, how long heat is applied, and how much force is applied to the faces depend on the thickness of the material and the ambient temperature at which the process is conducted. Operators follow temperature, time, and force criteria assigned by the equipment manufacturer for the model and material in use. These values are specific to the manufacturer and design of the butt fusion equipment and are not standardized across the industry.

Figure 5-8. Butt fusion tool used to join 2-in. HDPE supply and return lines for lake plate heat exchanger

5. Once the pipe attains the appropriate "melt" or "roll back" stipulated in the manufacturer's instructions, the clamp is separated and the heating iron removed. After the heating iron is completely removed from the carriage, the heated pipe ends are brought together using the force specified by the manufacturer. This force is maintained to attain the appropriate butt fusion "roll back." Following a recommended cool-down time, the fused pipe is removed from the fusion tool.

Figure 5-9 shows a completed butt fusion with proper "roll back" at the fusion face. Butt fusion connections have a greater wall thickness and are stronger than the base pipe. Destructive testing of butt fusion connections show that failure occurs in the base pipe with little or no distortion of the butt weld area.

Electrofusion is the fourth means by which HDPE pipe is joined. The electrofusion process may be used on almost any size of HDPE pipe. However, it is used most prevalently in commercial projects with large pipe connections and in locations where butt fusion equipment may not fit. The equipment for electrofusion, which may be purchased or rented from major pipe suppliers, consists of a computer-controlled power module that includes a bar-code reader and manual keypad for identifying the fusion fitting. The power module automatically sets the voltage and heat time for the fitting. Electrofusion fittings have embedded heating coils on the inner face and connection terminals on the outer body of the fitting. The procedure for making an electrofusion weld is as follows:

Figure 5-9. Completed butt fusion joint

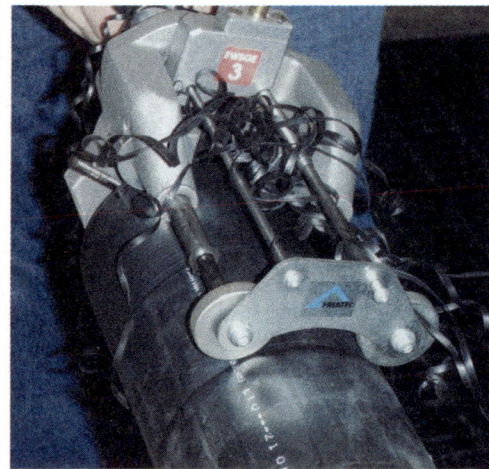

Figure 5-10. Preparing 4-in. HDPE pipe for electrofusion welding

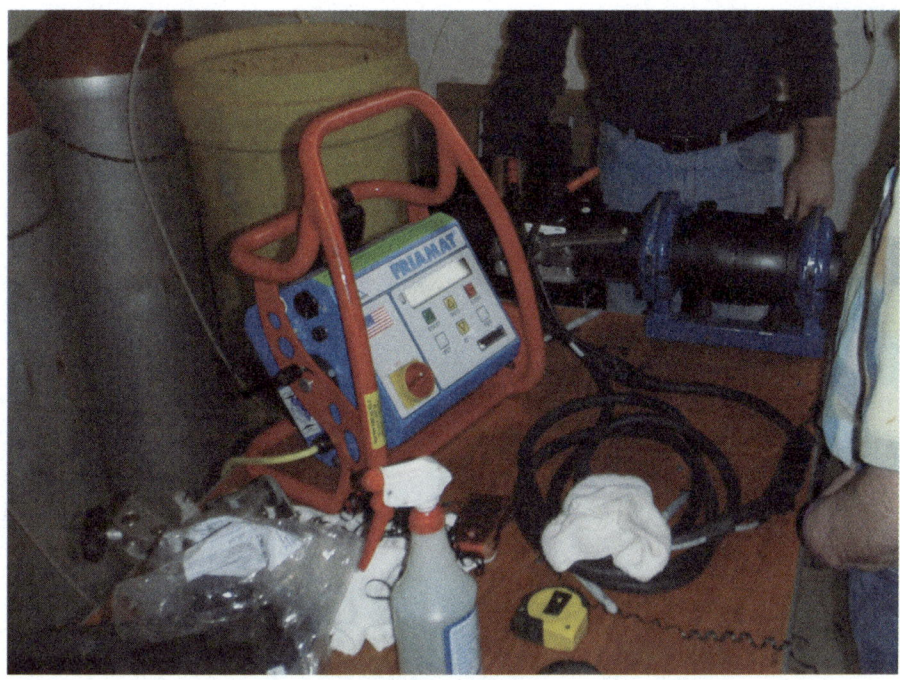

Figure 5-11. Setting up for electrofusion weld

1. The raw HDPE pipe must be surface-prepped to remove all signs of manufacturing "skin" left by the extrusion process and clean the pipe to its virgin PE resin body (see Figure 5-10).
2. Fitting insertion depth is marked on each line to be placed in the fusion coupling.
3. The coupling bar code is read and coded into the fusion power module.
4. The fitting is assembled, with both sides inserted into the coupling or fitting.
5. With the power module in run mode, the module checks for continuity and resistance of the heating element in the coupling. The resistance of the heating element also tells the power module the temperature of the coupling and allows the module to make adjustments in voltage and heat time needed to produce an effective fusion weld.
6. Once all system checks are OK, the fusion process begins. A cool-down period follows and a display notice appears indicating that the electrofusion weld is complete.

In Figure 5-11, the electrofusion control unit sits on the workbench. The voltage cable will attach to electrode fittings on the fusion coupling.

Closed-loop interior manifold piping

The most common closed-loop installation is a single loop dedicated to a single system. The geothermal loop lines pipe directly to the system flow center, with simple supply and return lines to the outdoor loop, as shown in Figure 5-12.

As application size increases and multiple geothermal systems are added, it's possible to operate two smaller-capacity systems in parallel from the same flow center (see Figure 5-13). The system controls produced by most manufacturers include a feature that provides for "pump slaving," which allows multiple systems to share a common pump or flow center. In order for parallel systems with a common flow center to be sized properly, the flow rate (gpm) for the loop and flow center must equal or exceed the combined flow for all connected geothermal units. If necessary, flow balancing between systems can be adjusted by restricting a ball valve on the outlet side of each unit until the measured pressure drop across the pressure-temperature ports matches the specified pressure drop for the required system flow.

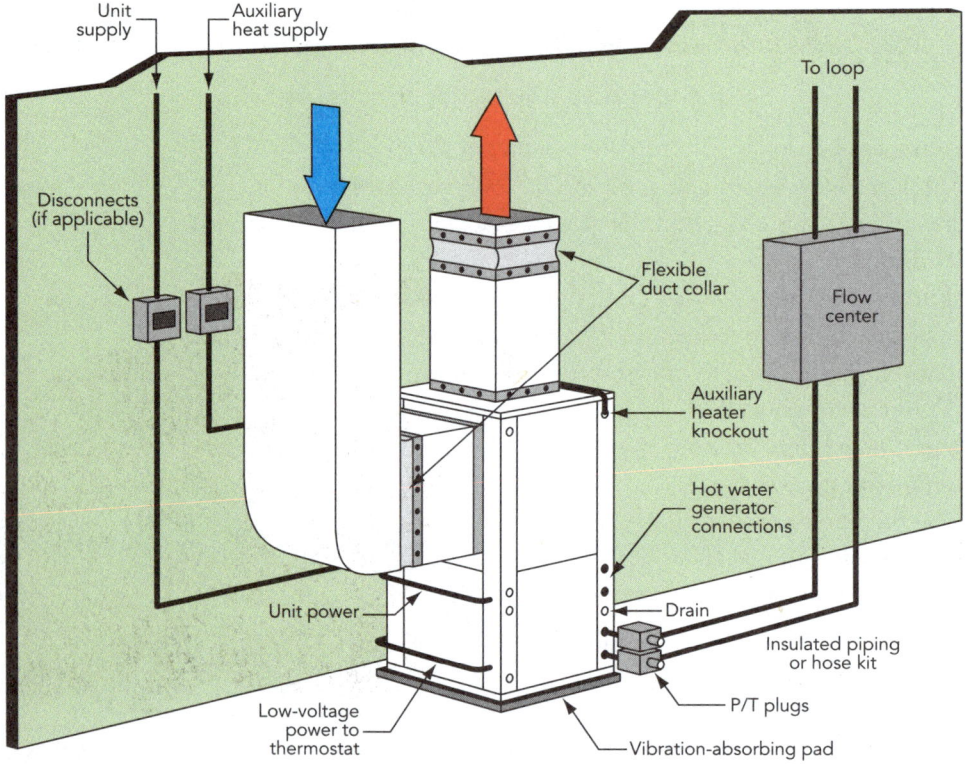

Figure 5-12. Simple closed-loop piping

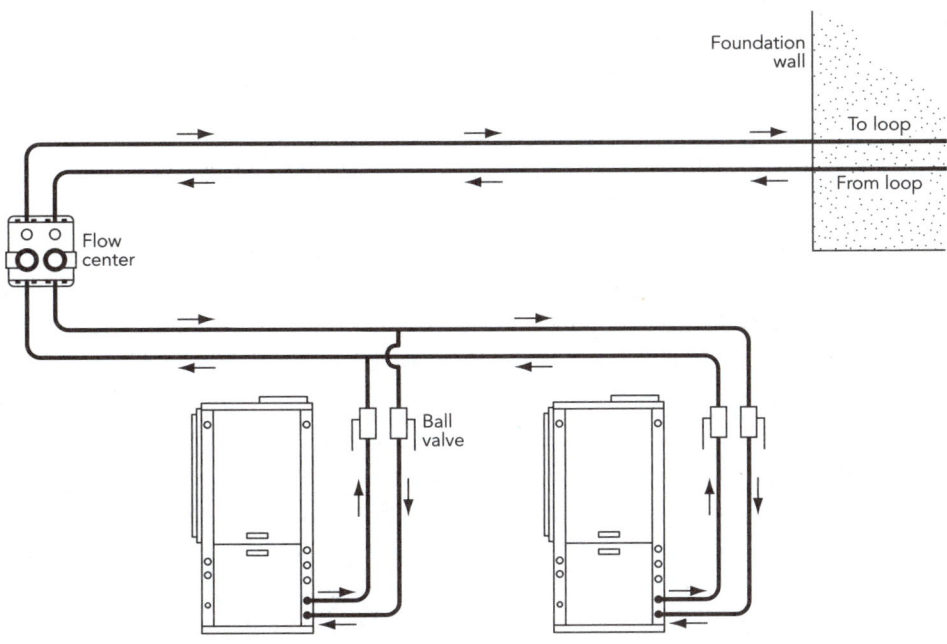

Figure 5-13. Parallel geothermal systems operating with single flow center

The energy penalty for running two geothermal units from a single flow center may seem relatively small—that is, until you take a closer look and realize that each pump is rated at 385 W. If the two geothermal units are fitted with zone valves and the pumps are staged to operate with their dedicated systems, the savings in reduced pumping power could amount to as much as $100 per year or more, depending on local utility rates. Recent innovations in flow center design allow for the use of variable-speed pumps like the one shown in Figure 5-14. Variable-speed pumping, when combined with a zone valve and flow regulator sized for each system, offers the lowest pumping cost and highest efficiency possible for a multiple-system installation.

Figure 5-14. Variable-speed pump used for geothermal fluid

When a single variable-speed pump supplies two or more systems, each system must be equipped with a motorized valve and flow regulator assembly. These controls are common to commercial installations and are readily available from most manufacturers. They can be incorporated directly into the manufacture of the system or field-installed later. Hose kits (see Figure 5-15) are available in common pipe diameters (from $1/2$ in. to 2 in.) to accommodate geothermal systems ranging from fractional-tonnage sizes to large commercial sizes of 20 to 30 tons. In a typical hose kit, a "Y" strainer captures any debris that may enter the system and ensures that the entering fluid is clean. The flow-regulating valve is connected to the outlet side of the geothermal system after the zone valve. A flow-regulating bobbin inside the flow control valve maintains constant flow with little more than a 2 to 3-psi pressure drop across the valve. A water solenoid valve or motorized zone valve (also incorporated into the outlet side of the hose kit) serves to close the discharge line whenever the system is not in operation, thereby reducing the fluid flow and pump capacity required by the variable-speed pump.

When multiple geothermal systems are connected and each has its own flow center, they can be configured in parallel, as shown in Figure 5-16. This arrangement works well when multiple geothermal units of similar capacity share a common loop. For proper operation at peak load, the loop design must accept the flow capacity of all of the connected systems. To operate effectively with a balanced pumping head, all flow centers must be identical.

If flow centers of differing head capacities are connected in parallel, the flow centers with higher head capacities will counteract the circulation of a low-head pump,

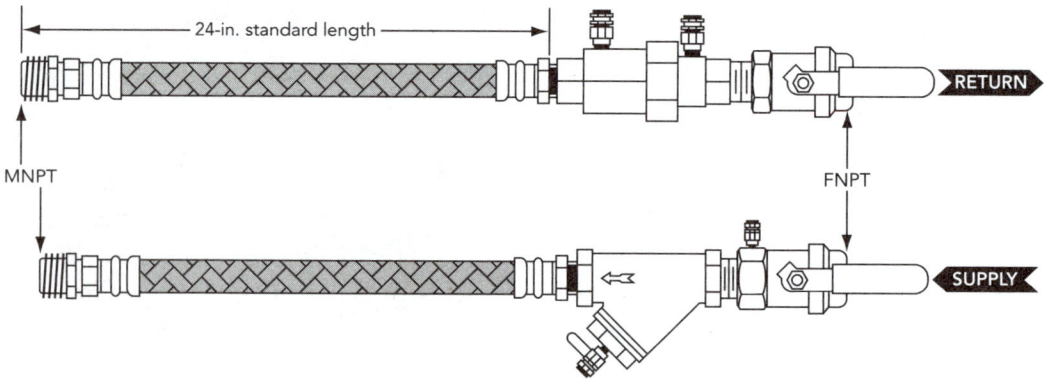

Figure 5-15. Hose kit

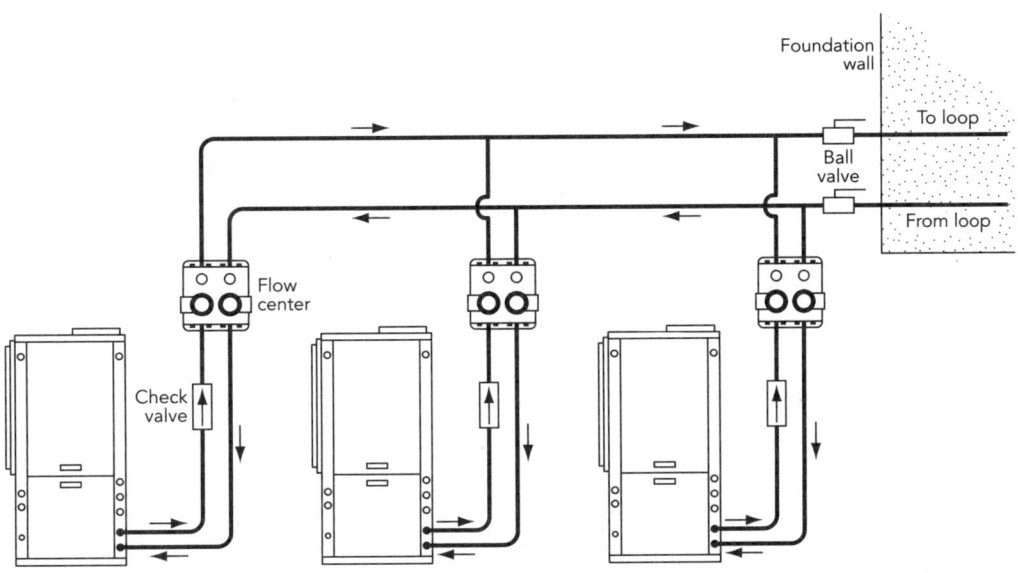

Figure 5-16. Multiple systems with matching flow centers share common loop

causing a reduction in flow for the low-head systems. To avoid counter-circulation through adjacent flow centers, each pumping unit incorporates a check valve. Check valve location is critical—each check valve must be located on the return line from the geothermal system and must point toward the flow center. The reason for this is to place the check valve in a section of line with low turbulence. If the valve were to be located directly after a pump discharge port, fluid turbulence in the line immediately after the pump would "rattle" the valve mechanism to the point of failure.

Open-loop interior piping

For open-loop interior piping, older water source systems often were piped with copper. However, recent market price increases for copper, fittings, and labor make PVC pipe the economical choice for most open-loop piping systems. Unlike closed-loop installations—which can undergo a wide range of temperatures between heating and cooling and which require the use of HDPE pipe—open systems have a much narrower and more controlled temperature range (typically between 40 and 70°F). PVC is not subject to issues of plastic deformation and embrittlement at these temperatures. Two grades of PVC pipe, Schedule 40 and Schedule 80, are in common use. Schedule 40 PVC with a diameter of 1 in. and a pressure rating of 270 psi at 73°F is used for a majority of residential installations. Schedule 80 PVC is specified for most commercial projects, and is rated at 378 psi at 73°F. Both pipe grades are well within the normal operating range of 40 to 60 psi for standard well pumps and domestic water systems.

As the diameter of PVC pipe increases, the working pressure rating decreases. When selecting a pipe size, be aware that PVC pipe will operate optimally if oversized. A larger-diameter pipe results in a greater volume of water (see Table 5-3) and a reduced water velocity within the pipe. Reduced water velocity has several benefits. It means less water flow noise, and less chance of "water hammer" when control valves open and close. The larger pipe size also allows for moderate mineral fouling of the piping without adverse effect to the equipment.

Pipe diameter	Flow rate
0.75 in.	5 gpm
1.00 in.	10 gpm
1.25 in.	20 gpm
1.50 in.	30 gpm
2.00 in.	50 gpm

Table 5-3. Maximum flow rates for PVC pipe

Larger pipe should always be insulated with $1/2$-in. soft rubber closed-cell insulation and hung or clamped so as to avoid any direct or rigid contact between the pipe and framing. Insulated and hung "loose," larger pipe leads to fewer complaints about the noise created by solenoid valves opening and closing and the cavitation sounds that can emanate from flow restrictors.

Working with PVC pipe

To help maintain a clean system, PVC pipe should *not* be cut with a saw. The preferred method of cutting PVC pipe is to use a ratchet cutter (see Figure 5-17). Cuts should be clean and square. In all cases, the raw cut edge should be beveled with a chamfering tool to remove the sharp outer edge on the pipe (see Figure 5-18). By beveling the square outer edges of slip fittings that are to be joined, using a PVC cleaning agent on both the male and female sides, and following that with a liberal coat of PVC cement, you can be assured that the cement will

Figure 5-17. Ratchet cutter

be retained in the interstitial space between the slip fittings (rather than squeegeed out by sharp edges) as the fittings are pressed together. The chamfering process is important on all sizes of PVC pipe and is considered a critical step in the well-drilling industry, where slip-joint PVC well casings must have a 100% bond between sections to maintain their integrity.

Perhaps the greatest hazard in assembling a PVC piping system is the issue of overtightening a threaded fitting. Slight differences in thread cut between fitting manufacturers make it essential for a combination of both non-stick tape and paste to be used on all threaded PVC fittings to ensure leak-free connections. Overtightened threaded connections are a primary source of leaks and failures in open-loop systems. Male PVC adapters may thread directly into female brass or stainless-steel fittings without issue, since the male fittings are compressed by the stronger, metal female base material. But problems occur when a metal or PVC male adapter is threaded into a female PVC fitting. Non-stick tape and paste offer very little resistance to tightening, making it easy to overtighten the male fitting into the female PVC section. As the tapered threads tighten, the leverage forces exerted on the female fitting can easily exceed its strength. The recommended method of tightening a PVC threaded fitting calls for hand-tightening, followed by little more than one extra turn with a wrench. An overtightened fitting typically requires several hours for the female side of the fitting to fracture. When it does, the water stream can quickly saturate everything within a 20-ft radius. After experiencing several such mishaps, most contractors have adopted the common practice of backing up every female PVC thread fitting with a band clamp *before* the threaded adapter is assembled (see Figure 5-19 on the next page). This recommendation applies to both Schedule 40 and Schedule 80 PVC fittings.

Figure 5-18. Chamfering tool

Managing flow restrictor noise

A typical open-loop system, regardless of the piping material used, includes a flow restrictor as a means of automatically maintaining a constant water flow when the system is in operation. Flow restrictors like the one shown in Figure 5-20 employ a soft rubber disk or stopper fitted against a fixed orifice. Water pressure acting against the rubber causes it to deflect and restrict the flow through the valve as pressure increases. A flow restrictor is designed to maintain a fixed flow with a fluctuating pressure differential across the valve ranging from as low as 15 psi to as high as 120 psi.

Flow restrictors are simple in construction and require no external attention. They are, however, subject to cavitation—a noise condition caused by dissolved gases that are released from solution as the raw well water passes from the high-pressure side to the low-pressure side of the valve. This cavitation can be heard as anything from a high-pitched scream to a lower, crackling sound. The best way to reduce the noise of cavitation is either to control the supply pressure (it should be maintained at a pressure near 40 psi) or to add back pressure to the outlet side of

Figure 5-19. Band clamp helps avoid stress split on female PVC fitting

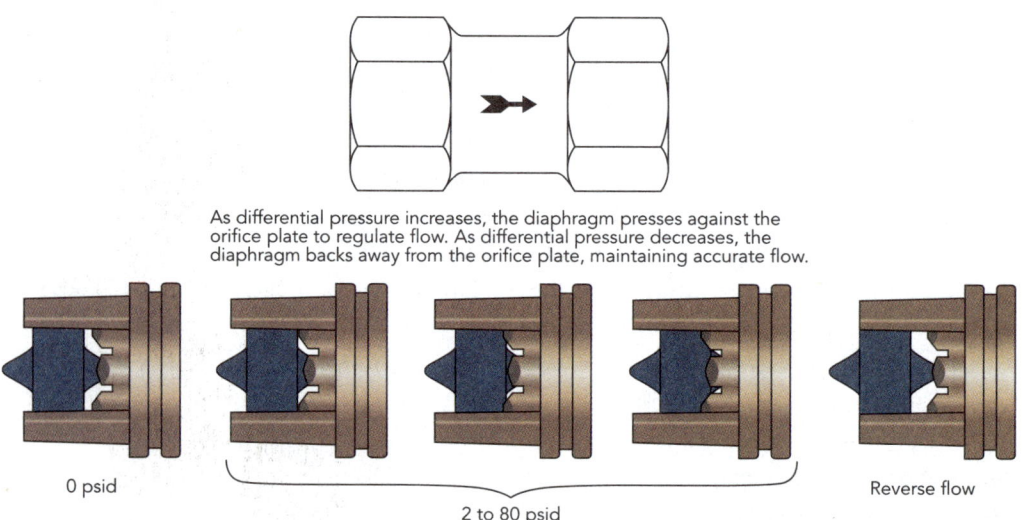

Figure 5-20. Typical flow restrictor

the flow valve. Control of the supply pressure can be managed with a pressure-regulating valve (see Figure 5-21 below). A pressure-regulating valve operates best if installed on the supply line close to the inlet of the geothermal unit, where it can be easily identified as a component of the geothermal system.

A pressure regulator typically has a small screen strainer in its inlet line. Strainers must be kept clean by prefiltering the water supply. Without a prefiltered supply, the thimble-size strainer tends to clog when debris is present, creating frequent low-flow or low-pressure lockouts of the geothermal system. It takes a perceptive technician to identify and correct the problem. As an alternative to the use of pressure regulators, many installers simply add back pressure by restricting a discharge-line ball valve. As the valve is closed, the back pressure helps to reduce the sound of cavitation to a tolerable level (but does not eliminate it entirely). Silencing a flow restrictor completely is an indication that the flow has been reduced below the specified size of the flow restrictor, which can create operational problems for the geothermal system.

Sound isolation for flow restrictors

Closed-loop systems use rubber hose to connect the flow center and the compressor section. A similar technique is used to isolate the cavitation vibrations created by a flow restrictor in an open-loop installation. To reduce sound transmission between water lines and the framing within the home, it is imperative for all water lines to be insulated and suspended from the floor joists. They should never be mounted in direct contact with the wood framing. The sound emitted by flow restrictors may be further reduced by isolating them from the rigid piping. Noise can be nearly eliminated by installing the flow restrictor between two 18-in. lengths of high-density rubber hose.

Substantial success has been achieved in installations that use heavy rubber hose with steel-reinforced braid rated for 400 psi (steam hose), and with the stainless-steel braided hose connectors intended for use with domestic hot water tanks. By isolating the flow restrictor within a flexible loop, vibrations that might be carried

Figure 5-21. Water pressure regulator

to floor joists are abated. Flow restrictors should be installed in the final discharge line after the water solenoid valve. By regulating the water flow and pressure on the outlet side of the geothermal system, the fluid inside the geothermal unit is always held at full pressure. Dissolved gases thus remain in solution and mineral precipitates are kept to a minimum.

ILLUSTRATION CREDITS
FIGURE 5-1: JEFF PERSONS
FIGURE 5-2: JEFF PERSONS
FIGURE 5-3: REHAU
FIGURE 5-4: JEFF PERSONS
FIGURE 5-5: JEFF PERSONS
FIGURE 5-6: JEFF PERSONS
FIGURE 5-7: JEFF PERSONS
FIGURE 5-8: JEFF PERSONS
FIGURE 5-9: JEFF PERSONS
FIGURE 5-10: JEFF PERSONS
FIGURE 5-11: JEFF PERSONS
FIGURE 5-12: CLIMATEMASTER
FIGURE 5-13: WATERFURNACE
FIGURE 5-14: GRUNDFOS
FIGURE 5-15: HAYS FLUID CONTROLS
FIGURE 5-16: WATERFURNACE
FIGURE 5-17: RIDGID
FIGURE 5-18: STANLEY VIRAX
FIGURE 5-19: JEFF PERSONS
FIGURE 5-20: HAYS FLUID CONTROLS
FIGURE 5-21: WATTS WATER TECHNOLOGIES

◄CHAPTER SIX►
Loop Fill Solutions

INTRODUCTION

Perhaps one of the most overlooked items in a geothermal installation is the quality and chemistry of the loop fill solution. The industry perception is that a loop can be filled and forgotten, that the original fill solution and piping components will last forever. Nothing could be further from the truth. With proper planning and execution, however, the correct water chemistry and solution fill will ensure the longevity of the geothermal system and the piping components through which the solution circulates.

Before embarking on a discussion of system fill solutions, it is necessary to understand the relationship among the various metals found in a geothermal system and in the flow center pumps that circulate the fluid. *Galvanic corrosion* is basically a reaction between two different metals. The reaction is both electrical and chemical in nature. Galvanic action requires three conditions:

➤ two dissimilar metals (metals with different electrochemical properties)
➤ an electrolyte (a solution through which an electric current can flow)
➤ an electron path to connect the two metals.

Many different metals are used to fabricate heating and cooling systems. Until two dissimilar metals come into contact, no galvanic action takes place. But add a solution containing ions, and you have an electrolyte that can bring the two dissimilar metals into electrical contact and set up an electron path. Take a look at the list of metals at the top of the next page. They are arranged in what is known as the *galvanic series*. Note that metals such as aluminum, zinc, and magnesium are at the bottom end of the scale ("active metals"), while silver, gold, and graphite are at the top end of the scale ("noble metals"). Steel, iron, copper, and brass are mid-scale metals. When dissimilar metals are immersed in a conductive solution, a weak voltage potential is created, essentially forming a battery cell. Whether the conductive solution bringing the metals in contact is antifreeze or water, electrons will move from the metal lower on the scale to one higher on the scale. As a result, the metal lower in the galvanic series is subjected to galvanic corrosion.

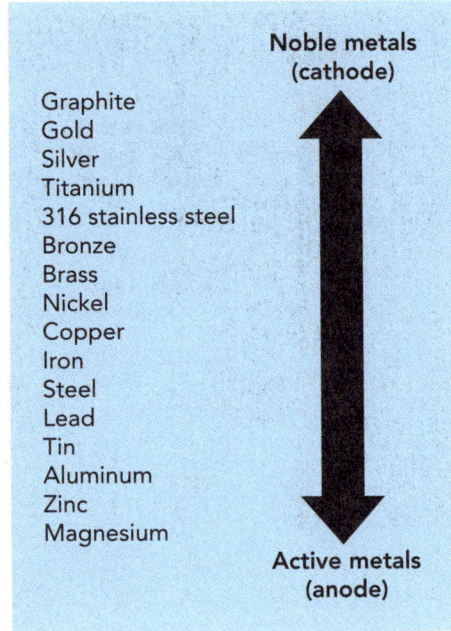

All water piping systems are exposed to galvanic corrosion. The water heaters used for domestic hot water are a prime example. The vast majority of hot water tanks are steel, with a glass lining that serves as short-term protection against corrosion and prevents "red iron" staining of the water supply. To add extra corrosion protection, the tank manufacturer installs a magnesium or aluminum rod in the tank to act as a "sacrificial anode."

Raw tap water is particularly aggressive toward metals that are on the lower end of the galvanic series. A common misconception is that softened water improves water quality. In fact, "soft" water simply replaces calcium and magnesium with sodium. In a catch-22 scenario, reducing the "scale formers" through the removal of calcium and magnesium actually makes the softened water *more* corrosive. Highly softened water supplies increase galvanic corrosion and the rapid depletion of the sacrificial anode in the water heater. Once the anode is consumed, there is about an 18-month time period until the tank itself starts to leak from corrosion around tank fittings and flaws in the glass lining.

How does this example relate to a geothermal system? In essence, almost all water solutions are corrosive or will allow some form of galvanic corrosion unless they are made chemically stable. Softened water may require less soap when you do laundry and is less likely to produce scale, but as mentioned in the preceding paragraph, it

Figure 6-1. Sodium carbonate salt crystals on brass purge valve installed in geothermal domestic hot water recirculation line

is far more corrosive than the original hard water. This is why it is common to find crusty white deposits on brass valves that distribute softened water. The corrosive nature of the softened water has depleted (less noble) zinc from the (more noble) brass, creating a porous metal. As sodium-rich water seeps through the brass, its evaporation forms the white crystals (see Figure 6-1).

The overall quality of the loop fill solution used in a geothermal system can have a long-lasting effect on the life expectancy of flow center pumps and piping components. Valves, like water heaters and plumbing fixtures, are frequently replaced, but few customers appreciate being told that a $1,500 geothermal flow center needs to be replaced. Understanding galvanic corrosion and how to avoid the problems that it causes can help contractors maintain happy customers and efficient operating systems.

WATER VS. ANTIFREEZE

In southern climates, cooling-dominant geothermal installations typically use domestic water as the system fill. Plumbers and well water industry tradespeople have long understood that black iron and galvanized metal are the first to begin leaking if used in a water distribution system. To avoid callbacks and leak problems, contractors instead choose pumps with bronze or stainless steel bodies. The primary metals on the "wet" side of a geothermal system are copper or cupronickel and brass. If the pump body of a geothermal flow center is made of cast iron, it becomes the sacrificial anode (because it is the only ferrous component in the entire piping system and has a lower rating in the galvanic series), and is therefore subject to the same life-span limitations as a water heater. A simple solution for avoiding flow center corrosion is to specify bronze body pumps on any flow center that uses "raw" water as the system fill. For larger systems, in which ferrous body pumps and steel piping are more common, commercial contractors who are familiar with water-conditioning procedures for boiler and cooling tower systems are likely to have an agreement with a "water system maintenance" company. Water treatment and conditioning for large closed systems is a science to itself and is best left to those with a strong background in water chemistry. An online search for boiler/tower water treatment services in your location should turn up a number of companies familiar with the process of testing and treating water supplies.

Specifying a bronze body flow center solves the majority of issues surrounding galvanic corrosion in "raw" water circulation systems. There is, however, one other condition that requires attention. A water supply that is low in hardness minerals, such as snowmelt, rainwater, distilled water, or in some cases water derived from a granite or igneous aquifer, is likely to have a low pH value. This kind of water is said to be "thirsty"—that is, it is looking for something to dissolve—and can be highly corrosive to metal piping systems.

Recall that the pH scale is used for measuring the acidity or alkalinity of a substance. It is a logarithmic scale numbered from 0 to 14. A pH value of 7 is considered neutral, 0 is highly acidic, and 14 is highly alkaline. The *alkalinity* of a water supply is defined as its capacity to neutralize acid. Alkalinity increases with the presence of hardness minerals (calcium and magnesium carbonate) in a water supply. Simple test kits for the measurement of pH and alkalinity, as well as chemicals needed to make adjustments to each, are available from pool and spa supply stores. Litmus paper test strips provide an easy way to check for both pH and alkalinity. If the pH of a water supply is less than 7.4, it is probable that the alkalinity is also low and needs to be adjusted. To correct for low pH, follow the instructions on the container and add pool or spa sodium carbonate (soda ash) or sodium bicarbonate (baking soda) as needed to increase the alkalinity and raise the pH. A final pH reading between 7.4 and 7.6 should place the solution within a range that will ensure a trouble-free circulation system. (A good target for total alkalinity is a reading of 80 to 140 ppm. The addition of 0.2 ounces of soda ash or baking soda per 100 gallons of fluid should raise the alkalinity by 10 ppm.) Remember: This process is intended for systems with bronze-body flow center pumps. Ferrous-body pumps are still likely to experience corrosion because of the presence of copper and brass within the geothermal system piping and valves.

In northern climates, heating-dominant systems spend a significant portion of their winter run hours with system loop temperatures near or below the freezing point. These systems require an antifreeze solution to accommodate winter operation. The ideal antifreeze should have three primary qualities:

> nontoxicity (to comply with local environmental and health codes)
> low viscosity (easily pumpable at temperatures between 24 and 110°F)
> compatibility (noncorrosive to metals within the geothermal system).

TYPES OF ANTIFREEZE SOLUTIONS

Table 6-1 on the next page lists nine antifreeze solutions that have been used with geothermal installations. The following paragraphs consider them individually and discuss the suitability of each for use in a geothermal system.

Calcium chloride

Calcium chloride is a relatively nontoxic, low-viscosity salt solution commonly used as a low-temperature pavement de-icer. Its hygroscopic nature (ability to absorb moisture) also makes it useful as an agent for holding down road dust. When combined with oxygen, calcium chloride is highly corrosive and will eat through metal containers (geothermal cabinets, flow center boxes, pump housings, etc.). Calcium chloride is commonly used to fill heavy-equipment tires and as an inexpensive antifreeze for hockey rink ice-mat systems. When used for hockey rinks, careful attention must be given to chemical maintenance and to the concentration of oxygen scavengers needed to prevent the solution from attacking metal components of the system. The slightest leak from a fitting or residue left on a cabinet or metal surface can lead to complete corrosion of the affected area. Most ground-loop heat pumps filled with calcium chloride are "retired" from service within 8 to 10 years of installation, due to cabinet corrosion and the failure of flow center pumps and piping components. Calcium chloride is not recommended for use with geothermal heat pumps.

Potassium acetate

Potassium acetate was considered an environmentally acceptable antifreeze for a brief period. Potassium acetate is a nontoxic, low-pH potassium salt that quickly biodegrades if released into the environment. At one time it was used as a plane de-icing agent for environmentally sensitive areas, but the solution proved to have a very low surface tension, which allowed it to leak through almost any threaded connection. Threaded pipe had to be carefully cleaned to remove any trace of oil or contaminant. Teflon tape and paste were ineffective at preventing seepage at threaded connections. Special compounds were needed to prevent seepage at pipe joints. When seepage did occur, the solution proved to be as aggressive to metals as calcium chloride. Cast-iron body pumps suffered numerous failures from corrosion and pump seal leaks. The only flow centers to survive were those with bronze pumps. The use of potassium chloride was

Solution	Characteristics	Suitability
Calcium chloride	• Highly corrosive if oxygen is present • Low cost • Low viscosity • Will rust most metals • Residue will draw moisture	Not recommended
Potassium acetate	• Low surface tension will leak past most connections • Low viscosity • Highly corrosive if oxygen is present • Will biodegrade in the environment	Not recommended
Methanol (racing alcohol)	• Low cost • Toxic fluid • Low viscosity • Highly corrosive to metals • Flammable vapors • Check compatibility with gaskets, "O" rings, and seals	Not recommended (but commonly used)
Inhibited ethanol	• Moderate to high cost • Nontoxic • Low viscosity • Flammable vapors • Check compatibility with gaskets, "O" rings, and seals	Good for low-temperature loops
Ethylene glycol (automotive)	• Moderate cost • Toxic fluid • Viscosity increases at higher concentrations and lower temperatures • Inhibitors may jell	Not recommended
Inhibited ethylene glycol	• Moderate cost • Toxic • Boiler and tower fill antifreeze • Viscosity increases at higher concentrations and lower temperatures	OK for use when permitted by local health codes
Propylene glycol (food grade)	• Moderate to high cost • Nontoxic • Corrosive • Viscosity increases at higher concentrations and lower temperatures	Not recommended due to corrosive nature of uninhibited solution
Inhibited propylene glycol	• Moderate to high cost • Nontoxic • Viscosity increases at higher concentrations and lower temperatures	Good for low-temperature loops*
Glycerine	• High cost • Nontoxic • Corrosive without inhibitors • Viscosity increases at higher concentrations and lower temperatures	Required by health codes in some areas**

* Viscosity becomes an issue at concentrations higher than 20% and temperatures lower than 20°F.
** Concentration of 25% provides protection to 20°F. Alkalinity and pH of mixed solution likely will determine if solution is corrosive.

Table 6-1. Comparing antifreeze solutions for use in geothermal systems

discontinued within one to two years of its introduction. Potassium chloride is *not recommended* for use with GLHPs.

Methanol

Methanol (racing alcohol) is listed in the loop pressure drop tables of nearly every manufacturer of geothermal equipment. As an alcohol, it is a low-cost antifreeze with low viscosity, making it easy to pump at low temperatures. Unfortunately, methanol has three negative factors:

➤ Its toxicity makes it a deadly hazard should it find a way to contaminate a water supply or be consumed.

➤ Methanol is a great solvent, which means that it is highly corrosive. It can quickly begin dissolving metals and rubber seals. An excellent example of the corrosive nature of methanol dates back to the early 1970s, when one brand of gasoline marketed a product with an "ice guard," backed by a pledge to pay your towing bill if your car's fuel line froze up. The "ice guard" additive was methanol. The solubility of water with methanol prevented the formation of ice in the fuel line. It was a great marketing tool and it did prevent fuel-line freeze-ups, but water in the gas tank was not the only thing that the methanol was dissolving. Its use led to an industry-wide failure of gas tanks, gas lines, fuel pumps, and carburetors. For the same reason, those who follow **NASCAR** or use methanol for racing know that it is necessary to replace their "fuel cells" (gas tanks) regularly due to corrosion

Figure 6-2. Methanol corrosion and perforation of pump body

and leakage. Because of its corrosive nature, methanol should *not* be stored in metal containers. Furthermore, methanol can lead to rapid corrosion of flow center pumps. In a geothermal installation, the ferrous metal pump bodies are the lowest metal in the galvanic series. In the presence of methanol, a pump body becomes the sacrificial anode for the piping system (see Figure 6-2).

> Methanol is flammable. A low vapor pressure and an ignition temperature create a hazard for handling methanol. Vapors may ignite (the flame is nearly invisible) with a simple spark from a light switch or cigarette, from static electricity, or from the careless use of an extension cord or drop light near a flush-and-purge pump. For proper handling of methanol, flush-and-purge equipment should be explosion-proof, and work spaces need to be well-ventilated. The safety of the structure and its occupants calls for concentrated solutions to be diluted outside the building, and piped or carried inside using closed containers. Most systems that use an alcohol solution as an antifreeze are designed for long periods of operation at subfreezing temperatures. These systems are likely to have a concentration adjusted for a freeze point of 15 to 17°F and an alcohol concentration of 20%. At this dilute concentration, the solution is not flammable—but this is no guarantee that the captive vapors in a covered container will not ignite. The possibility of ignition of methanol vapor increases as the temperature of the solution rises and the alcohol evaporates from the base solution.

Methanol, while in wide use as a geothermal system antifreeze, can be a major contributor to system leaks and the failure of ferrous body pumps. To date, no magical corrosion inhibitor has been found to neutralize methanol's aggressive behavior. The liability exposure created by methanol's toxicity, corrosiveness, and flammability should make geothermal installers think twice about its continued use.

Inhibited ethanol

Inhibited ethanol (vodka and water) is a nontoxic, low-viscosity antifreeze formulated from denatured ethyl alcohol and deionized water. The ethanol solution contains corrosion inhibitors to protect metals within the system and a flavoring agent to discourage its consumption. For safety's sake, inhibited ethanol solutions are best purchased as premixed solutions. This ensures that the mix water and the inhibitors are compatible with each other. The premix solution is 25% ethanol in deionized water for a freeze point of 10°F. As a dilute solution, the premix is less flammable and easier to handle than the concentrate.

Those who wish to work with concentrate must heed warnings always to use deionized water as a make-up solution. Raw well water or even city water is not recommended for mixing with an "inhibited antifreeze." Naturally occurring minerals in a raw water supply can combine with corrosion inhibitors, causing them to precipitate and leave the system without the needed corrosion protection. Deionized water is essentially the same as distilled water—it has no mineral content to interfere with maintaining inhibitor strength and protection for metals within the piping system. The concentrate is super-saturated with inhibitors, which may settle to the bottom of the drum. For effective mixing, the concentrate needs to be constantly agitated in order to suspend the inhibitors and make sure that they are mixed with the deionized water in the proper proportion. If mixed for a ratio of 20% concentrate to 80% deionized water, the resulting solution should have a freeze point of 20°F.

Inhibited ethanol has the advantages of low toxicity and low viscosity. When handled as a premixed solution, ignition hazards are reduced. Vapors still represent a potential danger, however, and require proper ventilation and safety precautions to avoid ignition. Inhibited ethanol antifreeze is an excellent nontoxic alternative to methanol solutions. Its denatured formulation with corrosion inhibitors helps to prevent the corrosion problems associated with methanol.

Ethylene glycol

Ethylene glycol (automotive antifreeze) is extremely toxic. If ingested, ethylene glycol can cause kidney failure. In some instances, commercial-grade inhibited ethylene glycol may be used in GLHP systems. However, its use requires complete isolation from domestic water sources, as well as posted safety precautions and warnings. When glycols are to be used, GLHP systems should be designed for a 20% solution in deionized water. System loop minimum design temperature should be set for 30°F or higher, with an antifreeze freeze point of 20°F. If ethylene glycol solutions are used in concentrations greater than 20%, the viscosity increases dramatically as the temperature decreases. As a result, pumping costs escalate and system efficiency drops.

Ethylene glycol formulated for automotive use contains corrosion inhibitors designed for use in high-temperature engines. These inhibitors are *not* intended for the metals (or the temperature range) found in GLHP systems, and should always be avoided. If inhibitors in the automotive blend start to react with hardness minerals in a make-up water solution, the antifreeze has been known to gel and produce mineral precipitates that hamper heat exchange. Automotive ethylene glycol is *not recommended* for use in geothermal systems.

Propylene glycol

Propylene glycol is a nontoxic, food-grade antifreeze with moderate to high viscosity. Propylene glycol has wide application as an agent in pharmaceuticals, soft drinks, and processed foods. In its "food-grade" condition, propylene glycol is corrosive to metals. For use with GLHP piping systems, propylene glycol must be specified as "inhibited."

Inhibitors added to the propylene glycol help to buffer the pH by adding controlled alkalinity to the fluid mixture. Propylene glycol is popular as a nontoxic antifreeze solution for loop designs with a minimum loop temperature of 30°F or higher. Like its toxic counterpart, ethylene glycol, propylene has issues related to viscosity when used in concentrations greater than 20% and at temperatures below 30°F. Solutions made from inhibited concentrate should always be made with deionized or distilled water. This ensures that the inhibitors will remain in solution and be effective at preventing corrosion of system metals.

Failure to maintain a clean system or to use deionized or distilled water as a make-up solution risks the potential for bacterial contamination of any glycol solution. Bacteria can utilize glycol as a food source. Should this occur, glycols can gel or become acidic and take on a sickeningly foul odor. The treatment for systems with contaminated glycol can be extensive. A complete system flush, sanitizing, and fluid replacement usually are required, combined with a compatible biocide agent specified by the glycol chemical supplier. Propylene glycol can be an excellent GLHP system antifreeze when used with loop designs that maintain operating temperatures above 30°F.

Glycerin

Glycerin is a nontoxic, pharmaceutical-grade antifreeze. In the 1920s, glycerin was the principal antifreeze for automotive systems. Its production cost at that time was several times greater than that of ethylene glycol. When automotive manufacturers made the change to ethylene glycol, glycerin fell out of favor. More recently, because it is a byproduct of biofuel production, glycerin is gaining a renewed market interest as a nontoxic antifreeze. To date, the major producers of glycerin make a product for pharmaceutical use only. Information on suitable inhibitors and inhibitor mixing procedures for glycerin appear to be lacking. Its concentration, freeze point, and viscosity are similar to those of the glycols. A glycerin concentration of 25% in deionized water is needed to attain a freeze point of 20°F. The viscosity of glycerin—again like that of the glycols—increases at higher concentrations and reduced temperatures.

Information obtained from field sources indicates that, in a few instances, local health departments have established their own standards for geothermal loop installations and have specified glycerin as the only acceptable antifreeze for their jurisdictions. This specification is probably well-intended but may be premature. It may be reasonably anticipated that if glycerin is mixed with distilled or deionized water, the resulting solution will be corrosive and will need buffering to increase the alkalinity and raise the pH. Glycerine has the ability to become an acceptable nontoxic antifreeze, but additional research and industry support is needed to develop an inhibited prepackaged product before it can gain wide acceptance.

When you are working with solutions for GLHP systems, the best advice is:

- For systems that utilize local tap water as a solution fill, use bronze-body pumps to avoid premature pump failure.
- For antifreeze-protected systems, always use a clean, demineralized solution as the mix water. This means using distilled or deionized water.
- Use an antifreeze that has corrosion inhibitors to protect the metals in the system.
- Mix the solution according to the manufacturer's instructions. *Never* combine antifreezes from different sources. Cross-mixing can cause the precipitation of inhibitors and create additional problems.
- Label or tag each flow center to identify the antifreeze type and manufacturer, so that those who follow will know what to expect when the system is open for service.
- When filling a system, leave a sample of the antifreeze mix in a sealed 5-gallon plastic container. Label the container with the antifreeze type, concentration, and purpose (geothermal loop fill solution). This will come in handy for technicians when service is required, or when "goosing the loop" is needed to raise the operating loop pressure (should the pressure slowly drop with changes in time and temperature).

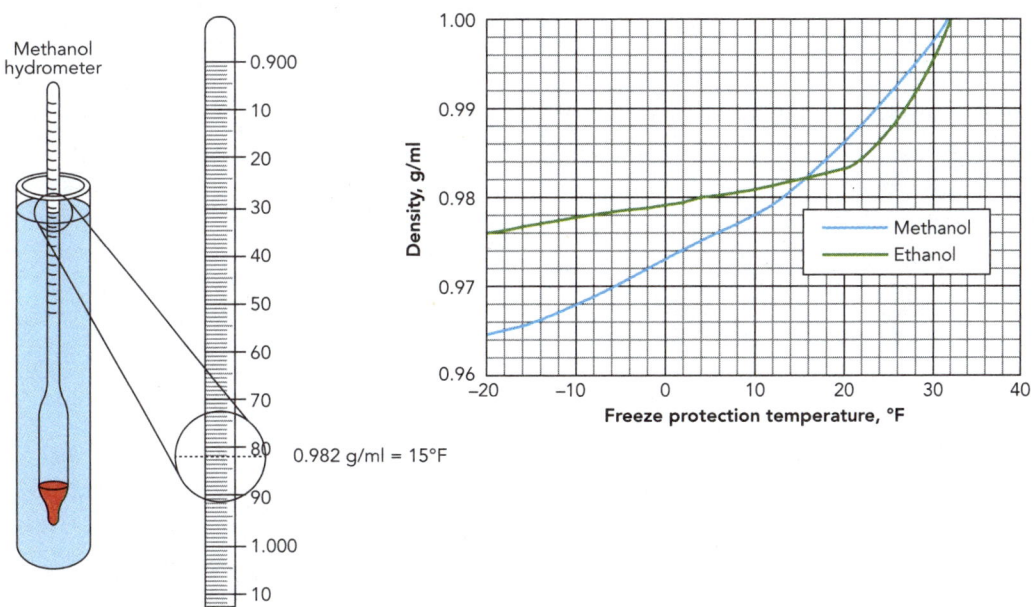

Figure 6-3. Methanol/ethanol freeze protection curves

CHECKING ANTIFREEZE CONCENTRATIONS

Two methods are employed for determining antifreeze concentration. Each is specific to the type of antifreeze in use. For alcohol solutions that are less dense than water, a *hydrometer* is used (see Figure 6-3 on the previous page). When you are working with alcohol solutions, it is important to know whether the solution being measured is methanol or ethanol. As you can see in Figure 6-3, the density and freeze point curves for the two solutions are different. Taking a hydrometer reading is relatively easy. A capped ¾-in. PVC pipe makes an excellent sample container. The hydrometer will float in the sample solution. As the concentration of alcohol in the solution increases, the density of the water is reduced and the hydrometer sinks. The density is read starting from the top of the hydrometer at a reading of 0.900. From the example shown in Figure 6-3, a density reading of 0.982 equates to a freeze point of approximately 15°F for both methanol and ethanol.

Glycol-based antifreezes are denser than water. Concentrations of ethylene glycol and propylene glycol are best measured with a *refractometer*. A refractometer operates on the principle that light is refracted,

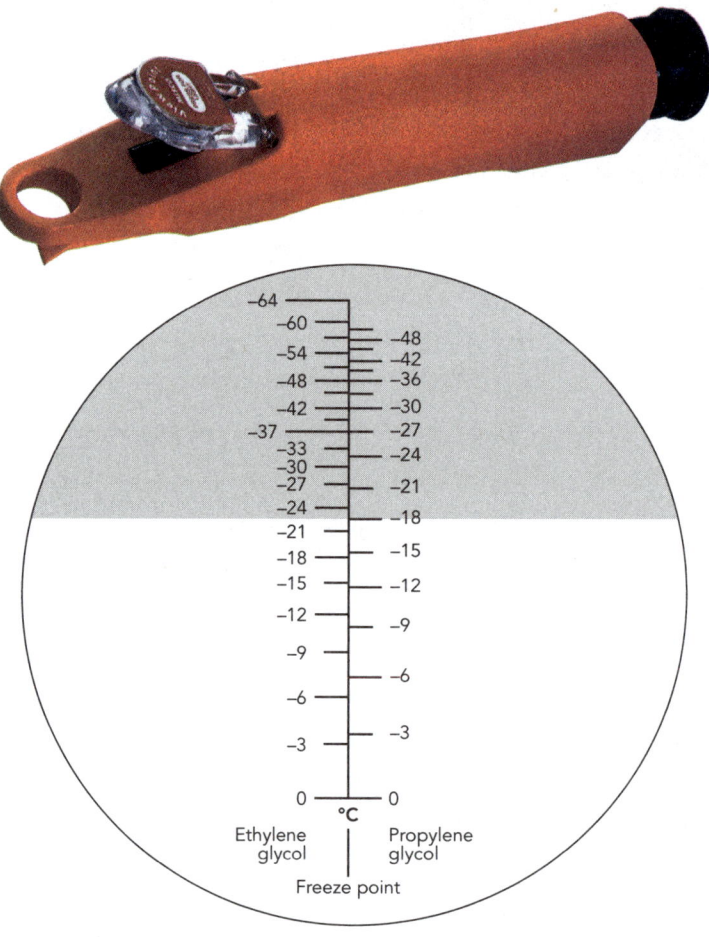

Figure 6-4. Glycol refractometer

or bent, as it passes through a fluid sample (just as a prism separates visible light into a spectrum of colors). The angle by which a ray of light bends when it passes through a solution is based on the density of the solution, and is directly related to the solution's freeze point. A few drops of antifreeze on the lens plate of a handheld refractometer (see Figure 6-4) produce a light/shadow pattern on the viewfinder's density scale that corresponds with the freeze point of the antifreeze sample being tested. The image at the bottom of Figure 6-4 illustrates the light/shadow pattern as seen through the sightglass of the refractometer. The line between the shaded and unshaded areas indicates the antifreeze density and corresponding freeze point. Refractometers that provide digital readouts are also available.

ADJUSTING ANTIFREEZE CONCENTRATIONS

When working with closed-loop systems, you sometimes may find it necessary to reconstitute an antifreeze solution that has been diluted due to the loss of fluid during service or equipment replacement. A good example comes from a customer with a leaky "single-pipe" loop. The leak was the result of pipe contraction caused by freezing temperatures and a sharp rock at the return bend of the $1^{1}/_{4}$-in. thin-wall, 65-psi PE earth loop (similar to the failure shown in Figure 5-1). In an effort to keep the system in operation until the leak could be located, the customer added an unknown quantity of distilled water to a solution pail connected to a fitting on the flow center. The solution pail allowed for the addition of fluid on the suction side of the pumps without artificially pressurizing the loop, thus causing increased fluid loss. Records left from the initial installation indicated a total installed length of 2,160 ft (2,000 ft of the $1^{1}/_{4}$-in. thin-wall pipe, plus another 160 ft for interior piping). The manufacturer's tables for the PE pipe stipulated a fluid volume of 9.45 gallons per 100 ft of pipe, for a total system volume of 204 gallons (9.45 gallons × 2,160 ft/100 ft). Following the repair and flushing operation to replace lost fluid with more distilled water, a measurement with the refractometer indicated a remaining concentration of only 15%. The challenge, once the system was known to be full, was:

How many gallons of concentrated propylene glycol need to be added to bring the final solution back up to a 20% concentration?

The equation used to solve this problem holds true for all concentrations and dilutions, provided that the amount of dilute fluid removed from the system is equal to the volume of concentrate added (so that the total system volume remains constant). In this case, the total system volume was 204 gallons of 15% solution, and you want to find out how many gallons of 100% propylene glycol need to be added as you decant (remove) the same volume of 15% solution. The equation can be stated as follows:

$$Q = \frac{V \times (P_d - P_t)}{(100 - P_t)}$$

where:
- Q = quantity of antifreeze to be added
- V = system volume, in gallons
- P_d = percent solution desired
- P_t = percent solution by test
- 100 = percent solution in the concentrate to be added (this value could be less than 100% if you are working with a premixed solution rather than a concentrate).

Substituting the known values into the equation:

$$Q = \frac{204 \text{ gallons} \times (20 - 15)}{(100 - 15)}$$

$$= \frac{204 \text{ gallons} \times 5}{85}$$

$$= \frac{1{,}020 \text{ gallons}}{85}$$

$$= 12 \text{ gallons}$$

The quantity of concentrated antifreeze that needs to be added is 12 gallons. As the concentrate is added, the same volume of 15% antifreeze is decanted from the return side of the loop into a clean container to be reconstituted for future reuse. The resulting loop solution will be at 20% as specified by the project design. ◆

ILLUSTRATION CREDITS
FIGURE 6-1: JEFF PERSONS
FIGURE 6-2: JEFF PERSONS
FIGURE 6-3: WATERFURNACE
FIGURE 6-4: MISCO

‹CHAPTER SEVEN›
Controls

ENERGY STAR RATINGS

As of May 2011, the list of Energy Star-rated geothermal systems included at least 27 manufacturing sources. The Energy Star rating is necessary if a geothermal system is to receive the 30% federal residential energy efficiency tax credit. The document, which can be found at the www.energystar.gov website, contains 123 pages of qualifying equipment model numbers listed by manufacturer, brand name, and model name. The geothermal industry is constantly changing—new products are introduced on a weekly basis. In many cases, a "new" offering is simply a "private label" product for an approved geothermal system that is already manufactured by one of several larger companies. The geothermal industry abounds with "look-alike" systems from different sources that share the same controls and piping configurations. While many of these systems have essentially the same parent company, warranty parts and technical support must be obtained via the supply chain that made the initial sale. This chapter examines standardized controls used by three major equipment manufacturers. The purpose is to highlight some of the most frequent installation oversights—and thereby help technicians avoid costly callbacks for repeat service on new systems. The three primary manufacturers account for 76% of the total number of systems included in the Energy Star listings. As for the remaining 24%, the number of variations and manufacturer-specific controls is far too great to cover in this chapter. *All* geothermal systems—those in the predominant 76% and those in the other 24%—require service technicians to obtain additional factory instruction to become competent with the necessary controls, operating procedures, programming, and set-up routines.

In exploring the Energy Star-rated geothermal systems listed online, be aware that some manufacturers allow open access to equipment manuals and installation literature, while others require registration and passwords to access service-related information. Energy Star guidelines are quite stringent and therefore are focused on the higher-efficiency models produced by the listed manufacturers. Most manufacturers are likely to have additional models that are very efficient, but do not meet the cut-off restrictions to qualify for tax credits. The Energy Star program has separate efficiency requirements for open-loop and closed-loop systems. For this reason, many of the listed geothermal systems may appear twice—once as a qualifying open-loop system, and a second time as a qualifying closed-loop system.

Tier 1 requirements (effective December 1, 2009)		
Product type	EER	COP
Closed-loop water-to-air	14.1	3.3
Open-loop water-to-air	16.2	3.6
Closed-loop water-to-water	15.1	3.0
Open-loop water-to-water	19.1	3.4
DGX	15.0	3.5
Tier 2 requirements (effective January 1, 2011)		
Product type	EER	COP
Closed-loop water-to-air	16.1	3.5
Open-loop water-to-air	18.2	3.8
Closed-loop water-to-water	15.1	3.0
Open-loop water-to-water	19.1	3.4
DGX	16.0	3.6
Tier 3 requirements (effective January 1, 2012)		
Product type	EER	COP
Closed-loop water-to-air	17.1	3.6
Open-loop water-to-air	21.1	4.1
Closed-loop water-to-water	16.1	3.1
Open-loop water-to-water	20.1	3.5
DGX	16.0	3.6

Note: The specifications in the charts above apply to single-stage models. Multistage models may be qualified based on:
EER = (highest-rated capacity EER + lowest-rated capacity EER) ÷ 2
COP = (highest-rated capacity COP + lowest-rated capacity COP) ÷ 2

Table 7-1. Energy efficiency requirements for geothermal heat pumps

In some instances, it may even happen that a system qualifies in the open-loop category but does not meet the efficiency level to qualify in the closed-loop category.

There are three tiers to the Energy Star guidelines for geothermal systems qualifying for federal tax credits. The effective dates and efficiency levels required for each type of geothermal system appear in Table 7-1. As you can see, Tier 1 requirements in the schedule went into effect on December 1, 2009. The efficiency requirements increased to Tier 2 on January 1, 2011, and increased again to Tier 3 on January 1, 2012. The January 1, 2012 standards will remain effective until the tax credit either expires on December 31, 2016, or is modified as the transition date approaches.

As of May 2011, there were 3,185 product listings in the Energy Star geothermal heat pump program. As stated before, the majority of these listings (76%) are derived from three primary equipment manufacturers.

Taken alphabetically and providing equipment marketed under the following brand names, they are:

1. **ClimateMaster, Inc.**
   - ClimateMaster
   - Bryant
   - Carrier
   - Century
   - Comfort-Aire
   - Rheem
   - Ruud
2. **FHP Manufacturing/Bosch Group**
   - Florida Heat Pump
   - Bosch Geo
   - GeoExcel
3. **WaterFurnace International, Inc.**
   - WaterFurnace
   - Eagle Mountain
   - GeoSmart
   - GeoStar
   - Johnson Controls
   - Trane/American Standard

> *Note:* Service and sales personnel who make a commitment to a customer regarding tax credits *must* be familiar with the Energy Star requirements and verify that the system model and application method comply with Energy Star guidelines. *Never* presume that all systems in a manufacturer's product lineup qualify for the tax credit. It's easy to make broad statements regarding tax credits. However, if a purchasing customer believes that he or she is entitled to a tax credit based on your recommendation, and it turns out that the system in question does *not* qualify under Energy Star criteria, some courts of law may regard this as a "breach of truth in advertising" and award triple damages to the plaintiff.

CONTROLS OVERVIEW

Some field technicians and system installers may be accustomed to the simple "set it and forget it" approach. This is definitely *not* the case with today's super-high-efficiency geothermal systems. These sophisticated systems require far more than a simple defrost board for their control. They use microprocessors to manage variable-speed fans, two-stage compressors, geothermal loop pumps, and domestic hot water pumps. Their controls sense refrigerant pressure and temperature at multiple points in the system, impose time delays, provide fan cfm readings, monitor condensate, and provide status outputs to assist with the diagnosis of system faults and service needs. The days of simple mechanical controls are over.

In the late 1980s and early 1990s, if a geothermal system did not run, there was no mechanism to tell the technician which control tripped or why the system faulted. Diagnostics were a matter of the technician's experience and familiarity with the system. Beginning in the early 1990s, however, geothermal manufacturers began using microprocessor control boards to monitor system operation and report the status of key functions. As the technology has advanced, several of these control boards have been configured to adapt and communicate with building automation systems and "smart home" technology. These controls add flexibility, provide operation history, report current status, and dramatically reduce the time required for service and diagnostics. Technicians who set up and maintain these systems must have total comprehension of the installation and troubleshooting procedures for proper commissioning and service.

Early mechanical controls

Early geothermal controls were very basic. Because many are still in use, technicians should have an understanding of their operation. Primary safety controls are limited to a conventional high- and low-pressure switch, plus one or more thermal sensors to protect the system from freezing. To prevent repeat cycling from the automatic reset of a safety limit, the safety controls are wired in series with the normally closed contact of a lockout relay (see Figure 7-1). The lockout relay consists of a high-impedance relay coil with normally closed contacts. (A high-impedance coil typically has a resistance of more than 200 Ω, as opposed to a normal 24-V compressor contactor coil with a resistance of 10 Ω.) The lockout relay coil is wired in parallel with the safety controls, so that whenever a safety control opens, all power to the compressor contactor must pass through the high-impedance coil of the lockout relay. This configuration places the two coils in a series circuit. The higher impedance (resistance) of the lockout relay coil—as opposed to the lower impedance of the compressor relay coil—allows the high-impedance coil to function as a resistor, reducing voltage to the compressor contactor and preventing the contactor from engaging the compressor.

As long as 24-V power is maintained from the thermostat, the lockout relay contacts are held open even if the high-pressure control, low-pressure control, or any additional safety control resets while in the lockout condition. To reset a system, it is necessary either to: satisfy the heat or cool signal from the thermostat, turn off the thermostat, or turn off the primary power supply. Any action that breaks the 24-V run signal to the

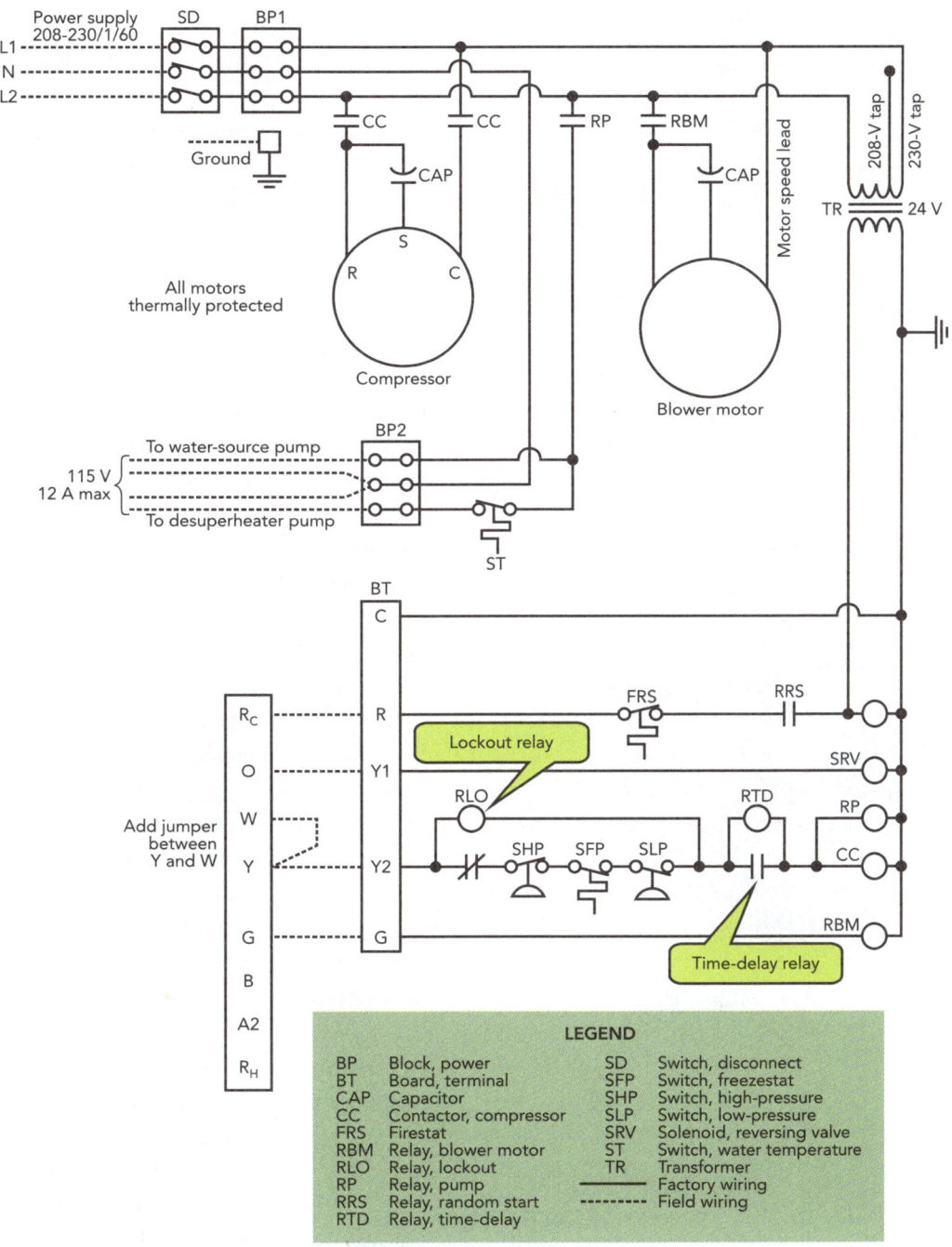

Figure 7-1. Early mechanical control wiring diagram

Note: To attain high efficiency across a wide range of entering fluid temperatures and also make the best use of available fin-coil heat exchange, geothermal systems utilize thermal expansion valves (TEVs) to regulate refrigerant flow. When a TEV is used, refrigerant pressures take much longer to equalize after a run cycle than is common with systems that use a simple flow orifice or capillary tube. This necessitated the need for 5-minute short-cycle delay timers to prevent damage to compressors from attempted locked-rotor restarts before refrigerant pressure had a chance to equalize.

compressor contactor circuit will allow the lockout relay to reset and permit the system to resume operation. In addition to the basic controls, solid-state time-delay relays sometimes were incorporated as a way to prevent short-cycling of the compressor contactor (such as might happen if the voltage was unstable during a storm or when short-cycling of a mechanical mercury-bulb thermostat occurred).

The most common time-delay relays are the two-wire variety, which must be wired into the circuit either *before* or *after* the lockout and safety control circuit. (A two-wire time-delay relay imposes a slight resistance in the control circuit to allow the solid-state timer to operate. If a two-wire timer is placed in the same series circuit with the high- and low-pressure switches and is wired in parallel with the high-impedance coil of the lockout relay, the resistance imposed by the timer will, in many instances, divert enough current through the lockout relay coil to cause a false lockout condition.) Technicians need to be aware of this condition when servicing or modifying older mechanical control systems.

High-pressure and low-pressure controls represent a key safety feature in geothermal system design. In nearly every manufacturer's control method, high-pressure and low-pressure

Figure 7-2. Early pressure cutout control

safety switches provide positive system shutdown in the event of a system imbalance in refrigerant pressure. Figure 7-2 shows a pressure control typical of many early geothermal systems. These controls are adjustable and may be obtained in both automatic and manual-reset versions for use as either high-pressure or low-pressure safety controls.

Freeze-up safety controls on early systems took the form of either adjustable manual-reset low-pressure switches, typically set to trip if the refrigerant evaporating temperature approached 27 to 30°F (50 psi for R-22), or expansion bulb/capillary devices characteristic of refrigeration equipment. The expansion bulb/capillary controls were inserted into sensing tubes placed in the outlet fluid lines of the loop-side heat exchangers, or wrapped around the common suction line to the compressor. These systems were universally shipped with sensors preset for open-loop conditions with a lockout temperature of 34°F. Fine-print footnotes on the electrical wiring diagrams and a one-line reference buried within the installation manual were the only references to the freeze sensor.

> *Service note:* There are only two ways to reset a freezestat that tests open and causes a system lockout (short of spending many hours warming up the cabinet). One is to remove the control and warm up the capillary tube. The other is to set the thermostat for AC and manually depress the compressor contactor to warm up the heat exchanger and sensing capillary, thereby resetting the freeze control.

Closed-loop installations that had antifreeze protection required a low-temperature sensor with an opening setting of 20 to 24°F. Low-temperature sensors were *not* shipped with the systems and needed to be ordered separately as an "option." Consequently, due to both administrative and technician oversight, countless closed-loop residential and commercial systems have been installed that fault on their low-temperature sensors by mid-November, when the leaving fluid temperature approaches 34°F. These systems will not reset until the sensor temperature rises by at least 20°F. Customers who have had this experience report fantastic air conditioning capacity, but question if they are saving anything, since—not surprisingly—the heating bills are substantially higher in winter. Some owners have tolerated this abuse for over 20 years and were led to believe that they were saving money. Figure 7-3 on the next page shows a low-temperature capillary sensor of the type used as a freeze control. It opens at 20°F and closes at 25°F. The open-loop sensor has a lockout at 34°F and resets, with a 20°F differential, at 54°F.

The scenario of forgotten low-temperature controls is not limited to older systems. *All* geothermal systems are shipped with controls set to conditions appropriate for open-loop installation. Every one of these systems will start up and operate as normal for at least a week or two, even in winter, until the loop temperature drops into the danger zone for an open system. Installation and service technicians need to be aware of system settings and set-up codes for each geothermal model they install or service. The customer may not realize that there is

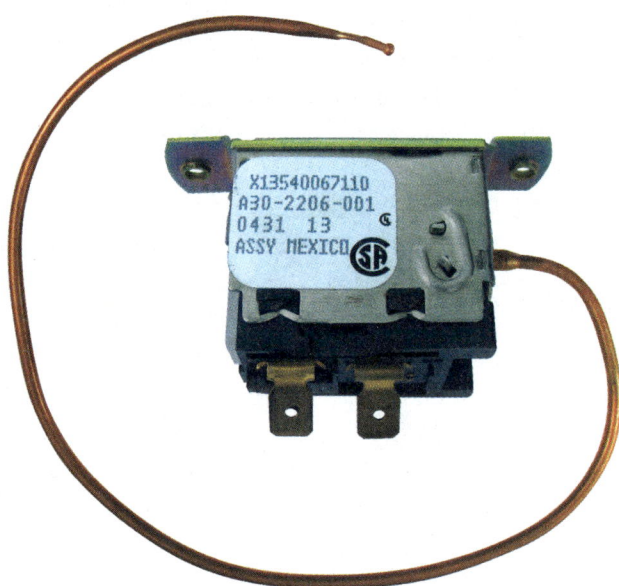

Figure 7-3. Low-temperature capillary sensor freeze control

a problem until one or two higher-than-normal electric bills have been received. An inexperienced technician may simply reset the system, find that everything checks out OK, and charge for the service call—only to repeat the same exercise the next month. For lack of reading the installation manual and paying attention to footnotes, some contractors have resorted to doubling the strength of the antifreeze and adding or replacing loop pumps to a system in an attempt to avoid freeze faults. Such situations result in a loss of consumer confidence.

The timer operation for time-delay controls may be either "delay-on-make" or "delay-on-break." The majority are of the delay-on-break design, which gives the compressor a 5-minute rest between cycles. Systems that provide multiple functions—such as dedicated domestic

Figure 7-4. Adjustable delay-on-make time-delay relay

hot water and radiant floor heat—have multiple relays, which need to change position for each function. In order to prevent compressor contact chatter as relays make and break, a delay-on-make time delay is used. Be aware that in such cases, system operation often requires a $2^{1}/_{2}$ to 5-minute delay from the moment a thermostat signal is received until system operation commences. Figure 7-4 shows a typical two-wire solid-state adjustable time-delay module.

CLIMATEMASTER CONTROLS

ClimateMaster systems currently operate using a CXM series control board. The CXM board has modular capability as a building block—expansion possibilities include control board modules for ECMs (variable-speed fans) and domestic hot water (desuperheater) pumps and temperature controls. Additional add-on modules allow for connection to building automation systems. The CXM boards are in wide use throughout the ClimateMaster product line and with all the "private label" systems produced by ClimateMaster. Figure 7-5 on the following two pages shows the typical layout for the ClimateMaster CXM control board. Frequently overlooked service areas are highlighted in yellow. Each of the highlighted areas is discussed below.

Ignoring Note 4, for example, is a common source of installer and commissioning errors (see Figure 7-6 on page 136 for an expanded view of the service notes). The technician working on a closed system with antifreeze protection must read the wiring diagram, identify the JW3 jumper, and be certain that the jumper is snipped to open the circuit. Another routine oversight is the failure to activate the domestic hot water pump, as indicated in Note 8. Likewise, Note 9 specifies that the hot water temperature must be kept at the factory default setting of 125°F, and that special accommodations must be made to allow the domestic hot water temperature to run up to 150°F.

WARNING: All service power to the geothermal system and control board must be off before you change switch settings or snip a jumper wire. The CXM control will not recognize a setting change while power is applied. The control board may be easily shorted by accidental contact between control circuits when you cut an exposed jumper wire. *Always be safe and turn the power off first.* Following restoration of power, the board will automatically impose a delay of five to eight minutes before start-up. This delay is designed to allow for the staggered start-up of multiple compressors when more than one system is installed in a building. On successive start-ups, the delay is set for five minutes from completion of the previous cycle.

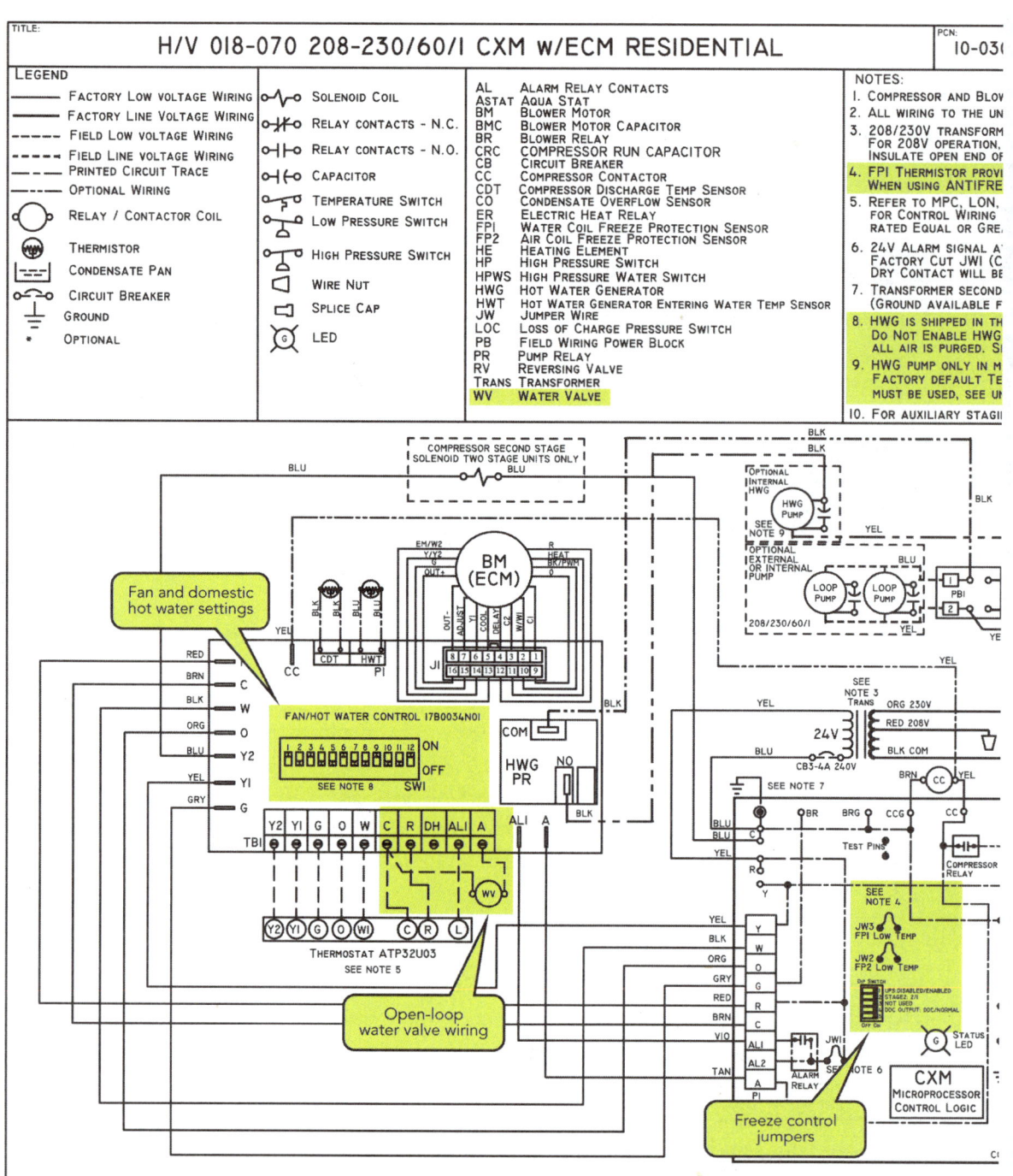

Figure 7-5. ClimateMaster CXM control board

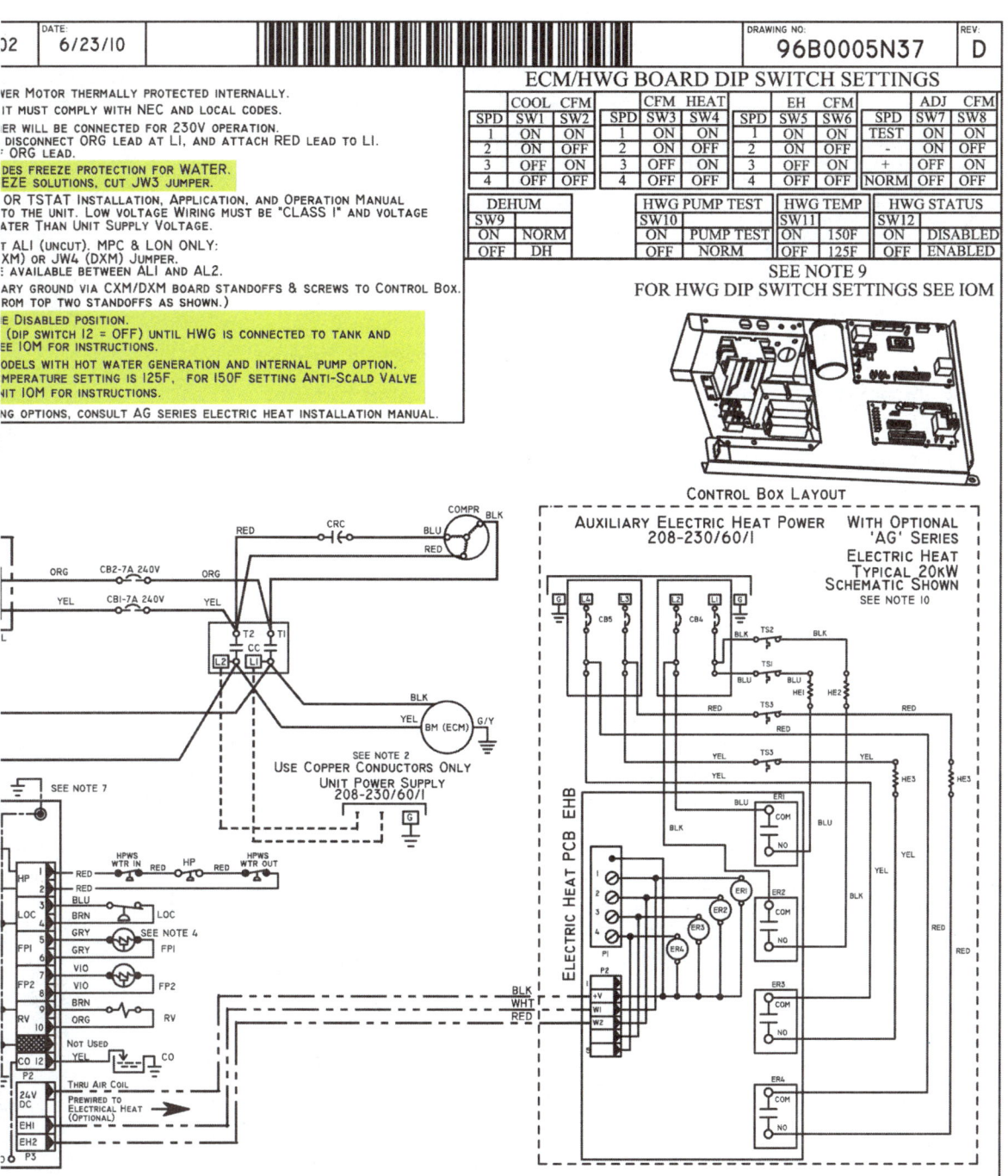

Figure 7-5. ClimateMaster CXM control board (continued)

NOTES:
1. Compressor and Blower Motor thermally protected internally.
2. All wiring to the unit must comply with NEC and local codes.
3. 208/230V transformer will be connected for 230V operation. For 208V operation, disconnect ORG lead at L1, and attach RED lead to L1. Insulate open end of ORG lead.
4. **FPI Thermistor provides freeze protection for WATER. When using ANTIFREEZE solutions, cut JW3 jumper.**
5. Refer to MPC, LON, or TSTAT Installation, Application, and Operation Manual for control wiring to the unit. Low voltage wiring must be "CLASS I" and voltage rated equal or greater than unit supply voltage.
6. 24V alarm signal at AL1 (uncut). MPC & LON only: Factory cut JW1 (CXM) or JW4 (DXM) jumper. Dry contact will be available between AL1 and AL2.
7. Transformer secondary ground via CXM/DXM board standoffs & screws to control box. (Ground available from top two standoffs as shown.)
8. **HWG is shipped in the Disabled position. Do Not Enable HWG (DIP switch 12 = OFF) until HWG is connected to tank and all air is purged. See IOM for instructions.**
9. **HWG pump only in models with hot water generation and internal pump option. Factory default temperature setting is 125F, for 150F setting Anti-Scald valve must be used, see unit IOM for instructions.**
10. For auxiliary staging options, consult AG series electric heat installation manual.

Figure 7-6. Expanded view of CXM installer notes

Look at Figure 7-7 below to see an expanded view of the DIP switch settings for the variable-speed ECM fan and domestic hot water generator (HWG) pump. The HWG status is highlighted in yellow. For proper commissioning, the service technician must identify the switch settings on the ECM/HWG control board. Each system model and fan drive option has its own specific settings. Be aware that the factory settings on the control board may not reflect the operating conditions needed in the field. Let's look at an example. From the codes provided in Figure 7-7 and the switch positions shown

ECM/HWG BOARD DIP SWITCH SETTINGS											
COOL	CFM		CFM	HEAT		EH	CFM		ADJ	CFM	
SPD	SW1	SW2	SPD	SW3	SW4	SPD	SW5	SW6	SPD	SW7	SW8
1	ON	ON	1	ON	ON	1	ON	ON	TEST	ON	ON
2	ON	OFF	2	ON	OFF	2	ON	OFF	-	ON	OFF
3	OFF	ON	3	OFF	ON	3	OFF	ON	+	OFF	ON
4	OFF	OFF	4	OFF	OFF	4	OFF	OFF	NORM	OFF	OFF
DEHUM			HWG PUMP TEST			HWG TEMP			HWG STATUS		
SW9			SW10			SW11			SW12		
ON	NORM		ON	PUMP TEST		ON	150F		ON	DISABLED	
OFF	DH		OFF	NORM		OFF	125F		OFF	ENABLED	

Figure 7-7. Expanded view of speed settings for variable-speed ECM fan and domestic hot water generator (HWG) pump

on the control board below, you can conclude that the fan and hot water controls are set as follows:

- Switch 1 = ON and 2 = OFF .... Fan is on 2nd speed for cooling.
- Switch 3 = ON and 4 = OFF .... Fan is on 2nd speed for heat.
- Switch 5 = OFF and 6 = ON .... Fan is on 3rd speed for emergency heat.
- Switch 7 = OFF and 8 = OFF ...... Fan is on "NORM" setting.
- Switch 9 = ON .... Fan runs at normal speed for AC (when Switch 9 is OFF, fan runs at reduced speed for AC).
- Switch 10 = OFF .... HWG pump will cycle with compressor when Switch 12 is OFF.
- Switch 11 = OFF .... Hot water generator is set for a 125°F limit.
- Switch 12 = ON .... Hot water pump function is disabled.

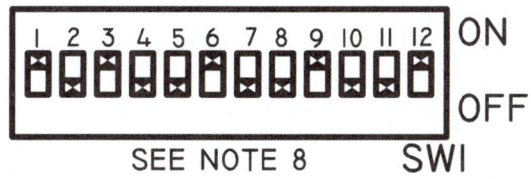

Note: All systems are shipped with the domestic hot water generator pump disabled to prevent pump burnout until the system is completely installed and the lines are flushed and free of all air pockets. Switch positions may be confusing. In this case, Switch 12 is in the factory-set, "ON" position. *The HWG pump is disabled and will not operate!*

Open-loop water valve connections

In Figure 7-5, a 24-V signal is provided at the ECM/HWG board terminals "C" and "A" for operation of a water solenoid valve. These terminals are wired in parallel with the compressor contactor and energize a standard 24-V sprinkler valve. This is the simplest means possible for the control of water flow with an open-loop system. Easily serviceable sprinkler valves such as the one shown in Figure 7-8 draw little more than 5.75 VA . The threaded jar-top

Figure 7-8. Heavy-duty PVC electric sprinkler valve

design allows for the removal of the cap over the solenoid for easy maintenance. When water pressure and velocity are correctly managed with proper pipe sizing, irrigation/sprinkler valves will close softly, with a minimum of audible water-line "thump."

If a quiet water shutoff is required, a motorized valve that opens and closes slowly should be used. This type of valve works via the action of either a heat motor or a mechanical motor linkage. Because the valve may take several minutes to open and close, it does not function in parallel with the compressor contactor, but rather must operate from the thermostat or an auxiliary control. To activate the compressor, the valve relies on an "end switch" (auxiliary contact inside the valve) to close before the power signal activates the compressor control circuit. Figure 7-9 shows a popular heat motor valve for geothermal applications.

The Taco geothermal valve pictured in Figure 7-9 is identified by its orange valve motor, which is different from the green or bronze valve motors traditionally intended for use with low-pressure hydronic systems that feed radiators and baseboard heaters. The heat motor for the valve shown in Figure 7-9 draws 0.9 to 1.3 A intermittently as the heat motor cycles to hold the valve open. If you add the contactor load of the geothermal system, which is also carried by the valve, the total current load can easily reach 1.5 to 1.7 A. This type of valve places a heavy load on thermostats. Older thermostats with adjustable anticipators must have the anticipator adjusted to take it out of the circuit or it will overheat and burn out. Digital thermostats have contacts

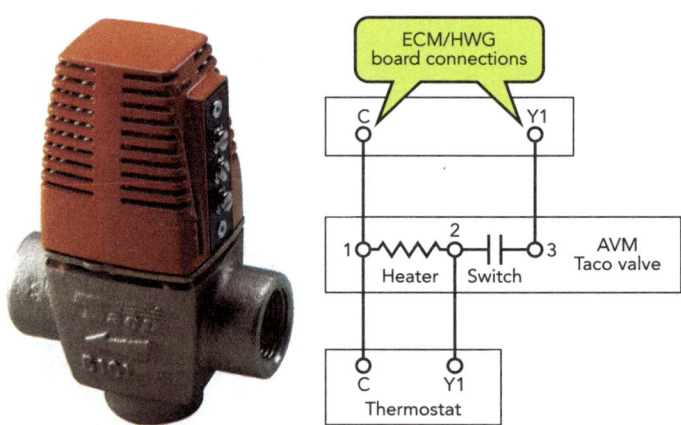

Figure 7-9. Geothermal heat motor valve

rated at 0.5 to 1.0 A. The added load imposed by this heat motor valve can cause premature failure of a digital thermostat. Installation instructions packaged with the valve show the valve powered directly from the thermostat. Most geothermal manufacturers, including ClimateMaster, show this valve wired according to the instructions packaged with the valve. Technicians who encounter thermostat failures when a heat motor valve is used will find that isolating the valve from the thermostat with a control relay greatly increases thermostat reliability.

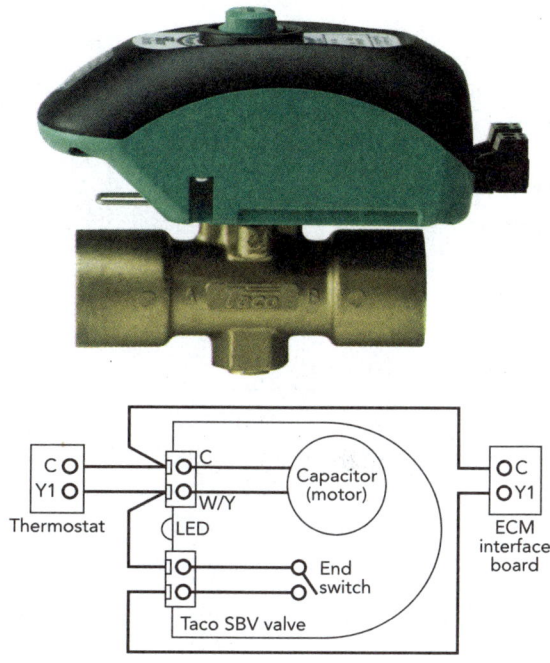

Figure 7-10. Bidirectional zone valve

Heat motor valves require replacement of the motor and valve operating assembly every few years. Aside from the heavy load imposed on digital thermostats, their main weakness is due to wear on exposed contact surfaces that regulate voltage to the heat motor. As the contacts wear from the continual cycling necessary to prevent the motor from overheating, they arc and begin to build up carbon. As deposits build, electrical resistance increases, causing a failure and a service call for no heat or air conditioning. This process can be accelerated by moisture and condensation when the valve is located in a moist environment. Typical heat motor life span depends on equipment operation hours, but generally ranges from 3 to 5 years.

More recently, Taco has developed a type of ball valve capable of closing against 125 psi (see Figure 7-10). This valve operates with 24 V at 0.48 A to charge the motor capacitor. The motor powers to open and charges an internal capacitor, which powers the valve closed once the 24-V signal is broken. An internal end switch closes to complete the power signal to turn on the compressor. This valve is relatively new to the geothermal market and shows promise as a reliable alternative to earlier heat motor valves.

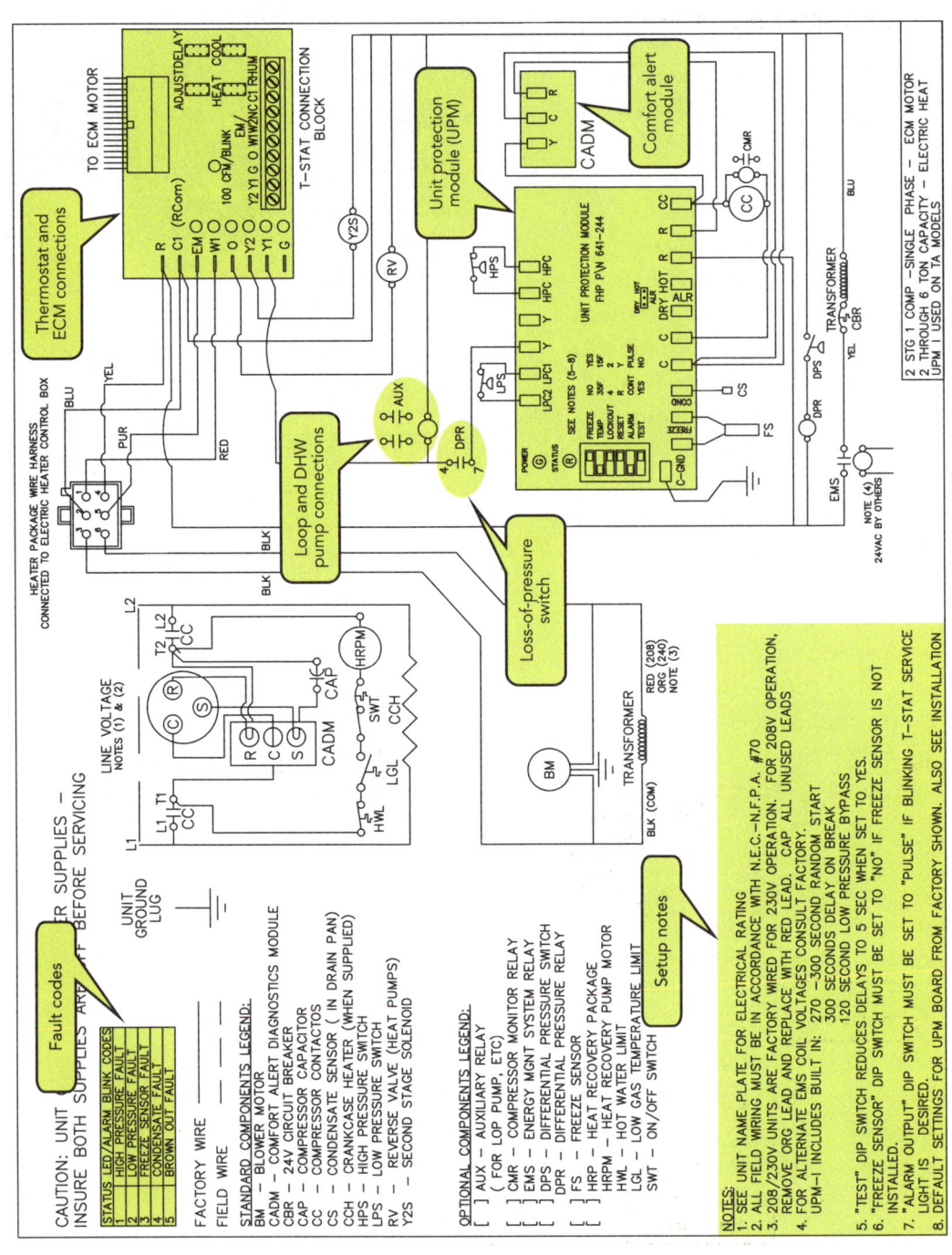

Figure 7-11. FHP/Bosch controls wiring diagram

FLORIDA HEAT PUMP/BOSCH CONTROLS

FHP/Bosch systems utilize a single "unit protection module" (UPM), which is common to all of their residential systems. The UPM accommodates single-stage and two-stage compressors, safety controls, freeze sensor settings, and fault report status. Domestic hot water controls are all factory-preset and controlled by a cabinet-mounted ON/OFF switch. Figure 7-11 reproduces the basic controls wiring diagram common to the FHP/Bosch product line. Key components discussed in the paragraphs below are highlighted.

Figure 7-12 shows an expanded view of the ECM interface board, which is standard with the Bosch 6000 Series systems. These systems have ECM variable-speed fans that utilize multiple fan settings for heating/cooling and constant fan operation. The 1000 and 3000 Series systems do not have this interface board and manage thermostat connections with a terminal strip and ECM control via dedicated terminal connections (see Note 10 on the wiring diagram).

For open-loop systems, FHP/Bosch recommends the use of a slow-closing water valve. A 24-V solenoid valve can be connected between terminals Y1 and C1 on the

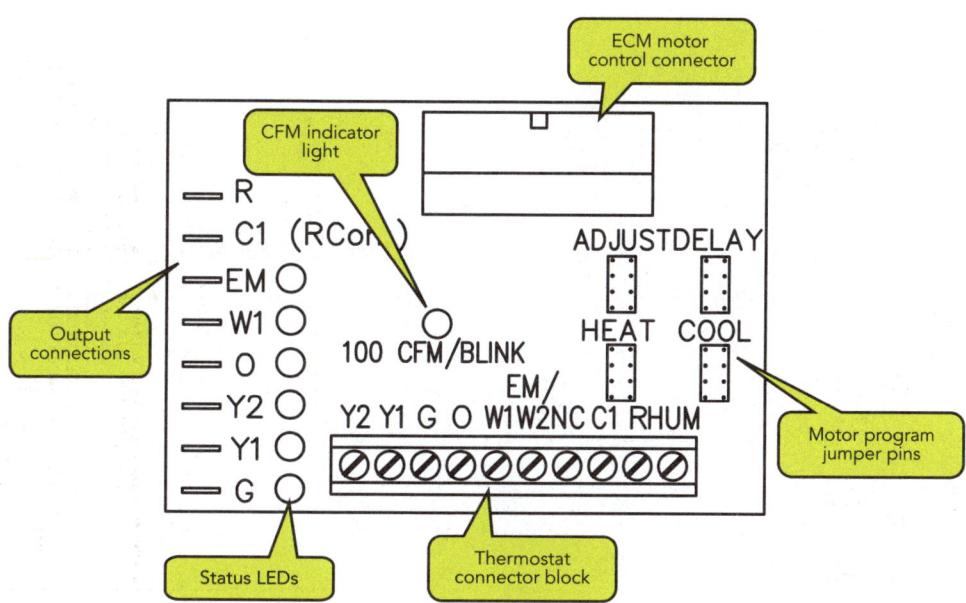

Figure 7-12. Expanded view of ECM interface board

CONTROLS **141**

interface board. As a precaution, FHP/Bosch notes that the VA rating of the solenoid valve must not exceed the contact VA rating of the thermostat. (Installers need to be cautious—the "total load VA" of a thermostat is greater than the individual contact rating and can be deceiving.) A heat motor slow-closing valve may exceed the contact rating of most digital thermostats.

Closed-loop connections are provided via a dry contact double-pole, single-throw (DPST) relay labeled "AUX" on the wiring diagram. Installers must provide a power source connection and line protection for loop and domestic hot water pumps that use this AUX relay as their control source.

The wiring diagram for the FHP/Bosch unit protection module (see Figure 7-13 below) is easy to interpret and leaves little to question. All switches are in the factory-preset position when the system is shipped. For applications that have antifreeze protection, the only change needed is to move the "TEMP" switch from the factory setting of 35°F to the closed-loop setting of 15°F. The instructions provide a warning that "freeze settings are limits only and will not prevent a system freeze-up." The factory setting for lockout retry attempts is set at "2," but the slide switch also can be set for "4" retries.

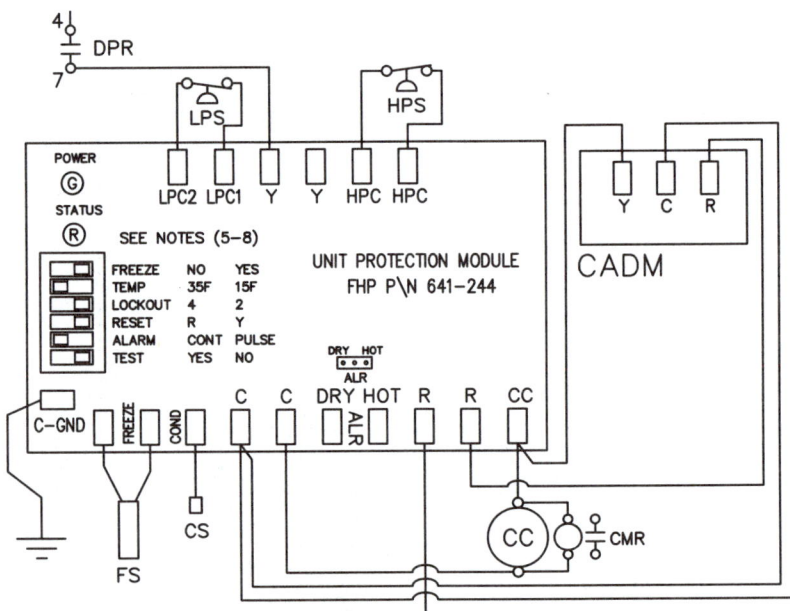

Figure 7-13. Expanded view of UPM wiring

If an open-loop system is permitted to recycle with a loss of water flow, freeze-up is possible. As added protection against loss of flow, the manufacturer recommends the use of an external differential pressure control or flow switch on the water line. However, the FHP/Bosch manual leaves the selection of a "loss of flow" device to the installer. A good example is the Square D reverse-acting/loss-of-pressure well pump switch shown in Figure 7-14, which is set to open its two-pole contact at pressures below 20 psi and close at pressures above 40 psi. This switch has seen wide industry use as a loss-of-pressure safety switch with open-loop installations. When connected in series with the "Y" signal between the thermostat and compressor, the 20-psi lockout condition will interrupt geothermal operation during times of peak water usage or water softener regeneration, or when problems occur with a well or pump that cause a loss of water pressure. The two-pole feature of the switch allows for interruption of both stages of two-stage compressors. When installed to also break the control signal to a water valve, the control can assist in managing peak water loads by turning off flow through the geothermal system until the pressure rises back above 40 psi.

Figure 7-14. Reverse-acting pressure switch

A cautionary note: Whenever imposing an auto-recycling device in the system control circuit, test the device while in use to ensure that it will not cause the compressor to short-cycle when under load. If short-cycling occurs, try a two-wire delay-on-break short-cycle delay timer in series with the control signal and the pressure switch.

Technicians who service equipment with a loss-of-pressure switch must be aware that conditions such as a clogged water strainer or "waterlogged" water pressure tank can cause short-cycling of the switch and system controls. One symptom of a problem related to water pressure is a momentary start of the geothermal system, followed by a shutdown, followed by a restart after the short-cycle delay period elapses. This cycling does not report as a fault to the system controls and typically will not show up until it becomes so chronic that the customer complains of a loss of heat or air conditioning. Technicians who service open-loop systems need to be well-versed on the operation of water pressure tanks and controls in order to diagnose issues related to the water side of the system properly.

NOTES:
1. SEE UNIT NAME PLATE FOR ELECTRICAL RATING
2. ALL FIELD WIRING MUST BE IN ACCORDANCE WITH N.E.C.-N.F.P.A. #70
3. 208/230V UNITS ARE FACTORY WIRED FOR 230V OPERATION. FOR 208V OPERATION, REMOVE ORG LEAD AND REPLACE WITH RED LEAD. CAP ALL UNUSED LEADS
4. FOR ALTERNATE EMS COIL VOLTAGES CONSULT FACTORY.
   UPM-I INCLUDES BUILT IN: 270 -300 SECOND RANDOM START
                            300 SECONDS DELAY ON BREAK
                            120 SECOND LOW PRESSURE BYPASS
5. "TEST" DIP SWITCH REDUCES DELAYS TO 5 SEC WHEN SET TO YES.
6. "FREEZE SENSOR" DIP SWITCH MUST BE SET TO "NO" IF FREEZE SENSOR IS NOT INSTALLED.
7. "ALARM OUTPUT" DIP SWITCH MUST BE SET TO "PULSE" IF BLINKING T-STAT SERVICE LIGHT IS DESIRED.
8. DEFAULT SETTINGS FOR UPM BOARD FROM FACTORY SHOWN. ALSO SEE INSTALLATION

Figure 7-15. Expanded view of FHP/Bosch installer notes

Notes for the FHP/Bosch UPM are straightforward (see Figure 7-15). Small print makes it easy to miss the instruction in Note 6 to set the freeze sensor DIP switch to "No" if a freeze sensor is not installed. Failing to use a freeze sensor—and overlooking the instructions regarding the freeze sensor DIP switch setting—are among the most common setup errors that installers make in many residential and commercial open-loop systems. Complete installation manuals and specification sheets are available for download from the FHP/Bosch website.

WATERFURNACE CONTROLS

WaterFurnace manufactures systems that employ several control board variations. The most prevalent are the "Premier 2" and the "E Series" logic boards, which are designed for full-function operation of both single-stage and two-stage compressors used, most recently, in the "Legend" and "Envision" model lines. However, the basic control board spans a period of over 20 years, and new versions are backward-compatible with earlier systems. Installation and service technicians working with WaterFurnace equipment are strongly advised to attend a factory training class and carefully read the installation manual. Make a habit of highlighting key sections and notes for future quick reference as an aid for field setup and commissioning. Complete specifications and installation manuals for current systems are available in the "Residential Products" section of the WaterFurnace website. Archived manuals for older systems, technical notes, and bulletins require permission to enter the "Secure Dealer" portion of the website.

The diagram reproduced in Figure 7-16 identifies six key areas of the control board, including the setup switches, an 8-LED panel for displaying system status and fault diagnostics, and the Comfort Alert compressor status codes. Such diagrams normally are provided on 11 × 17-in. adhesive-backed prints attached to the back side of the system's mechanical access door. Additional copies of the same diagram, fault code diagnostics, and system operation parameters are printed in the system installation

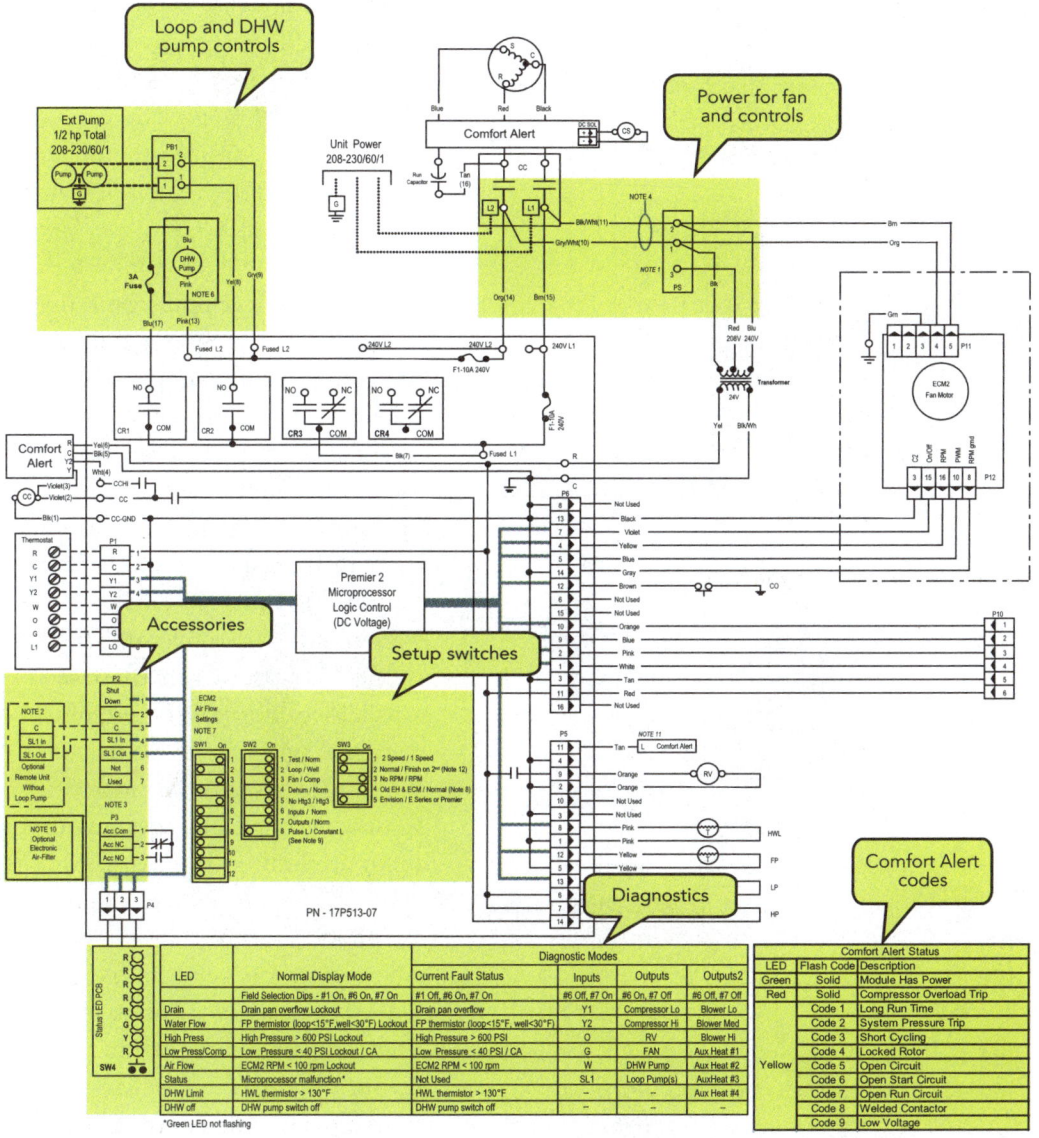

Figure 7-16. *WaterFurnace Premier 2 logic control board*

CONTROLS **145**

manual. The manual should be enclosed in a plastic zip-lock pouch attached to the exterior or packaged inside the system. Due to the overall size of the wiring diagram, each area discussed in the paragraphs below has been enlarged for easy viewing.

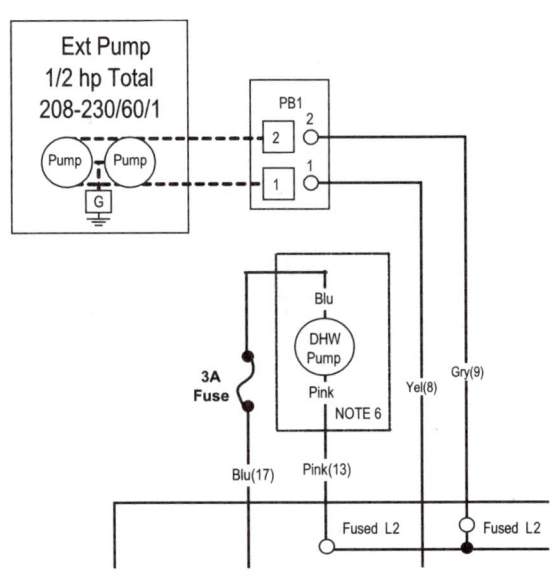

Figure 7-17. Flow connections

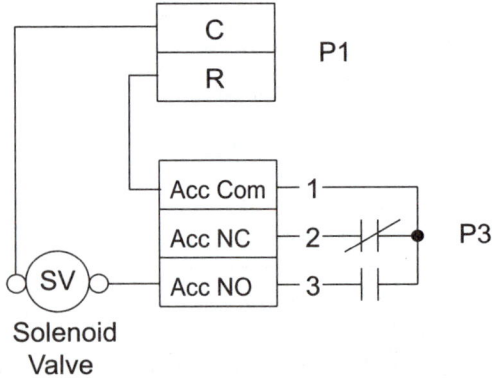

Note: *SW2-3 should be in the Comp "ON" position.*

Figure 7-18. Open-loop two-wire solenoid valve wiring

Flow center connections

Loop pump and domestic hot water pump wiring is provided by internal fused connections (see Figure 7-17). Two 10-A tower fuses mounted on the control board serve as protection for both loop and domestic hot water pumps. A smaller 3-A inline fuse acts as additional protection for an internally mounted domestic hot water pump. System pumps are controlled by independent relays on the control board and will stage "ON" several seconds before the compressor. If the system is operating as a closed loop, technicians responding to a "water flow" fault in the heating season or a "high-pressure" fault in the AC season are advised to check for a blown fuse as the first step in diagnosing the problem. If a fuse is open, trace the wiring to discover the cause and repair before replacing the fuse.

Open-loop connections

Open-loop water valve wiring connections are not shown on the master wiring diagram, but are detailed within the installation manual. The 24-V connections for a fast-acting, two-wire water

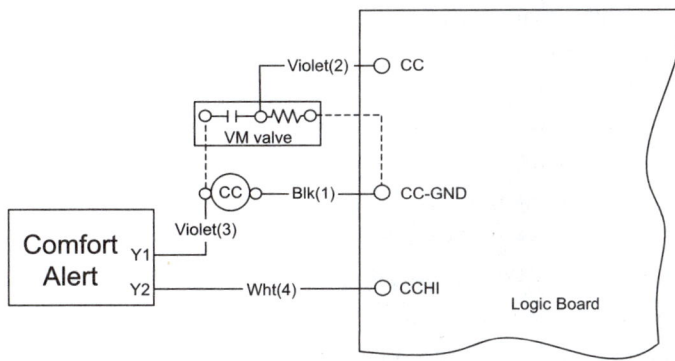

Figure 7-19. Three-wire motorized water valve wiring

valve are made using the accessory relay P3 "C" and "NO" terminals, as shown in Figure 7-18. Set switch SW2-3 to the compressor "ON" position, as instructed in the note beneath the drawing. This will cycle the accessory relay with the compressor and apply power to the solenoid valve.

Three-wire heat motor valves must be wired to break the run signal "CC" wire between the logic board and the compressor contactor. In Figure 7-19, the three-wire valve is powered by an isolated control relay on the logic board. The relay prevents the high current load of the valve from damaging electronic thermostats. A compressor run signal is provided by terminal "CC" on the logic board. Instead of applying it directly to the contactor coil, the signal is diverted to terminal 2 on the water valve. A new, field-supplied wire is used as a jumper between valve terminal 1 and "CC-GND." A second field-supplied wire connects terminal 3 and the compressor contactor's low-voltage coil terminal (where the violet wire previously was connected). By using this control method, the high current load of a heat motor valve is isolated from the thermostat and operates directly from a control relay on the circuit board. The same wiring technique may be used for the zone valve shown in Figure 7-10.

Wiring changes when adding auxiliary heat

A common installer error relates to a "red-tagged" jumper wire. Turn to the next page and look at the portion of the wiring diagram magnified in Figure 7-20. The "black with white" and "gray with white" jumpers between the compressor contactor (CC) and the power strip (PS) that provides power to the control transformer and ECM fan motor allow the entire geothermal system to operate from a single power source. These jumpers are left in place for two possible situations:

CONTROLS **147**

> The system is installed without electric auxiliary heat.
> The system is set to operate the "compressor only" from a whole-house generator.

If electric auxiliary heat is installed, its load will exceed the generator's capacity and therefore must be isolated as a separate circuit. The auxiliary heat circuit is connected to the "electric utility" side of the household electrical panel and is *not* powered by the generator. One of the most common installer errors is a failure to read the red tag and remove the jumper wires when installing a system that has electric auxiliary heat (Note 4, highlighted in Figure 7-20, can be seen in Figure 7-28 on page 154). In order to provide added security for system operation and continuity of backup/emergency heat in the event of a compressor circuit breaker fault, the electric auxiliary heat wiring harness is used to power the fan and system controls as well (see Figure 7-21). If the jumpers are *not* removed when the wiring harness connections are changed, the dual connection can create either a dead short with the electrical panel, or a dangerous parallel voltage feed to the compressor section—a condition that represents a shock hazard for service technicians and will overload either circuit if the other is turned off. *Failure to remove the jumper wires is a critical error.* The red tag and related warning

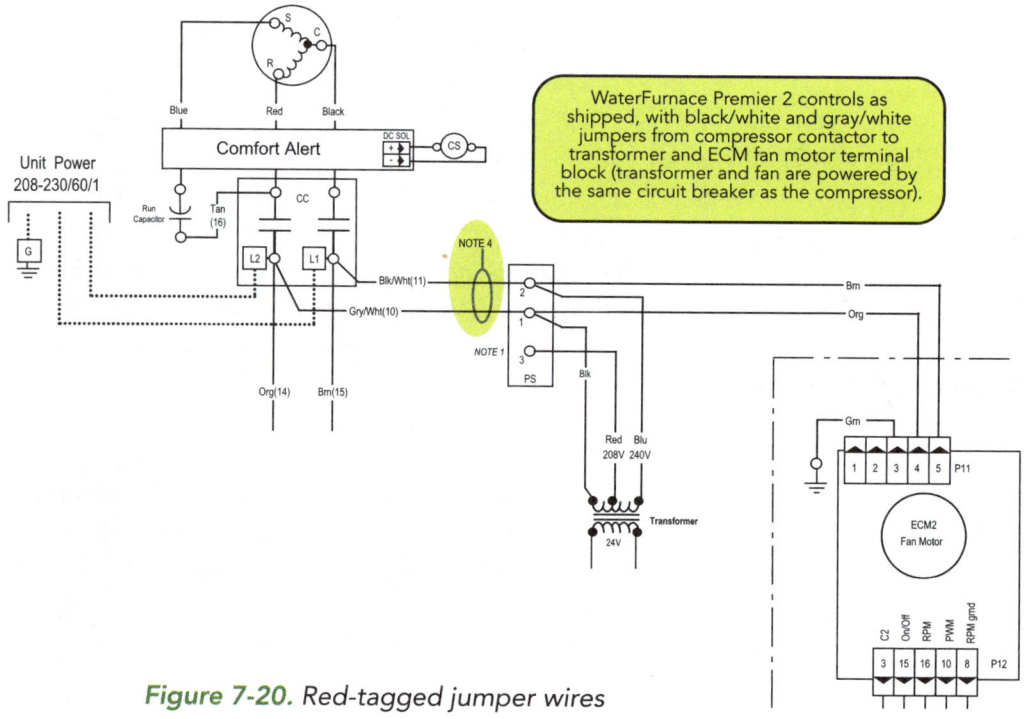

Figure 7-20. Red-tagged jumper wires

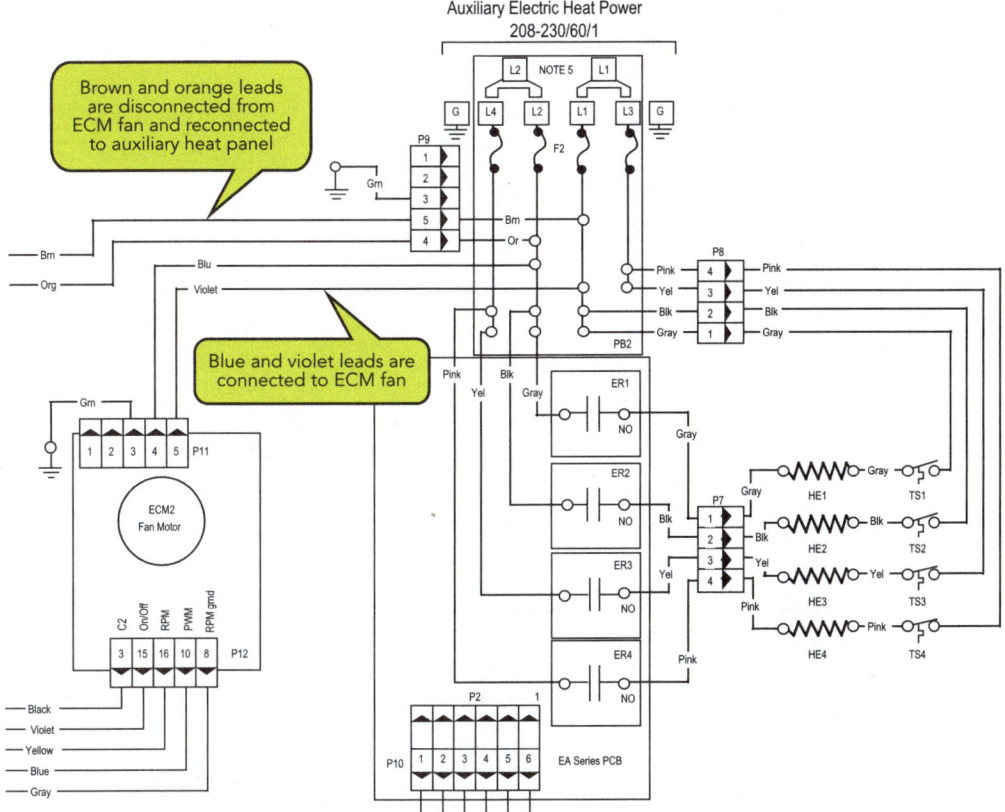

Figure 7-21. Wiring harness changes for installation of auxiliary heat

notes are easily identified in the heat pump installation manual, in the auxiliary heat installation manual, and on the equipment's "red-tagged" wiring diagram.

Setting up the control board

The WaterFurnace control board setup conditions relate primarily to three circuit board switches. They are labeled as SW1, SW2, and SW3 (see Figure 7-22 on the next page). Switch SW1 has twelve switch positions and is used to set the speed for the ECM fan motor. Each geothermal model has a fan table attached inside the control panel door. The fan table provides the cfm setting for each switch position and a range of cfm settings for the system configuration. The fan control will accept only three "ON" settings—constant-fan operation as "LOW," first-stage compressor operation as "MEDIUM," and second-stage compressor operation as "HIGH." If a technician makes

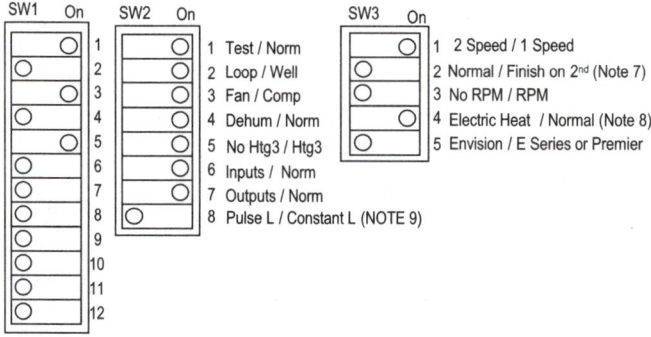

Figure 7-22. Identification of switch functions

an error when changing fan settings in the field and leaves a fourth setting in an "ON" position, the control will recognize only the lower three settings, resulting in a lower-than-design air volume and reduced performance of the system.

FIELD SELECTION DIP SWITCHES (SW2)				
DIP SWITCH NUMBER		DESCRIPTION	OFF POSITION	ON POSITION
SW 2-	1	**Service Test Mode** On the control, allows field selection of "NORMAL" or "TEST" operational modes. Test mode accelerates most timing functions 16 times to allow faster troubleshooting. Test mode also allows viewing the "CURRENT" status of the fault inputs on the LED display.	Test Mode	Normal Speed Operation
SW 2-	2	**Freeze Protection Setting** Allows field selection of freeze thermistor fault sensing temperatures for well water (30°F) or antifreeze-protected (15°F) earth loops.	Loop Water Freeze Protection 15° F	Well Water Freeze Protection 30° F
SW 2-	3	**Accessory Relay** Allows field selection of the accessory relay to operate with the compressor or fan.	Acc Relay Tracks Fan	Acc Relay Tracks Compressor
SW 2-	4	**Fan Speed Control** Allows field selection of reduced fan speed (85% of selected medium and high speed – ECM only) for cooling in the dehumidification mode.	Dehumidification Fan Speeds	Normal Fan Speeds
SW 2-	5	**Auxiliary Off** Disables 3rd-stage Heating. Full emergency heat would still be available if needed.	Disable Heating Stage 3	Enable Heating Stage 3
SW 2-	6	**Diagnostics Inputs** Allows viewing the inputs from the thermostat to the control board such as Y1, Y2, O, G, W, SL1-In on the LED display.	Diagnostic Inputs Viewed at LEDs	Normal Display Viewed at LEDs
SW 2-	7	**Diagnostics Outputs** Allows viewing the outputs from the control board such as compressor, reversing valve, blower, hot water pump, and loop pump on the LED display.	Diagnostic Outputs Viewed at LEDs	Normal Display Viewed at LEDs
SW 2-	8	**Thermostat Selection** Configures the control for a pulsed lockout signal (ComforTalk and FaultFlash thermostats) or continuous 5 VAC lockout signal.	Pulsed "L" signal	Continuous "L" signal

Figure 7-23. SW2 DIP switch selections

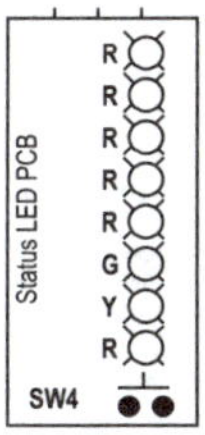

			Diagnostic Modes		
LED	Normal Display Mode	Current Fault Status	Inputs	Outputs	Outputs2
Field Selection Dips - #1 On, #6 On, #7 On		#1 Off, #6 On, #7 On	#6 Off, #7 On	#6 On, #7 Off	#6 Off, #7 Off
Drain	Drain pan overflow Lockout	Drain pan overflow	Y1	Compressor Lo	Blower Lo
Water Flow	FP thermistor (loop<15°F, well<30°F) Lockout	FP thermistor (loop<15°F, well<30°F)	Y2	Compressor Hi	Blower Med
High Press	High Pressure > 600 PSI Lockout	High Pressure > 600 PSI	O	RV	Blower Hi
Low Press/Comp	Low Pressure < 40 PSI Lockout / CA	Low Pressure < 40 PSI / CA	G	FAN	Aux Heat #1
Air Flow	ECM2 RPM < 100 rpm Lockout	ECM2 RPM < 100 rpm	W	DHW Pump	Aux Heat #2
Status	Microprocessor malfunction*	Not Used	SL1	Loop Pump(s)	AuxHeat #3
DHW Limit	HWL thermistor > 130°F	HWL thermistor > 130°F	–	–	Aux Heat #4
DHW off	DHW pump switch off	DHW pump switch off	–	–	–

*Green LED not flashing

Figure 7-24. Diagnostic modes and fault status LEDs

As shown in Figure 7-23, switch SW2 provides for the following system setup options:

➤ SW2-1 (Service Test Mode) must be kept in the "NORMAL" position for normal system operation. If accidentally left in the "TEST" position, there will be a slow continuous fault flash at the thermostat but no fault display at the system status panel. The delay timer is sped up 16 times, which may result in short-cycle stress to the system.

➤ SW2-2 must be switched to the "OFF "position for closed-loop installations with antifreeze protection. Without this change, a closed-loop system will experience repeated "water flow" faults as the entering fluid temperature cools to 40°F or less.

➤ SW2-6 and SW2-7 relate to the diagnostic codes listed on the 8-LED status display panel (see Figure 7-24).

➤ SW2-8 controls how system faults are displayed at the thermostat. Faults also are displayed via status lights on the equipment panel and are held in system memory until the main power service is interrupted to "reboot" the microprocessor board and erase any resident faults.

All faults (with the exception of those from the Comfort Alert compressor protection module) can be reset by turning the thermostat off and then back on. This is called a "soft reset." Soft resets allow the system to operate, but retain the fault indication on the LED status panel. This feature permits the customer to restart the system when necessary, yet saves the fault data to assist the service technician in locating the cause of the fault. Faults retained on the status panel may be erased by powering the system off from the main breakers to reboot the control board.

Comfort Alert faults (see Figure 7-25 at the top of the next page) operate in series with the "low-pressure" fault LED on the status panel. Low-pressure faults may be reset by cycling the thermostat to the "OFF" position, and then back to "ON" for either heat or

AC. Comfort Alert faults can be reset only by interrupting the primary power supply to the system from the main circuit breaker.

Switch SW3 is factory-set to match the system as it is shipped (see Figure 7-26). Changes to SW3 are likely only when a technician is changing control boards or must match a new control board to an older system.

Comfort Alert Status		
LED	Flash Code	Description
Green	Solid	Module Has Power
Red	Solid	Compressor Overload Trip
Yellow	Code 1	Long Run Time
	Code 2	System Pressure Trip
	Code 3	Short Cycling
	Code 4	Locked Rotor
	Code 5	Open Circuit
	Code 6	Open Start Circuit
	Code 7	Open Run Circuit
	Code 8	Welded Contactor
	Code 9	Low Voltage

Figure 7-25. Comfort Alert compressor protection module codes

Accessory connections

The accessories terminals highlighted in Figure 7-27 provide connection points for added system flexibility. Accessory connections to the logic control board allow for thermostat inputs via plug terminal P1. P1 is a removable, low-voltage connector that enables the service technician to make low-voltage connections at a comfortable viewing angle and then insert the connector plug back onto its circuit board pins. A total of eight conductors is needed for full-function operation.

FACTORY SETUP DIP SWITCHES (SW3)				
DIP SWITCH NUMBER		DESCRIPTION	OFF POSITION	ON POSITION
SW 3-	1	**Dual Capacity/Single-Speed** Configures the control for single-speed compressor operation or dual capacity operation.	Dual Capacity Operation	Single-Speed Operation
SW 3-	2	**Zoned/Finish on Second Stage** This switch allows the unit to down stage with the thermostat when off and finish with second stage when on. Finish on second stage reduces stage changing in reciprocating dual capacity compressors.	Normal - All Other Systems	Finish on 2nd - Unzoned Dual Capacity E Series or Premier 2 Speed
SW 3-	3	**No RPM/RPM** Configures the control to monitor the RPM output of an ECM/ECM2 blower motor. When using IntelliZone or a PSC fan motor, the control should be configured for "NO RPM" sensing.	PSC Fan/RPM Monitoring Disabled	ECM-ECM2 Fan/RPM Monitoring Enabled
SW 3-	4	**Electric heat and ECM2** Allows backward compatibility with older Premier Series. In the Off position this switch allows older electric heat board (17P501A01) and older ECM (square end) compatibility. On is for all newer EH board (17P514A01) and ECM2 (round end).	Old EH & Old ECM	Normal
SW 3-	5	On dual capacity units this switch allows stage change: on the fly when off, and 1 minute delay when on. A delay is required on all reciprocating dual capacity units.	Envision	E-Series or Premier

Figure 7-26. Factory-set SW3 DIP switches

Connector P2 has a "Shut Down" terminal that allows for automatic shutdown when tied into a building fire alarm system. Terminals "C,"" SL 1 In," and "SL 1 Out" make it possible for several systems to communicate with each other and share a common geothermal flow center or loop pump. When system size and flow center capacity allow for a single pump, this feature simplifies pumping, piping, and controls wiring, and reduces installation cost.

Connector P3 provides a single-pole, double-throw (SPDT) dry-contact relay for interfacing 24-V accessories, such as an electronic air cleaner, 24-V UV lamp, water solenoid valve, or humidifier. The accessory relay is *not* intended for line voltage. It is suitable for switching low-voltage loads only. The contacts may be powered by the internal transformer with a jumper wire between the control board "R" and the "Acc-Com" terminal, or by an auxiliary transformer and external power supply. Operation of the accessory relay is set to cycle with either the compressor or fan via switch SW2-3.

Figure 7-28 on the next page reproduces the notes for the WaterFurnace electrical wiring diagram. The two errors that installers make most frequently in setting up the logic board and controls are: 1) the failure to set the freeze protection switch SW2-2 properly, and 2) the failure to remove the jumper wires between the contactor and the power strip for the fan and low-voltage transformer when auxiliary heat is installed.

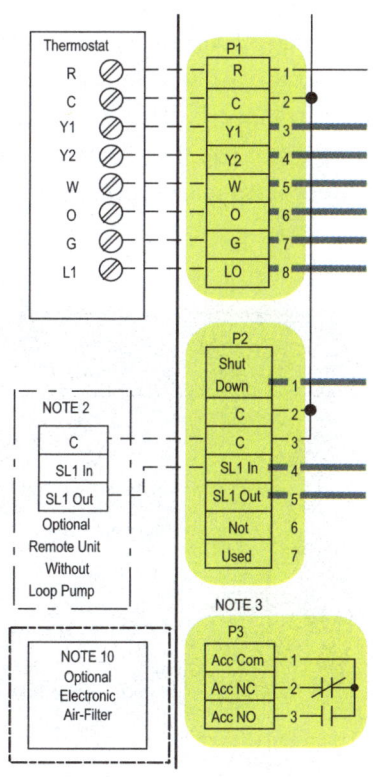

Figure 7-27. Accessory connections

NEXT-GENERATION LOGIC CONTROLS

In the spring of 2011, WaterFurnace began phasing in a "next-generation" logic board. The new logic board is called the Aurora Base Control (ABC). The Aurora Base Control and an accessory Aurora Expansion Board (AXB) serve as a communication platform for a wide variety of automation systems. This capability allows a system to interface with a multitude of home and building automation controls, and permits

NOTES
1. Switch Blue and Red wires for 208V operation.
2. Connection of remote unit that does not have a loop pump for slave operation.
3. 24V Accessory relay (see SW2 -3 for description of operation).
4. The blk/wh and gray/wh wires are removed when Aux Heat is installed.
5. Buss lugs L1 and L2 can be removed and dual power wire sets connected directly to box lugs L1, L2, and L3, L4.
6. DHW pump only in models with hot water generation option.
7. Air Flow Configuration Example: SW1 configured for dip 1 as low, dip 3 as medium, and dip 5 as high speed ECM2 fan.
8. SW3-4 should be in the OFF position when using ECM motor and 17P501A01 electric heat board and should be ON when using ECM2 with 17P514A01 electric heat board.
9. SW2-8 must be in the OFF position for pulsed "L" lockout signal and in the ON position for constant "L" lockout signal.
10. When optional electronic air-filter is installed, power for the electronic air-filter is provided by P2-2 and 24 VAC.
11. Comfort Alert fault output to Premier Control Board.
12. This switch allows the unit to down stage with the t-stat when off and finish with second stage when on. Finish on second stage reduces stage changing in recip dual capacity compressors and should be ON for unzoned Dual Cap E Series or Premier 2 Speed.

Figure 7-28. Wiring diagram notes

global access where required. While the Aurora controls are relatively straightforward, their capability far exceeds the majority of standard controls. Technicians working with these controls must receive manufacturer-provided instruction on their proper operation and setup. The Aurora control is factory-set for operation with the system as it is shipped. Only fully trained, knowledgable technicians should attempt to modify a program routine or change a fan cfm setting. This is *not* a control that allows fan cfm adjustments with simple DIP switch settings. To assist with troubleshooting and service, contractors who receive training on the Aurora control may purchase a portable access point called an "Aurora Interface and Diagnostics" (AID) tool, shown in Figure 7-29.

Field technicians working with commercial projects—and, in particular, with the Versatec Ultra series of geothermal systems—will be the first to gain experience with the Aurora controls. (*Note:* the Versatec Ultra series is a commercial system and does not normally include options for a loop pump

Figure 7-29. Aurora interface and diagnostics (AID) tool

or auxiliary heat). In the future, Aurora controls will be included in a wide range of systems produced by WaterFurnace.

The Aurora control board features a clean layout with well-identified setup switches located near the top center of the board, as shown in Figure 7-30 below. Note that for

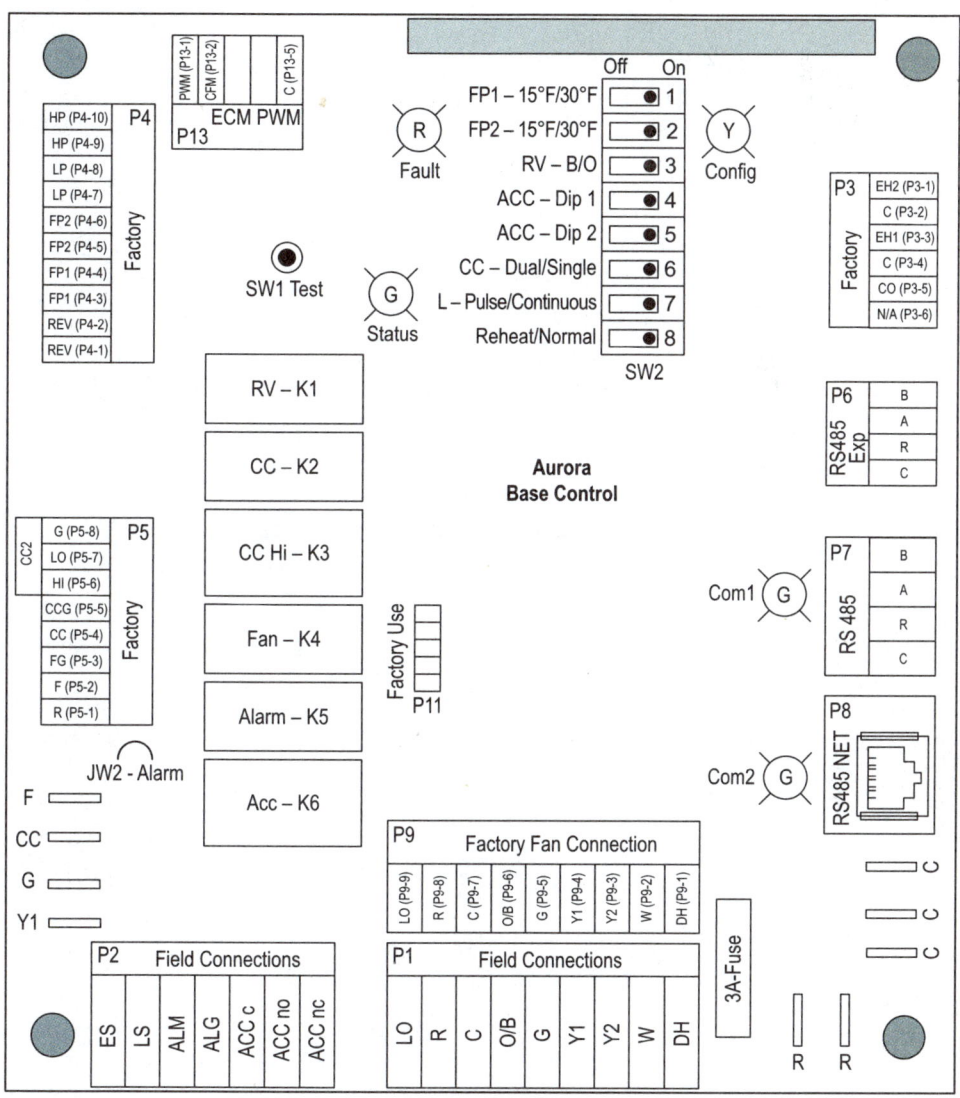

Figure 7-30. Aurora base control (ABC) board layout

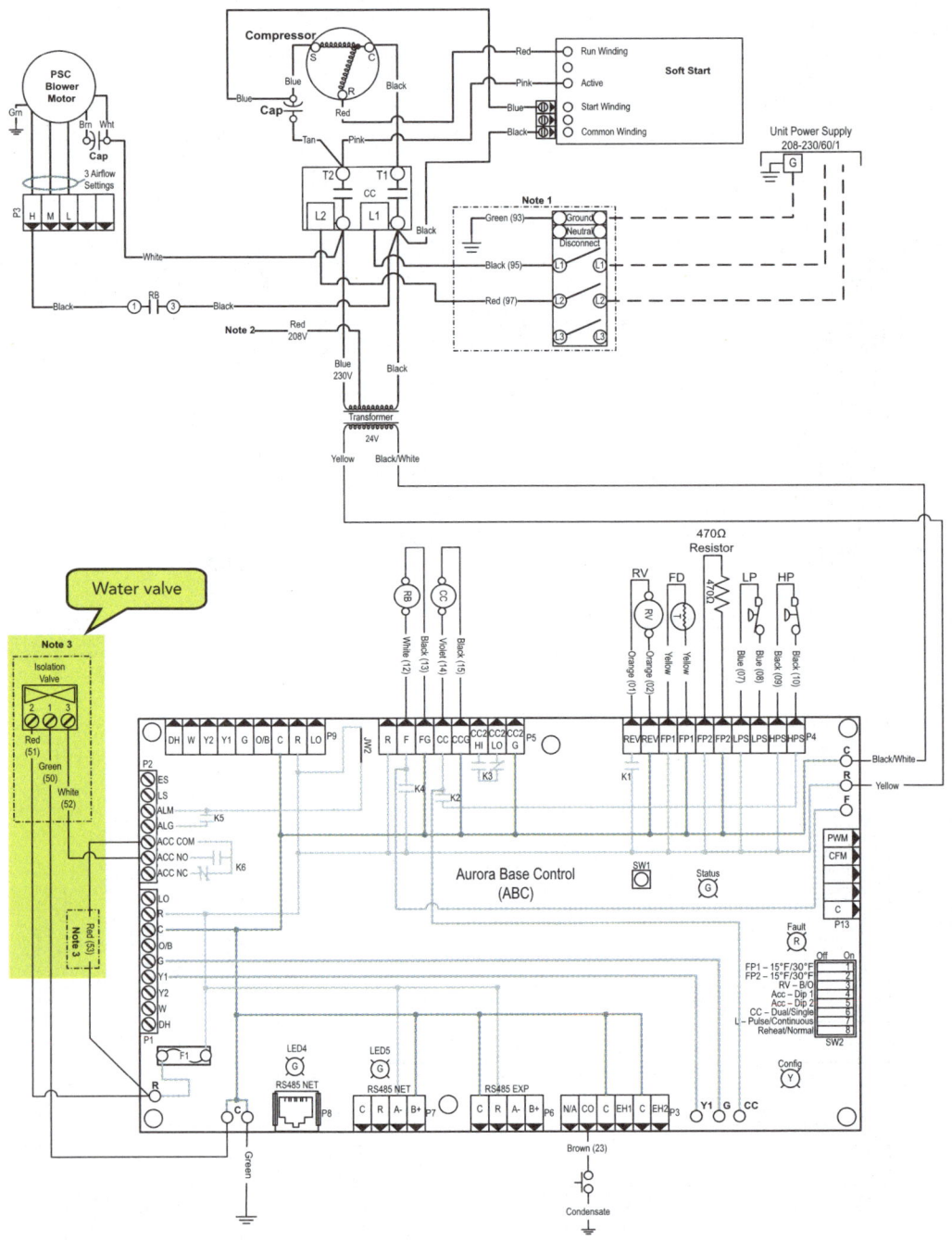

Figure 7-31. ABC board wiring diagram

closed-loop applications with antifreeze protection, switch SW2-1 needs to be shifted to the "OFF" position for a 15°F sensor setting. Switch SW2-2 has the same temperature indication as SW2-1, but is not associated with the loop freeze point and is reserved for future use. Switches SW2-4 and SW2-5 control the operation of the accessory relay. Open-loop and water valve connections for multiple-system commercial piping configurations are provided via the accessory relay, which is highlighted at the left side of Figure 7-31. Adjusting switches SW2-4 to "ON" and SW2-5 to "OFF" allows 90 seconds for a motorized water valve to open before the compressor stages on. Figure 7-32 provides a magnified view of the system's time-delay settings.

Accessory Relay		
Operation	SW2-4	SW2-5
Cycle with Blower	On	On
Cycle with Compressor	Off	Off
Water Valve Slow Open	On	Off
Outdoor Air Damper	Off	On

Aurora Timing Events		
Event	Normal Mode	Test Mode
Random Start Delay	5 to 80 seconds	1 second
Compressor On Delay	5 seconds	< 1 second
Compressor Minimum On Time	2 minutes	5 seconds
Compressor Short Cycle Delay	4 minutes	15 seconds
Blower Off Delay	30 seconds	2 seconds
Fault Recognition Delay – High Pressure	Less than 1 second	Less than 1 second
Start-Up Bypass – Low Pressure	2 minutes	30 seconds
Fault Recognition Delay – Low Pressure	30 seconds	30 seconds
Start-Up Bypass – Low Water/Air Coil Limit	2 minutes	30 seconds
Fault Recognition Delay – Low Water/Air Coil Limit	30 seconds	30 seconds
Fault Recognition Delay – Condensate Overflow	30 seconds	30 seconds
Thermostat Call Recognition Time	2 seconds	2 seconds
Auxiliary Heat Staging Delay	5 minutes	20 seconds
Emergency Heat Staging Delay	2 minutes	7.5 seconds
Water Valve Slow Open Delay	90 seconds	90 seconds
Reheat Delay	30 seconds	30 seconds

Figure 7-32. ABC board time-delay settings

Aurora LED Flash Codes	
Slow Flash	1 second on and 1 second off
Fast Flash	100 milliseconds on and 100 milliseconds off
Flash Code	100 milliseconds on and 400 milliseconds off with a 2 second pause before repeating

Random Start Delay	
Status LED (LED1, Green)	Fast Flash
Configuration LED (LED2, Yellow)	Fast Flash
Fault LED (LED3, Red)	Fast Flash

Status LED (LED1, Green)		Configuration LED (LED2, Yellow)		Fault LED (LED3, Red)	
Normal Mode	ON	No Software Overide	Flash ECM Setting	Normal Mode	OFF
Control is Non-Functional	OFF	DIP Switch Overide	Slow Flash	Input Fault Lockout	Flash Code 1
Test Mode	Slow Flash	ECM Configure Mode	Fast Flash	High Pressure Lockout	Flash Code 2
Lockout Active	Fast Flash	Reset Configure Mode	Off	Low Pressure Lockout	Flash Code 3
Dehumidification Mode	Flash Code 2			Low Air Coil Limit Lockout - FP2	Flash Code 4
Reserved	Flash Code 3			Low Water Coil Limit Lockout - FP1	Flash Code 5
Reserved	Flash Code 4			Reserved	Flash Code 6
Load Shed	Flash Code 5			Condensate Overflow Lockout	Flash Code 7
ESD	Flash Code 6			Over/Under Voltage Shutdown	Flash Code 8
Reserved	Flash Code 7			Reserved	Flash Code 9
				Reserved	Flash Code 10
				Air/Water Coil Limit Sensor Error	Flash Code 11

Figure 7-33. LED flash codes for ABC board

The Aurora LED flash codes are interpreted via communicating thermostats, which are matched to install with the ABC system. Service technicians who are equipped with the AID tool shown in Figure 7-29 will be able to read system status and faults in "plain English." For those lacking the AID tool, the flash code chart reproduced in Figure 7-33 at the bottom of the previous page provides a means to interpret and diagnose system faults. ◆▶

ILLUSTRATION CREDITS
FIGURE 7-1: COMMAND-AIRE
FIGURE 7-2: JOHNSON CONTROLS
FIGURE 7-3: JEFF PERSONS
FIGURE 7-4: ICM CONTROLS
FIGURE 7-5: CLIMATEMASTER
FIGURE 7-6: CLIMATEMASTER
FIGURE 7-7: CLIMATEMASTER
FIGURE 7-8: IRRITROL
FIGURE 7-9: TACO INC.
FIGURE 7-10: TACO INC.
FIGURE 7-11: FHP/BOSCH
FIGURE 7-12: FHP/BOSCH
FIGURE 7-13: FHP/BOSCH
FIGURE 7-14: SQUARE D
FIGURE 7-15: FHP/BOSCH
FIGURE 7-16: WATERFURNACE
FIGURE 7-17: WATERFURNACE
FIGURE 7-18: WATERFURNACE
FIGURE 7-19: WATERFURNACE
FIGURE 7-20: WATERFURNACE
FIGURE 7-21: WATERFURNACE
FIGURE 7-22: WATERFURNACE
FIGURE 7-23: WATERFURNACE
FIGURE 7-24: WATERFURNACE
FIGURE 7-25: WATERFURNACE
FIGURE 7-26: WATERFURNACE
FIGURE 7-27: WATERFURNACE
FIGURE 7-28: WATERFURNACE
FIGURE 7-29: WATERFURNACE
FIGURE 7-30: WATERFURNACE
FIGURE 7-31: WATERFURNACE
FIGURE 7-32: WATERFURNACE
FIGURE 7-33: WATERFURNACE

◀CHAPTER EIGHT▶
Putting It All Together

START-UP PROCEDURES AND CHECKLISTS

A geothermal contractor with more than 30 years of experience has observed that 90% of problems occurring within the first six months of a system's operation can be attributed to installer oversight. If the installers had followed the manufacturer's recommended start-up procedures, the majority of these problems might have been avoided. This responsibility applies directly to the installation team and to the start-up technicians. Both groups need to be thoroughly familiar with the design requirements of the installation as set forth in the manufacturer's instruction manual. Geothermal systems, despite their "unitary, self-contained" design, are *not* simple "plug-and-play" appliances. There is much more to the setup and operation of a geothermal system than simply applying water and power and setting the thermostat. Sadly, many residential and commercial systems *are* "set up" simply by turning on the power and setting the thermostat—if it runs, everything is assessed as OK, the tools get packed away, and the crew heads to the next project.

The problem is this: Systems that get turned on without the documentation of a commissioning report, or "birth certificate," have no baseline from which to evaluate their subsequent performance. A well-executed start-up checklist will identify installation issues and help avoid costly callbacks in the future. The following pages provide a series of start-up checklists. The examples shown in Figures 8-1, 8-2, 8-3, and 8-4 are drawn from the installation and maintenance manuals of the three major equipment manufacturers. Spending a few extra minutes to complete a start-up

Unit Start-Up and Operating Conditions

Unit and System Checkout
BEFORE POWERING SYSTEM, please check the following:

UNIT CHECKOUT
- Balancing/shutoff valves: Insure that all isolation valves are open and water control valves are wired.
- Line voltage and wiring: Verify that voltage is within an acceptable range for the unit and wiring and fuses/breakers are properly sized. Verify that low voltage wiring is complete.
- Unit control transformer: Insure that transformer has the properly selected voltage tap. Residential 208-230V units are factory wired for 230V operation unless specified otherwise.
- Loop/water piping is complete and purged of air. Water/piping is clean.
- Antifreeze has been added if necessary.
- Entering water and air: Insure that entering water and air temperatures are within operating limits of Table 8.
- Low water temperature cutout: Verify that low water temperature cut-out on the CXM/CXM control is properly set.
- Unit fan: Manually rotate fan to verify free rotation and insure that blower wheel is secured to the motor shaft. Be sure to remove any shipping supports if needed. DO NOT oil motors upon start-up. Fan motors are pre-oiled at the factory. Check unit fan speed selection and compare to design requirements.
- Condensate line: Verify that condensate line is open and properly pitched toward drain.
- HWG pump is disconnected unless piping is completed and air has been purged from the system.
- Water flow balancing: Record inlet and outlet water temperatures for each heat pump unit upon startup. This check can eliminate nuisance trip outs and high velocity water flow that could erode heat exchangers.
- Unit air coil and filters: Insure that filter is clean and accessible. Clean air coil of all manufacturing oils.
- Unit controls: Verify that CXM field selection options are properly set. Low voltage wiring is complete.
- Blower speed is set.
- Service/access panels are in place.

SYSTEM CHECKOUT
- System water temperature: Check water temperature for proper range and also verify heating and cooling set points for proper operation.
- System pH: Check and adjust water pH if necessary to maintain a level between 6 and 8.5. Proper pH promotes longevity of hoses and fittings (see Table 3).
- System flushing: Verify that all air is purged from the system. Air in the system can cause poor operation or system corrosion. Water used in the system must be potable quality initially and clean of dirt, piping slag, and strong chemical cleaning agents. Some antifreeze solutions may require distilled water.
- Flow Controller pump(s): Verify that the pump(s) is wired, purged of air, and in operating condition.
- System controls: Verify that system controls function and operate in the proper sequence.
- Low water temperature cutout: Verify that low water temperature cut-out controls are set properly (FP1 - JW3).
- Miscellaneous: Note any questionable aspects of the installation.

⚠ CAUTION! ⚠
CAUTION! Verify that ALL water control valves are open and allow water flow prior to engaging the compressor. Freezing of the coax or water lines can permanently damage the heat pump.

⚠ CAUTION! ⚠
CAUTION! To avoid equipment damage, DO NOT leave system filled in a building without heat during the winter unless antifreeze is added to the water loop. Heat exchangers never fully drain by themselves and will freeze unless winterized with antifreeze.

Unit Start-up Procedure
1. Turn the thermostat fan position to "ON." Blower should start.
2. Balance air flow at registers.
3. Adjust all valves to their full open position. Turn on the line power to all heat pump units.
4. Room temperature should be within the minimum-maximum ranges of Table 8b. During start-up checks, loop water temperature entering the heat pump should be between 30°F [-1°C] and 95°F [35°C].
5. Two factors determine the operating limits of water source heat pumps, (a) return air temperature, and (b) water temperature. When any one of these factors is at a minimum or maximum level, the other factor must be at normal level to insure proper unit operation.
   a. Adjust the unit thermostat to the warmest setting. Place the thermostat mode switch in the "COOL" position. Slowly reduce thermostat setting until the compressor activates.
   b. Check for cool air delivery at the unit grille within a few minutes after the unit has begun to operate. Note: Units have a five minute time delay in the control circuit that can be bypassed on the CXM/CXM control board as shown below in Figure 27. See controls description for details.
   c. Verify that the compressor is on and that the water flow rate is correct by measuring pressure drop through the heat exchanger using the P/T plugs and comparing to Tables 9a through 9b.
   d. Check the elevation and cleanliness of the condensate lines. Dripping may be a sign of a blocked line. Check that the condensate trap is filled to provide a water seal.

Figure 8-1. ClimateMaster start-up checklist

Unit Start-Up Procedure

e. Refer to Table 10. Check the temperature of both entering and leaving water. If temperature is within range, proceed with the test. If temperature is outside of the operating range, check refrigerant pressures and compare to Tables 11 through 12. Verify correct water flow by comparing unit pressure drop across the heat exchanger versus the data in Tables 9a through 9b. Heat of rejection (HR) can be calculated and compared to catalog data capacity pages. The formula for HR for systems with water is as follows: HR = TD x GPM x 500, where TD is the temperature difference between the entering and leaving water, and GPM is the flow rate in U.S. GPM, determined by comparing the pressure drop across the heat exchanger to Tables 9a through 9b.
f. Check air temperature drop across the air coil when compressor is operating. Air temperature drop should be between 15°F and 25°F [8°C and 14°C].
g. Turn thermostat to "OFF" position. A hissing noise indicates proper functioning of the reversing valve.

6. Allow five (5) minutes between tests for pressure to equalize before beginning heating test.
   a. Adjust the thermostat to the lowest setting. Place the thermostat mode switch in the "HEAT" position.
   b. Slowly raise the thermostat to a higher temperature until the compressor activates.
   c. Check for warm air delivery within a few minutes after the unit has begun to operate.
   d. Refer to Table 10. Check the temperature of both entering and leaving water. If temperature is within range, proceed with the test. If temperature is outside of the operating range, check refrigerant pressures and compare to Tables 11 through 12. Verify correct water flow by comparing unit pressure drop across the heat exchanger versus the data in Tables 9a through 9b. Heat of extraction (HE) can be calculated and compared to submittal data capacity pages. The formula for HE for systems with water is as follows: HE = TD x GPM x 500, where TD is the temperature difference between the entering and leaving water, and GPM is the flow rate in U.S. GPM, determined by comparing the pressure drop across the heat exchanger to Tables 9a through 9b.
   e. Check air temperature rise across the air coil when compressor is operating. Air temperature rise should be between 20°F and 30°F [11°C and 17°C].
   f. Check for vibration, noise, and water leaks.

7. If unit fails to operate, perform troubleshooting analysis (see troubleshooting section). If the check described fails to reveal the problem and the unit still does not operate, contact a trained service technician to insure proper diagnosis and repair of the equipment.

8. When testing is complete, set system to maintain desired comfort level.

9. BE CERTAIN TO FILL OUT AND RETURN ALL WARRANTY REGISTRATION PAPERWORK.

Note: If performance during any mode appears abnormal, refer to the CXM section or troubleshooting section of this manual. To obtain maximum performance, the air coil should be cleaned before start-up. A 10% solution of dishwasher detergent and water is recommended.

⚠ WARNING! ⚠

WARNING! When the disconnect switch is closed, high voltage is present in some areas of the electrical panel. Exercise caution when working with energized equipment.

⚠ CAUTION! ⚠

CAUTION! Verify that ALL water control valves are open and allow water flow prior to engaging the compressor. Freezing of the coax or water lines can permanently damage the heat pump.

Figure 8-1. ClimateMaster start-up checklist (continued)

UNIT CHECK-OUT SHEET **BOSCH**

Customer Data
Customer Name _____   Date _____
Address _____
_____
Phone _____   Unit Number _____

Unit Nameplate Data
Unit Make _____
Model Number _____   Serial Number _____
Refrigerant Charge (oz) _____
Compressor: RLA _____ LRA _____
Blower Motor: FLA (or NPA) _____ HP _____
Maximum Fuse Size (Amps) _____
Minimum Circuit Ampacity (Amps) _____

Operating Conditions

	Cooling Mode	Heating Mode
Entering / Leaving Air Temp	_____ / _____	_____ / _____
Entering Air Measured at:	_____	_____
Leaving Air Measured at:	_____	_____
Entering / Leaving Fluid Temp	_____ / _____	_____ / _____
Fluid Flow (gpm)	_____	_____
Source Fluid Type	_____	_____
Fluid Flow (gpm)	_____	_____
Fluid Side Pressure Drop	_____	_____
Suction / Discharge Pressure (psig)	_____ / _____	_____ / _____
Suction / Discharge Temp	_____ / _____	_____ / _____
Suction Superheat	_____	_____
Entering TXV / Cap Tube Temp	_____	_____
Liquid Subcooling	_____	_____
Compressor Volts / Amps	_____ / _____	_____ / _____
Blower Motor Volts / Amps	_____ / _____	_____ / _____

Auxiliary Heat
Unit Make _____
Model Number _____   Serial Number _____
Max Fuse Size (Amps) _____
Volts / Amps _____ / _____
Entering Air Temperature _____
Leaving Air Temperature _____

Figure 8-2. FHP/Bosch start-up checklist

Unit Startup

Before Powering Unit, Check The Following:

Note: Remove and discard the two compressor hold down shipping bolts located at the front and rear of the compressor mounting bracket. The bolts can then be discarded.

- High voltage is correct and matches nameplate.
- Fuses, breakers and wire size correct.
- Low voltage wiring complete.
- Piping completed and water system cleaned and flushed.
- Air is purged from closed loop system.
- Isolation valves are open, water control valves or loop pumps wired.
- Condensate line open and correctly pitched.
- Transformer switched to 208V if applicable.
- Black/white and gray/white wires in unit control box have been removed if auxiliary heat has been installed.
- Dip switches are set correctly.
- DHW pump switch is "OFF" unless piping is completed and air has been purged.
- Blower rotates freely – foam shipping support has been removed.
- Blower speed correct (dip switch is set correctly).
- Air filter/cleaner is clean and in position.
- Service/access panels are in place.
- Return air temperature is between 50-80°F heating and 60-95°F cooling.
- Check air coil cleanliness to insure optimum performance. Clean as needed according to maintenance guidelines. To obtain maximum performance the air coil should be cleaned before startup. A 10-percent solution of dishwasher detergent and water is recommended for both sides of coil, a thorough water rinse should follow.

Startup Steps

Note: Complete the Equipment Start-Up/Commissioning Check Sheet during this procedure. Refer to thermostat operating instructions and complete the startup procedure.

1. Initiate a control signal to energize the blower motor. Check blower operation.
2. Initiate a control signal to place the unit in the cooling mode. Cooling setpoint must be set below room temperature.
3. First stage cooling will energize after a time delay.
4. Be sure that the compressor and water control valve or loop pump(s) are activated.
5. Verify that the water flow rate is correct by measuring the pressure drop through the heat exchanger using the P/T plugs and comparing to unit capacity data in specification catalog.
6. Check the temperature of both the supply and discharge water (see pages 35-36).
7. Check for an air temperature drop of 15°F to 25°F across the air coil, depending on the fan speed and entering water temperature.
8. Decrease the cooling set point several degrees and verify high-speed blower operation.
9. Adjust the cooling setpoint above the room temperature and verify that the compressor and water valve or loop pumps deactivate.
10. Initiate a control signal to place the unit in the heating mode. Heating set point must be set above room temperature.
11. First stage heating will energize after a time delay.
12. Check the temperature of both the supply and discharge water (see pages 35-36).
13. Check for an air temperature rise of 20°F to 35°F across the air coil, depending on the fan speed and entering water temperature.
14. If auxiliary electric heaters are installed, increase the heating setpoint until the electric heat banks are sequenced on. All stages of the auxiliary heater should be sequenced on when the thermostat is in the Emergency Heat mode. Check amperage of each element.
15. Adjust the heating setpoint below room temperature and verify that the compressor and water valve or loop pumps deactivate.
16. During all testing, check for excessive vibration, noise or water leaks. Correct or repair as required.
17. Set system to desired normal operating mode and set temperature to maintain desired comfort level.
18. Instruct the owner/operator in the proper operation of the thermostat and system maintenance.

Note: Be certain to fill out and forward all warranty registration papers.

Figure 8-3. WaterFurnace start-up procedures

Preventive Maintenance

Water Coil Maintenance
1. Keep all air out of the water. An open loop system should be checked to ensure that the well head is not allowing air to infiltrate the water line. Lines should always be airtight.
2. Keep the system under pressure at all times. It is recommended in open loop systems that the water control valve be placed in the discharge line to prevent loss of pressure during off cycles. Closed loop systems must have positive static pressure.

Note: On open loop systems, if the installation is in an area with a known high mineral content (125 PPM or greater) in the water, it is best to establish with the owner a periodic maintenance schedule so the coil can be checked regularly. Should periodic coil cleaning be necessary, use standard coil cleaning procedures which are compatible with either the cupronickel or copper water lines. Generally, the more water flowing through the unit the less chance for scaling.

Other Maintenance
Filters
Filters must be clean to obtain maximum performance. They should be inspected monthly under normal operating conditions and be replaced when necessary. Units should never be operated without a filter.

Condensate Drain
In areas where airborne bacteria produce a slime in the drain pan, it may be necessary to treat chemically to minimize the problem. The condensate drain can pick up lint and dirt, especially with dirty filters. Inspect twice a year to avoid the possibility of overflow.

Blower Motors
ECM blower motors are equipped with sealed ball bearings and require no periodic oiling.
PSC blower motors should only be lubricated if dry operation is suspected.

Desuperheater Coil
See Water Coil Maintenance section above.

Air Coil
The air coil must be cleaned to obtain maximum performance. Check once a year under normal operating conditions and, if dirty, brush or vacuum (with a brush attachment) clean. Care must be taken not to damage the aluminum fins while cleaning.

 CAUTION: Fin edges are sharp.

Replacement Procedures

Obtaining Parts
When ordering service or replacement parts, refer to the model number and serial number of the unit as stamped on the serial plate attached to the unit. If replacement parts are required, mention the date of installation of the unit and the date of failure, along with an explanation of the malfunctions and a description of the replacement parts required.

In-Warranty Material Return
Material may not be returned except by permission of authorized warranty personnel. Contact your local distributor for warranty return authorization and assistance.

Figure 8-4. WaterFurnace maintenance procedures

checklist like one of these can make the difference between a system that cuts energy consumption by 80% and one that consumes thousands of dollars in auxiliary heat.

Look at the sample start-up/troubleshooting form and the companion data sheet shown in Figure 8-5. Such documents are used industry-wide by technical support departments when assisting with field service questions. The collection of system operation data helps to establish a baseline to which future readings may be compared. The data sheet also helps to identify any deviation in system operation during start-up and allows for its diagnosis and correction before it becomes a serious problem.

Customary start-up procedures from most geothermal manufacturers call for field technicians to check air-side and water-side temperature and pressure differences *before* placing refrigerant gauges on the system. This instruction may seem counterproductive and a waste of time to the many technicians who "live by their gauges." Keep in mind, however, the many "hidden" factors that can influence refrigerant pressures in a geothermal system—including fluid pressure drop, fluid flow rate and temperature change, air flow rate and temperature change, evaporating and suction temperatures, discharge-line and liquid-line temperatures. If these factors are not identified first, a technician who simply sees a low suction pressure is likely to add refrigerant and overcharge the system. The technician thereby creates a whole new series of problems that disguise the initial problem and make diagnosis a greater challenge.

INITIAL "TOUCH TEST"

A good start-up begins with a cursory touch test to see how the system feels. Check the temperature of the suction line where it returns to the compressor. Is it cold? A cold suction line indicates that the suction vapor is saturated and operating no more than about 10°F above the evaporating temperature. Is the compressor wall cool to cold at the suction-line fitting and warm to hot at the oil sump? If so, the windings are getting cool refrigerant vapor to keep them from overheating. Does the temperature rise across the condenser meet the manufacturer's specifications? As long as these conditions all fall within the manufacturer's recommendations, the system likely will operate without any issues—in which case, the manufacturer would prefer that the refrigerant system *not* be opened. In some instances, adding gauges to check pressures can introduce contaminants or allow the loss of a critical "O"-ring from a service valve cap. Manufacturers see this type of "service" as a potential future warranty claim, since everything might have been fine if the refrigerant system had not been opened to check pressures.

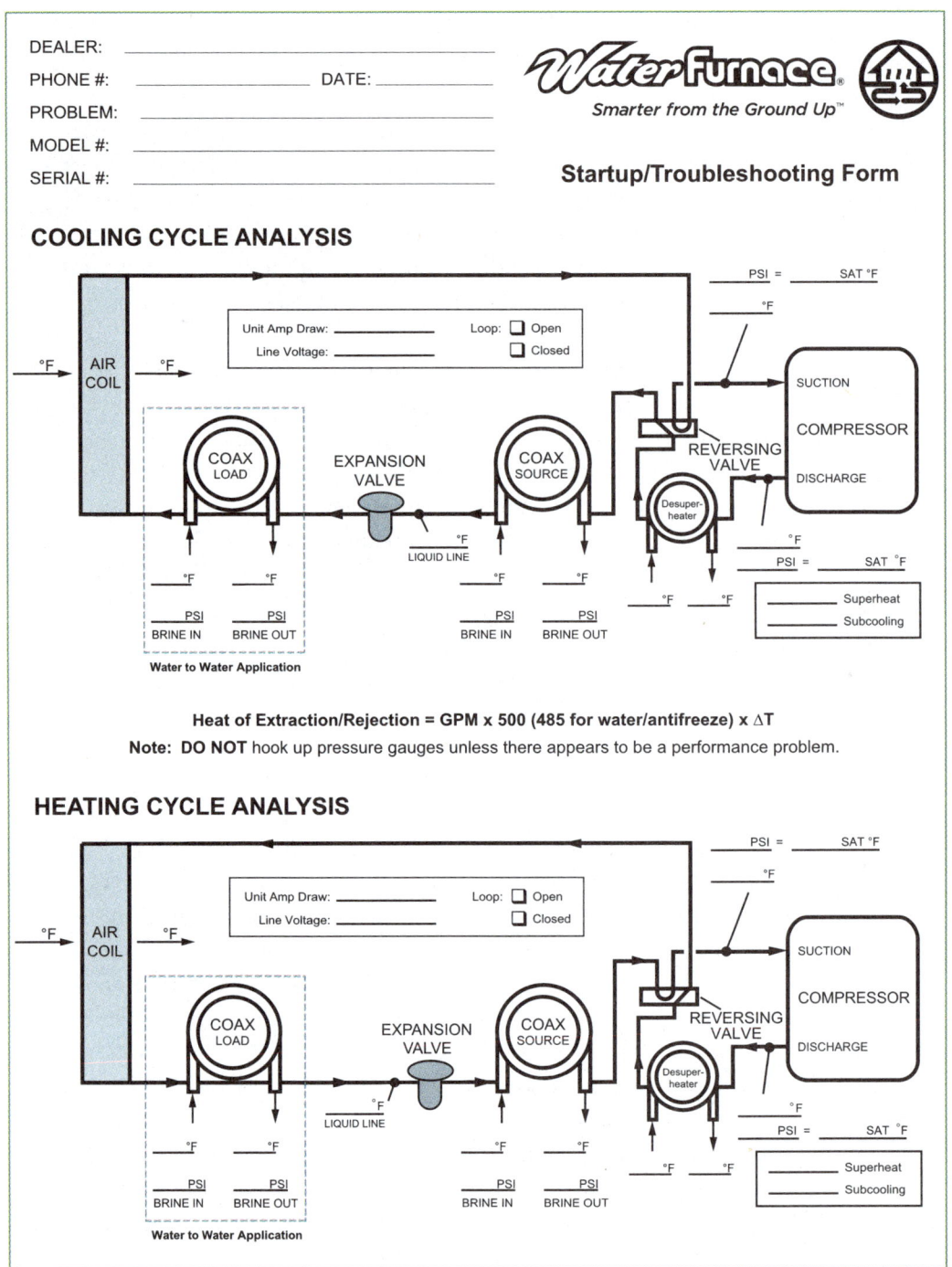

Figure 8-5. WaterFurnace start-up/troubleshooting form

1. JOB INFORMATION

WFI Model #: _____ Job Name: _____ Loop: Open / Closed
WFI Serial #: _____ Install. Date: _____ Desuperheater: Y / N

2. FLOW RATE IN GPM

	SOURCE COAX		LOAD COAX (WATER TO WATER)	
	COOLING	HEATING	COOLING	HEATING
WATER IN Pressure:	a. _____ PSI	a. _____ PSI	a. _____ PSI	a. _____ PSI
WATER OUT Pressure:	b. _____ PSI	b. _____ PSI	b. _____ PSI	b. _____ PSI
Pressure Drop = a - b	c. _____ PSI	c. _____ PSI	c. _____ PSI	c. _____ PSI
Look up flow rate in table:	d. _____ GPM	d. _____ GPM	d. _____ GPM	d. _____ GPM

3. TEMPERATURE RISE / DROP ACROSS COAXIAL HEAT EXCHANGER*

	COOLING	HEATING
WATER IN Temperature:	e. _____ °F	e. _____ °F
WATER OUT Temperature:	f. _____ °F	f. _____ °F
Temperature Difference:	g. _____ °F	g. _____ °F

*Steps 3 - 9 should be conducted with the desuperheater disconnected.

4. TEMPERATURE RISE / DROP ACROSS AIR COIL

	COOLING	HEATING	LOAD COAX (WATER TO WATER)	
			COOLING	HEATING
SUPPLY AIR Temperature:	h. _____ °F	h. _____ °F	LWT: h. _____ °F	h. _____ °F
RETURN AIR Temperature:	i. _____ °F	i. _____ °F	EWT: i. _____ °F	i. _____ °F
Temperature Difference:	j. _____ °F	j. _____ °F	j. _____ °F	j. _____ °F

5. HEAT OF REJECTION (HR) / HEAT OF EXTRACTION (HE)

Brine Factor*:   k. _____

* Use 500 for pure water, 485 for methanol or Environol™. (This constant is derived by multiplying the weight of one gallon of water (8.34) times the minutes in one hour (60) times the specific heat of the fluid.

Water has a specific heat of 1.0

	COOLING (HR)	HEATING (HE)
HR / HE = d x g x k	l. _____ BTU / HR	l. _____ BTU / HR

STEPS 6 - 9 NEED ONLY BE COMPLETED IF A PROBLEM IS SUSPECTED

6. WATTS

	COOLING	HEATING
Volts:	m. _____ VOLTS	m. _____ VOLTS
Total Amps (Comp. + Fan)*:	n. _____ AMPS	n. _____ AMPS
Watts = m x n x 0.85	o. _____ WATTS	o. _____ WATTS

* If there is only one source of power for the compressor and fan, Amp draw can be measured at the source wiring connections.

7. CAPACITY

	COOLING	HEATING
Cooling Capacity = l - (o x 3.413)	p. _____ BTU / HR	p. _____ BTU / HR
Heating Capacity = l + (o x 3.413)		

8. EFFICIENCY

	COOLING	HEATING
Cooling EER = p / o	q. _____ BTU / W	q. _____ BTU / BTU
Heating COP = p / (o x 3.413)		

9. SUPERHEAT (S.H.) / SUBCOOLING (S.C.)

	COOLING	HEATING
Suction Pressure:	r. _____ PSI	r. _____ PSI
Suction Saturation Temperature:	s. _____ DEG. F	s. _____ DEG. F
Suction Line Temperature:	t. _____ DEG. F	t. _____ DEG. F
S.H. = t - s	u. _____ DEG. F	u. _____ DEG. F
Head Pressure:	v. _____ PSI	v. _____ PSI
High Pressure Saturation Temperature:	w. _____ DEG. F	w. _____ DEG. F
Liquid Line Temperature*:	x. _____ DEG. F	x. _____ DEG. F
S.C. = w - x	y. _____ DEG. F	y. _____ DEG. F

* Liquid line is between the coax and the expansion device in the cooling mode; between the air coil and the expansion device in the heating mode.

Figure 8-5. WaterFurnace start-up/troubleshooting form (continued)

If the suction line to the compressor is icy cold to the touch and the compressor wall is chilled from the suction port to the base, the diagnosis could be either poor heat exchange at the evaporator (coaxial heat exchanger or fin coil) or an overcharged system. An accurate diagnosis cannot be made without first measuring the fluid pressure and temperature drop across the coaxial heat exchanger and matching it with the manufacturer's tables. The same principle applies to measuring air flow and temperature change across a fin coil. Countless refrigeration systems have met an early demise due to poor service procedures and the simple solution of "treating the symptom" by adding a few pounds of refrigerant to get the correct suction pressure reading. Geothermal systems are no different. An overcharge in the winter may produce a reasonable suction pressure. But excess refrigerant can flood the compressor and dilute the oil with liquid refrigerant, causing a loss of lubrication and reducing system efficiency. In addition, the system is now overcharged for the air conditioning cycle, which means that a whole new set of problems will emerge with the onset of summer weather.

The majority of mechanical compressor failures can be avoided by observing proper start-up service procedures and checking system parameters before adding refrigerant. This can be particularly useful when servicing open-loop systems, in which low water pressure, restricted flow, and iron or mineral fouling can create the perception of a low refrigerant charge, when in truth the problem is a fouled heat exchanger. Closed-loop systems are not immune to the same issues, but the cause is more likely to relate to the

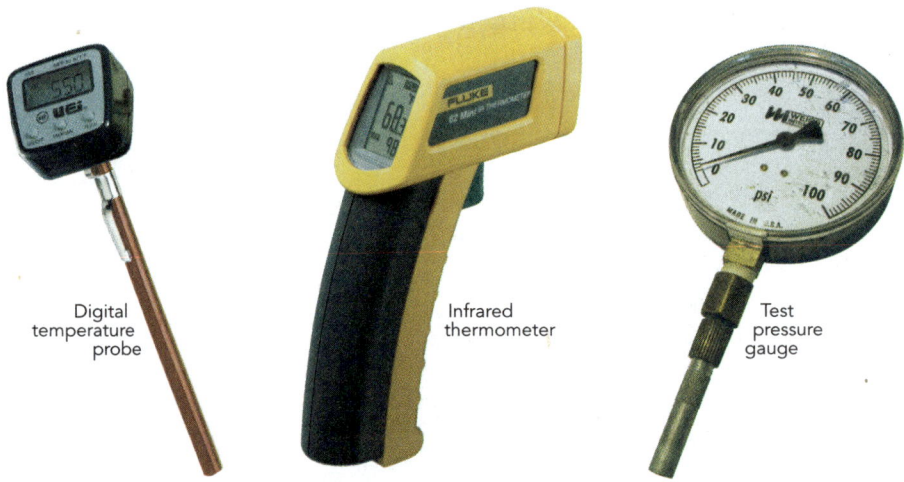

Figure 8-6. Common service tools

Figure 8-7. "Geo-Gooser"

operation of one or both loop pumps in a two-pump system, entrained air in a poorly flushed loop, pump impellers plugged with debris left inside a loop after an improper flush-and-fill process, or insufficient antifreeze causing a heat exchanger to ice up. Finding the sources of these problems requires the skill of a patient and diligent service technician. Often, the best way to discover the source of a problem is to measure the pressure and temperature differential across the heat exchanger. And the simplest way to take such measurements is to use a geothermal system test pressure gauge with a P/T needle, an insertion-type digital temperature probe, or a simple infrared temperature sensor or contact thermistor used in combination with digital meters or refrigerant manifolds (see Figure 8-6). A useful tool for reading and adjusting loop pressure ("goosing the loop") is shown in Figure 8-7.

An old adage frequently shared among service technicians is that "Checking compressor health is a lot like taking a child's temperature." If you feel the compressor wall at the suction intake and it has a high fever or is icy cold, there is a good chance that something needs attention and that more diagnostics will be necessary. If, on the other hand, the compressor wall around the suction intake feels cool (or "body temperature") and if the compressor's oil sump area (typically the lower third of the compressor shell) is in the warm-to-hot range, then chances are that the refrigerant side of the system is in good health.

FREEZE SENSOR SETTINGS

Of the three start-up checklists reproduced earlier in this chapter, the ClimateMaster document is the only one to state directly: "Verify that low water temperature cut-out controls are set properly." Even this instruction can be easily overlooked during start-up if the technician is not familiar with the process, or if the system appears to operate as it should on command from the thermostat. The WaterFurnace checklist contains a simple reference to check that "DIP switches are set correctly," presuming that the start-up technician is aware of the proper settings for well water or open-loop installations vs. antifreeze-protected closed-loop installations. FHP/Bosch makes no mention of the freezestat sensor settings on its unit check-out sheet. To find this information for FHP/Bosh systems, the start-up technician must be familiar with the system wiring diagram—and with the footnotes that accompany the diagram.

While all three manufacturers include excellent start-up checklists and data entry information in their installation manuals, remember that these checklists are made by engineers who are familiar with all aspects of a system's operation. Small details that come automatically to system designers may escape the understanding of the installing technicians who have not had the experience of "living with the controls." The vast majority of start-up problems relate directly to a lack of familiarity on the part of technicians with the "small print" instructions contained in the installation manuals. The footnotes at the bottom of wiring diagram pages are a good example of important but easy-to-miss information.

ELECTRIC AUXILIARY HEAT

Each manufacturer has its own process for wiring the auxiliary heat and compressor sections of the geothermal system. ClimateMaster and FHP/Bosch provide diagrams for separate, isolated line-voltage supply circuits for the compressor and auxiliary heat sections of the system. Thermostat controls, the main control board, and the fan motor are all powered by the circuit breaker dedicated to the compressor section of the system.

If the system is to operate from a home generator system, the compressor section can be powered from the generator panel and the auxiliary heat tied to a separate circuit breaker, which is powered by the utility side of the power distribution panel. The separation of wiring for the two sections is straightforward and relatively easy to interpret from the diagrams provided. Service technicians will note that in this case, "control power" is provided by the compressor side of the controls. Consequently, any system fault that may require a system reset will need to be addressed either by a "soft reset" (turning the thermostat on and off, which may retain the fault signal on the control board's LED status panel), or by a "hard reset," which erases the fault memory and returns the system to normal operation when the 230-V circuit breaker for the compressor section is turned off and then back on.

WaterFurnace systems allow for some variation in how system controls are powered when electric auxiliary heat is used. The controls and the fan may be powered from either the compressor circuit breaker or the auxiliary heat circuit breaker. If the compressor is to operate from an emergency power generator for heat and AC, and if the electric auxiliary heat is to remain connected to the utility side of the circuit panel, then the base unit wiring harness must remain "as shipped." When shipped, a black-with-white and gray-with-white (red-tagged) jumper wire is connected between the compressor contactor and a 230-V power distribution block for the control system and fan. An orange and brown power lead connects the fan to the power distribution block. If the system is *not* installed to operate from a generator, the suggested connection method is as follows:

1. Remove the (red-tagged) black-with-white and gray-with-white jumper.
2. Move the orange and brown fan control wire from the fan motor connection to a "Molex®" plug connector on the back of the auxiliary heat module.
3. Connect a blue and purple fan control wire (provided with the auxiliary heat kit) to the fan motor plug, where the orange and brown wire was connected previously.

This shift of control and fan wiring places the thermostat system controls and the fan on the auxiliary heat circuit breaker and provides an extra measure of safety. Should there ever be an event that causes the compressor circuit breaker to trip, the system will maintain heat (by using the auxiliary heat) and possibly prevent a "cold" or "frozen" service problem.

Installers who are not aware of these features and neglect to remove the jumper wires or fail to follow the instructions for reconnecting the orange/brown and blue/purple fan power wires risk burning out the 24-V transformer or shorting out the main electric panel breakers. Verification of the wire harness connections *must* be part of every system start-up procedure when you work with WaterFurnace systems that are installed with auxiliary heat modules.

CONDENSATE MANAGEMENT

Start-up checklists refer to condensate lines as "open and pitched to the drain." Currently produced geothermal systems typically have a vinyl hose fashioned with a "P" trap inside the system cabinet. Once the condensate water leaves the system, it must flow by gravity to a floor drain. Any second trap in the line doubles the hydrostatic head and is likely to cause the drain pan to overflow or to trigger a drain fault sensor that will turn the system off. Vertical geothermal installations seldom have any trouble with initial condensate removal. Horizontal systems, however, can experience several problems, since lines cannot be internally trapped and must rely on field-installed condensate traps.

Whenever possible, horizontal systems should be trapped at a substantially lower elevation rather than directly at the system outlet (as is customary with many installers, especially for attic installations). Trapping the line in a basement or at an accessible location on the main floor of the home allows for considerable head to build up inside the condensate line before it can impact and cause a coil pan to overflow. Condensate lines that can be trapped at elevations lower than the horizontal unit are far less likely to create drain pan overflow issues.

Problems with condensate drainage on horizontal installations begin to occur when "P" traps are placed at the equipment outlet. Variable-speed ECM fans used in high-efficiency geothermal systems modulate to maintain the proper air volume as air filters load and start to restrict the air flow. The suction force created by a variable-speed fan can be sufficient to draw air up a dry or shallow trap and prevent the condensate pan from draining. When this occurs, a drain pan overflow and possible ceiling damage are immanent. This problem typically does not present itself until the system is faced with an air conditioning demand sustained over a lengthy period of time and/or a clogged air filter (as might be expected when the system is switched from heat to AC on the first hot day of spring). Start-up technicians are advised to pre-prime the condensate drains on horizontal systems and test the drain pans for proper drainage.

CLEANING FIN COILS

In an ideal world, geothermal systems are never operated during construction. Unfortunately, few installers have ever experienced this "ideal" condition, and the fact is that the majority of systems do end up being operated during construction. Manufacturers are aware of this, and many have issued written notifications stating that the manufacturer's warranty will be considered void if the system is operated during construction.

From the manufacturer's standpoint, the lanced-fin air exchange coils and variable-speed fan motors are particularly susceptible to clogging and overheating from construction and drywall dust. Every effort must be made to ensure that return air vents are sealed off, and that the return air trunk line is not connected to the system until the structure is thoroughly cleaned before occupancy. With the return air duct disconnected and system fan in operation, high-efficiency pleated air filters must be used and cleaned frequently during construction. These actions will help keep the return air ducts clean and should allow for easier cleaning of the system fin coil at start-up time.

Both ClimateMaster and WaterFurnace recommend spraying the fin coil with a 10% solution of dishwashing detergent and water, followed by a thorough rinse with clean water. The use of compressed air is not mentioned in any of the manufacturers' start-up procedures, but depending on the situation, compressed air may be a prudent precursor to a soap solution for cleaning the coils.

Horizontal remote air handlers that use "A" coils require special note. Construction dust that collects on a horizontal "A" coil is likely to prevent proper condensate drainage, with the result that moisture drips off the elevated areas of the coil. That moisture can easily become suspended in the airstream and "carry over" into the fan section of the air handler. Washing the coils with soapy water helps break the surface tension and allows for better condensate migration from coil to drain pan. Condensate carryover with horizontal air handlers can be an issue during extended periods of high-humidity operation. Typically, the second-floor or attic system provides 70% of the AC capacity required by a two-story home. Continuous AC operation at a high fan speed setting is a "given" condition for these systems.

Applications that normally require high air volumes may be faced with issues of condensate mist carryover as moisture drips off the manifold and return bends of the horizontal "A" coils. It is not uncommon for moisture to be ingested by the fan and ejected into the supply air plenum, creating condensate leaks in places never anticipated. Most condensate carryover problems can be avoided by proper coil cleaning and, where possible, by using thermostat controls that allow for fan cfm reduction when humidity is high. If there is any carryover while a horizontal system is running—especially during the summer—setting the fan for continuous operation provides an opportunity to dry the cabinet and ducting during the OFF cycle.

PRE-INSTALLATION CHECKLISTS

While the major manufacturers' start-up checklists focus on post-installation procedures, the best time to make a materials checklist is *before* installation. Time spent chasing after a forgotten minor item is a profit loss, costing far more in labor than the component is worth. The checklists reproduced in Figures 8-8, 8-9, and 8-10 on the following pages are provided as a suggestion for materials that are likely to be needed for open-loop and closed-loop exterior and interior geothermal installations. These checklists may not apply to all situations, but should provide a good starting point and serve as a reminder for items that are needed when you are preparing for an installation. ◆▸

JOB NAME _____ PHONE # _____
ADDRESS _____
         _____

WATER WELL INSTALLATION MATERIALS

( ) HEAT PUMP MODEL # _____ SINGLE-SPEED/2-SPEED
( ) BASE PAD
( ) AUX HEAT
( ) THERMOSTAT
( ) THERMOSTAT WALL MOUNT (RETROFIT ONLY)
( ) FLOW REGULATOR VALVE/S .... 1-2 QTY
( ) SOLENOID VALVE/S .... 1-2 QTY
( ) SCREEN STRAINER W/SCREEN .... 1 QTY
( ) REVERSE-ACTING PRESSURE SWITCH .... 1 QTY
( ) 1" SCHEDULE 40 PVC WATER PIPE .... 60 FT
( ) 1" SCHEDULE 40 PVC 90° ELLS .... 15 QTY
( ) 1" SCHEDULE 40 PVC TEES .... 4 QTY
( ) 1" SCHEDULE 40 PVC MALE ADAPTERS .... 2 QTY
( ) 1" PVC STREET 90° MALE ADAPTERS .... 2 QTY
( ) WATTS DOUBLE CHECK VALVE $3/4$" WHERE REQUIRED .... 1 QTY
( ) 1" SCHEDULE 40 PVC TO $3/4$" MALE ADAPTERS .... 2 QTY
    (FOR WATTS DOUBLE CHECK VALVE)
( ) 1" SLIP BUSHINGS TO $3/4$" FPT PVC .... 6 QTY
( ) 1" SLIP BUSHINGS TO $1/2$" FPT PVC .... 2 QTY
( ) 1" SLIP BUSHING TO $3/4$" SLIP AS NEEDED TO ADAPT TO OLD PIPING .... 2 QTY
( ) $3/4$" MALE PT TO $3/4$" INSERT CONNECTORS (BRASS) .... 4-8 QTY
    (SINGLE-SPEED 4 QTY, 2-SPEED 8 QTY)
( ) 1" SLIP FIT PVC BALL VALVES .... 4 QTY
( ) $3/4$" SCHEDULE 40 PVC PIPE (CONDENSATE LINE) .... 20 FT
( ) $3/4$" PVC 90° ELLS .... 8 QTY
( ) BRASS THREADED BUSHING $3/4$" X $1/4$" (FOR RAPS SWITCH) .... 1 QTY
( ) 2" BRASS THREADED NIPPLE (FOR RAPS SWITCH) .... 1 QTY
( ) BLACK INDUSTRIAL HOSE APPROX. 18" (FOR FLOW VALVE/S) .... 2-4 QTY
( ) STAINLESS BAND CLAMPS 2" OD .... 12 QTY
( ) BRASS $1/2$" BOILER DRAINS FOR FLUSH PORTS AT UNIT .... 2 QTY
( ) PIPE "J" HOOKS 2" SIZE
    (NEED 2 QTY PER 10 FT OF HORIZONTAL RUN ON EACH LINE)
( ) PIPE INSULATION $1 5/8$" ID (AS NEEDED TO COVER 1" PVC) .... 1 BOX
( ) THERMOSTAT WIRE 8 CONDUCTOR MIN
( ) THERMOSTAT WIRE 2 CONDUCTOR
( ) ROMAX CLAMPS $3/4$"
( ) ROMAX CLAMPS 1"
( ) SE CABLE WIRE FOR HEAT PUMP WIRE GAUGE SIZE .... _____ FT
( ) SE CABLE WIRE FOR AUX HEAT WIRE GAUGE SIZE .... _____ FT
( ) WIRE TIES .... 1 BAG
( ) DUCTBOARD FOR RETURN AIR AND SCRAPS .... ±2 SHEETS
( ) DUCTBOARD TOOLS/TAPE BOX WITH STAPLE GUN
( ) DUCTBOARD "T" SQUARE

Figure 8-8. Open-loop checklist

COPPER FOR DOMESTIC HOT WATER PIPING KIT

TURN OFF ELECTRIC TO HOT WATER TANK FIRST

- ( ) $3/4"$ STRAIGHT COPPER (SCRAPS IN CASE NEEDED) .... 3 FT
- ( ) $1/2"$ STRAIGHT COPPER .... 3 FT
- ( ) $1/2"$ INLINE SADDLE TEES (BRASS) .... 2 QTY
- ( ) $1/2"$ BOILER VALVES .... 2 QTY
- ( ) COPPER $3/4"$ X $3/4"$ X $1/2"$ TEE .... 1 QTY
- ( ) BRASS $3/4"$ X $3/4"$ X $3/4"$ THREADED TEE .... 1 QTY
- ( ) GALVANIZED STEEL $3/4"$ DIELETRIC NIPPLE .... 1 QTY
- ( ) $3/4"$ BRASS BOILER DRAIN VALVE .... 1 QTY
  (INCLUDED INSIDE WATERFURNACE DHW PIPING KIT)
- ( ) $1/2"$ STOP WASTE VALVES (COMPRESSION FIT) .... 2 QTY
- ( ) COPPER $3/4"$ MPT X $1/2"$ SWEAT MALE ADAPTER .... 1 QTY
- ( ) $1/2"$ 90° STREET ELLS .... 4 QTY
- ( ) $1/2"$ MALE PEX ADAPTERS W/CRIMP RINGS .... 4 QTY
- ( ) $1/2$ 90° ELLS .... 4 QTY
- ( ) $1/2"$ PEX (AS NEEDED FOR DISTANCE TO TANK) .... _____ FT
- ( ) $1/2"$ PEX CRIMP TOOL
- ( ) PEX PIPE STAPLE-UP TOOL AND STAPLES
- ( ) 1 ROLL TEFLON TAPE
- ( ) 1 CAN PIPE DOPE
- ( ) BRASS SWING CHECK VALVE (IF SYSTEM IS ON A HOT WATER RECIRCULATION LOOP)

Figure 8-8. Open-loop checklist (continued)

JOB NAME _____   PHONE # _____
ADDRESS _____
         _____

CLOSED-LOOP INSTALLATION, EXTERIOR WORK

TOOLS:

( ) HAMMER DRILL WITH WALL BIT
( ) AIR COMPRESSOR
( ) GENERATOR
( ) GAS FOR GENERATOR
( ) OIL FOR GENERATOR
( ) HEAVY 100' EXTENSION CORD
( ) PVC SAW
( ) 2 SPADE SHOVELS
( ) 2 TRENCHING SHOVELS
( ) 2 RAKES
( ) 2 HOES
( ) 1 SPUD BAR
( ) BOOTS
( ) RAIN GEAR
( ) TRASH PUMP W/SUCTION HOSE & STRAINER (2 CYCLE FOR HIGH WATER)
( ) 2 CYCLE GAS

FUSION EQUIPMENT:

( ) FUSION TOOL BOX
( ) FUSION IRON WITH SOCKET FACES (SIZE: _____)
( ) HOT AIR GUN
( ) TEST PLUG WITH PRESSURE GAUGE & BALL VALVES FOR AIR PRESSURE TEST

FUSION FITTINGS:

( ) +2 SPARES $1^1/_4$ X $1^1/_4$ X $^3/_4$ TEES
( ) +2 SPARES $1^1/_4$ X $^3/_4$ X $^3/_4$ TEES
( ) 1 BAG $1^1/_4$ X $1^1/_4$ COUPLINGS - 1 BAG (10 COUNT)
( ) 1 BAG $^3/_4$ X $^3/_4$ COUPLINGS - 1 BAG (10 COUNT)
( ) 1 BAG $1^1/_4$ X $1^1/_4$ 90° ELLS - 1 BAG (10 COUNT)
( ) HOSE CLAMPS $1^1/_{16}$ - 2"
( ) DUCT TAPE

PIPE:

( ) _____ ROLLS OF $^3/_4$ X _____ FEET
( ) _____ ROLLS OF $1^1/_4$ X _____ FEET
( ) _____ STICKS $1^5/_8$ ID INSULATION
( ) 2" PVC WALL SLEEVE
( ) PREMIER WALL SLEEVE COUPLINGS
( ) CAULKING GUN WITH CONCRETE CAULK

Figure 8-9. Closed-loop exterior checklist

JOB NAME _____   PHONE # _____
ADDRESS _____
         _____

CLOSED-LOOP INSTALLATION MATERIALS, INTERIOR WORK ONLY

( ) HEAT PUMP MODEL # _____ SINGLE-SPEED/2-SPEED
( ) BASE PAD
( ) AUX HEAT
( ) THERMOSTAT
( ) THERMOSTAT WALL MOUNT (RETROFIT ONLY)
( ) PUMP PACK
( ) CONNECTION KIT CK4L
( ) BRASS ADAPTORS TO LOOP PIPE FROM PUMP PACK 1" MPT/$1^{1}/_{4}$"
( ) FUSION TOOL BOX
( ) FUSION HEATING TOOL
( ) $1^{1}/_{4}$" POLYETHELENE PIPE - STRAIGHT SECTIONS .... _____ FT
( ) $1^{1}/_{4}$" PE ELLS .... 1 BOX
( ) $1^{1}/_{4}$" PE 45° ELLS .... 4 QTY
( ) $1^{1}/_{4}$" PE COUPLINGS .... 1 BOX
( ) PIPE INSULATION $1^{5}/_{8}$" ID (AS NEEDED FOR $1^{1}/_{4}$" PE PIPE) .... _____ BOX
( ) PURGE PUMP AND FITTINGS
( ) DI WATER TANKS/DI COLUMN
( ) PROPYLENEGLYCOL IN 5-GALLON PAILS - PREMEASURED FOR SYSTEM
( ) $3/_{4}$" SCHEDULE 40 PVC PIPE (CONDENSATE LINE) .... 20 FT
( ) $3/_{4}$" 90° PVC ELLS .... 8 QTY
( ) STAINLESS BAND CLAMPS 2" OD .... 1 BOX
( ) PIPE "J" HOOKS 2" SIZE (AS NEEDED, 2 HOOKS PER 10 FT OF LINE)
( ) THERMOSTAT WIRE 8 CONDUCTOR MIN
( ) THERMOSTAT WIRE 2 CONDUCTOR
( ) ROMEX CLAMPS $3/_{4}$"
( ) ROMEX CLAMPS 1"
( ) BX CABLE FOR LOOP PUMP CONNECTIONS
( ) 90° BX CABLE CLAMPS FOR LOOP PUMPS .... 2-4 QTY
( ) SE CABLE WIRE FOR HEAT PUMP WIRE GAUGE SIZE.................... _____ FT
( ) SE CABLE WIRE FOR AUX HEAT WIRE GAUGE SIZE..................... _____ FT
( ) WIRE TIES... 1 BAG
( ) DUCTBOARD FOR RETURN AIR AND SCRAPS............................. ±2 SHEETS
( ) DUCTBOARD TOOLS/TAPE BOX WITH STAPLE GUN
( ) DUCTBOARD "T" SQUARE
( ) 2-CYCLE PUMP, SUCTION HOSE, 2-CYCLE GAS CAN
( ) HEAT GUN

Figure 8-10. Closed-loop interior checklist

COPPER FOR DOMESTIC HOT WATER PIPING KIT

TURN OFF ELECTRIC TO HOT WATER TANK FIRST

( ) 3/4" STRAIGHT COPPER (SCRAPS IN CASE NEEDED)	3 FT
( ) 1/2" STRAIGHT COPPER	3 FT
( ) 1/2" INLINE SADDLE TEES (BRASS)	2 QTY
( ) 1/2" BOILER VALVES	2 QTY
( ) COPPER 3/4" X 3/4" X 1/2" TEE	1 QTY
( ) BRASS 3/4" X 3/4" X 3/4" THREADED TEE	1 QTY
( ) GALVANIZED STEEL 3/4" DIELETRIC NIPPLE	1 QTY
( ) 3/4" BRASS BOILER DRAIN VALVE	1 QTY
(INCLUDED INSIDE WATERFURNACE DHW PIPING KIT)	
( ) 1/2" STOP WASTE VALVES (COMPRESSION FIT)	2 QTY
( ) COPPER 3/4" MPT X 1/2" SWEAT MALE ADAPTER	1 QTY
( ) 1/2" 90° ELLS	4 QTY
( ) 1/2" 90° STREET ELLS	4 QTY
( ) 1/2" MALE PEX ADAPTERS W/CRIMP RINGS	4 QTY
( ) 1/2" PEX PIPE	_____ FT
( ) 1/2" PEX CRIMP TOOL	
( ) PEX PIPE STAPLE-UP TOOL AND STAPLES	
( ) 1 ROLL TEFLON TAPE	
( ) 1 CAN PIPE DOPE	
( ) 1/2" BRASS SWING CHECK VALVE	
(IF SYSTEM IS ON A HOT WATER RECIRCULATION LOOP)	

Figure 8-10. Closed-loop interior checklist (continued)

ILLUSTRATION CREDITS
FIGURE 8-1: CLIMATEMASTER
FIGURE 8-2: FHP/BOSCH
FIGURE 8-3: WATERFURNACE
FIGURE 8-4: WATERFURNACE
FIGURE 8-5: WATERFURNACE
FIGURE 8-6, L–R: UEi, FLUKE CORPORATION, JEFF PERSONS
FIGURE 8-7: GEO-FLO PRODUCTS CORPORATION
FIGURE 8-8: GEO SOURCE ONE INC.
FIGURE 8-9: GEO SOURCE ONE INC.
FIGURE 8-10: GEO SOURCE ONE INC.

‹APPENDIX›
Information Resources

INTRODUCTION

This Appendix has been assembled as a reference tool to guide geothermal contractors and loop designers to common sources of information that may assist in the assessment of geological conditions within the area of interest for a given project. Keep in mind that addresses and web links are subject to change. Those seeking information about soils and subsurface conditions for a specific location are encouraged to conduct additional online searches for their project areas. For locations lacking public records, a working association with knowledgeable local contractors may prove useful. Whenever conditions are unknown, it is always prudent to include a contract clause for "final drilling/trenching expenses pending verification of a test well or excavation."

Common sources of subsurface information include:
- state geological surveys
  http://www.stategeologists.org/index.php
- Departments of Natural Resources
- Departments of Health
- state well-drilling associations
- IGSHPA
  http://www.igshpa.okstate.edu
- National Ground Water Association
  http://www.ngwa.org
- U.S. Department of Energy Geothermal Technologies Program
  http://www1.eere.energy.gov/geothermal/heatpumps.html

A state-by-state listing follows.

UNITED STATES

Alabama
Geological Survey of Alabama
Box O, University Station
Tuscaloosa, AL 35486
205/349-2852

➤ Alabama Water Quality Program
http://www.aces.edu/waterquality/index.php3

Alaska
Alaska Division of Mining & Geologic Survey
Box 7028
Anchorage, AK 99510
907/762-2177

➤ Alaska Department of Natural Resources
http://www.dnr.state.ak.us/mlw/water/index.htm

Arizona
Arizona Geological Survey
845 North Park Avenue
Tucson, AZ 85719
602/621-7906

➤ Arizona Water Well Association
http://www.azwwa.org
➤ Arizona Department of Water Resources
http://www.water.az.gov/adwr

Arkansas
Arkansas Geological Commission
Vardelle Parham Geology Center
3851 West Roosevelt Road
Little Rock, AR 72204
501/371-1488

> Arkansas Soil & Water Conservation Commission
  http://www.aswcc.arkansas.gov

California

California Division of Mines and Geology
Room 1341
1416 Ninth Street
Sacramento, CA 95814
916/445-1923

> California Groundwater Association
  http://www.groundh2o.org
> California Department of Water Resources
  http://www.dpla2.water.ca.gov

Colorado

Colorado Geological Survey
Room 715
1313 Sherman Street
Denver, CO 80203
303/866-2611

> Colorado Water Well Contractors Association
  http://www.cwwca.org
> Colorado Division of Water Resources
  http://water.state.co.us

Connecticut

Connecticut Geological & Natural History Survey
Room 553, State Office Building
165 Capitol Avenue
Hartford, CT 06106
203/566-3540

> Connecticut Well Construction Rules
  http://www.geoexchange.org/regulations/pages/states/ct/ct_well.html
> Connecticut Department of Public Health
  http://www.dph.state.ct.us/BRS/Water/DWD.htm

Delaware
Delaware Geological Survey
University of Delaware
101 Penny Hall
Newark, DE 19716
302/451-2833

- Delaware Licensing Regulations
  http://www.dnrec.state.de.us/water2000/Sections/WatSupp/Library/Final1998LicRegs.PDF

Florida
Florida Bureau of Geology
903 West Tennessee Street
Tallahassee, FL 32304
904/488-4191

- Florida Ground Water Association
  http://www.fgwa.org
- Florida Water Management District
  http://www.flwaterpermits.com

Georgia
Georgia Geologic Survey
Department of Natural Resources
Room 400
19 Martin Luther King Jr. Drive SW
Atlanta, GA 30344
404/656-3214

- Georgia Drillers Association
  http://gawelldrillingcontractors.org

Hawaii
Hawaii Division of Water & Land Development
Box 373
Honolulu, HI 96809
808/548-7539

- Hawaii Commission on Water Resource Management
  http://www.hawaii.gov/dlnr/cwrm/code.htm

Idaho
Idaho Geological Survey
Morrill Hall, Room 332
University of Idaho
Moscow, ID 83843
208/885-7991

- Idaho Ground Water Association
  http://www.igwa.info
- Idaho Department of Environmental Quality
  http://www.deq.state.id.us/water

Illinois
Illinois Geological Survey
Natural Resources Building
615 East Peabody Drive
Champaign, IL 61820
217/344-1841

- Illinois Association of Groundwater Professionals
  http://www.iagp.org
- Illinois Department of Public Health - Water Wells
  http://www.idph.state.il.us/envhealth/waterwells.htm

Indiana
Indiana Geological Survey
611 North Walnut Grove
Bloomington, IN 47405
812/335-2863

- Indiana Ground Water Association
  http://www.indianagroundwater.org

Iowa

Iowa Geological Survey
123 North Capitol Street
Iowa City, IA 52242
319/338-1173

- Iowa Water Well Association
  http://www.iwwa.org
- Iowa DNR - Geological Survey
  http://www.igsb.uiowa.edu

Kansas

Kansas Geological Survey
University of Kansas
Campus West
1930 Constant Avenue
Lawrence, KS 66046
913/864-3965

- Kansas Ground Water Association
  http://www.kgwa.org
- Kansas Department of Health and Environment
  http://www.kdhe.state.ks.us/water

Kentucky

Kentucky Geological Survey
University of Kentucky
311 Breckinridge Hall
Lexington, KY 40506
606/257-5863

- Kentucky Groundwater Association
  http://www.kygroundwater.org
- Kentucky Division of Water
  http://www.water.ky.gov/gw/gwtech/gwdrill/default.htm

Louisiana
Louisiana Geological Survey
Box G, University Station
Baton Rouge, LA 70893
504/342-6754

- Louisiana Department of Public Works - Water Resources Section
  http://www.dotd.state.la.us/intermodal/wells/mission_page.asp
- Louisiana DOTD - Water Resources Section
  http://www.dotd.state.la.us/intermodal/wells/home.asp

Maine
Maine Geological Survey
Department of Conservation
State House Station 22
Augusta, ME 04333
207/289-2801

- Maine Department of Environmental Protection
  http://www.state.me.us/dep/blwq/gw.htm

Maryland
Maryland Geological Survey
2300 St. Paul Street
Baltimore, MD 21218
301/554-5500

- Baltimore County Groundwater Management
  http://www.co.ba.md.us/Agencies/environment/ep_wellseptic.html
- Maryland Department of the Environment
  http://www.mde.state.md.us/Programs/WaterPrograms/Water_Supply/index.asp

Massachusetts
Massachusetts Department of Environmental Quality Engineering
1 Winter Street, 7th Floor
Boston, MA 02108
617/292-5690

- Massachusetts Water Resources - Well Drillers Program
  http://www.mass.gov/dcr/waterSupply/welldril/index.htm
- Massachusetts Geothermal Well Regulations
  www.mgwa.net/documents/DEPNEWWA032610.pdf

Michigan
Michigan Geological Survey Division
Box 30028
Lansing, MI 48909
517/373-1256

- Michigan Department of Environmental Quality
  http://www.michigan.gov/deq/0,1607,7-135-3307_4131_4155---,00.html
- Michigan Ground Water Association
  http://michigangroundwater.com

Minnesota
Minnesota Geological Survey
2642 University Avenue
St. Paul, MN 55114
612/373-3372

- Minnesota Water Well Association
  http://www.mwwa.org
- Minnesota Department of Health
  www.health.state.mn.us/divs/eh/groundwater/programs.html

Mississippi
Mississippi Bureau of Geology
Box 5548
Mackson, MS 39216
601/354-6228

- Mississippi Department of Environment Quality - Water Well Contractors
  http://www.deq.state.ms.us/MDEQ.nsf/page/L&W_Water_Well_Contractors_(Drillers)?OpenDocument

Missouri
Missouri Division of Geology & Land Survey
Box 250
Rolla, MO 65401
314/364-1752

➤ Missouri Water Well Association
http://www.wavecomputers.net/jsommer

Montana
Montana Bureau of Mines & Geology
Montana College of Mineral Science & Technology
Butte, MT 59701
406/496-4179

➤ Montana DNR - Board of Water Well Contractors
http://www.dnrc.state.mt.us/wrd/home.htm

Nebraska
Nebraska Conservation & Survey Division
University of Nebraska
113 Nebraska Hall
Lincoln, NE 68588
402/472-3471

➤ Nebraska Health & Human Services
http://www.hhs.state.ne.us/crl/crlindex.htm
➤ Nebraska Well Drillers Association
http://www.nebraskawelldrillers.org

Nevada
Nevada Bureau of Mines & Geology
University of Nevada
Reno, NV 89557
702/784-6691

➤ Nevada Division of Water Resources
http://www.water.nv.gov

New Hampshire
New Hampshire Department of Resources and Economic Development
University of New Hampshire
117 James Hall
Durham, NH 03824
603/862-1216

➤ New Hampshire Department of Environmental Service
http://des.state.nh.us

New Jersey
New Jersey Geological Survey
CN-029
Trenton, NJ 08625
609/292-1185

➤ New Jersey Department of Environmental Protection
http://www.state.nj.us/dep/dwq/groundw.htm
➤ New Jersey Ground Water Association
http://www.njgwa.org

New Mexico
New Mexico Bureau of Mines & Mineral Resources
Campus Station
Socorro, NM 87801
505/835-5420

➤ New Mexico Ground Water Association
http://www.nmgwa.org
➤ New Mexico Office of the State Engineer
http://www.seo.state.nm.us/water-info/index.html

New York
New York State Geological Survey
3136 Cultural Education Center
Empire State Plaza
Albany, NY 12230
518/474-5816

- Empire State Well Drillers Association
  http://www.nywelldriller.org
- New York Department of Environmental Conservation
  http://www.dec.state.ny.us/website/dow/index.html

North Carolina
North Carolina Department of Natural Resources & Community Development
Division of Land Resources
Box 27687
Raleigh, NC 27611
919/733-3833

- North Carolina Division of Water Quality
  http://gw.ehnr.state.nc.us
- Groundwater Professionals of North Carolina
  http://www.gwpnc.org

North Dakota
North Dakota Geological Survey
University Station
Grand Forks, ND 58202
701/777-2231

- North Dakota Department of Health
  http://www.health.state.nd.us/wq/gw/gw.htm

Ohio
Ohio Division of Geological Survey
Fountain Square, Building B
Columbus, OH 43224
614/265-6605

- Ohio Water Well Association
  http://www.ohiowaterwell.org
- Ohio Department of Health
  http://www.odh.state.oh.us/ODHPrograms/WATER/water1.htm
- Ohio Department of Natural Resources
  http://www.dnr.state.oh.us/water/maptechs/wellogs/app/default.asp

> Ohio Recommendations for Geothermal Systems
  http://wwwapp.epa.ohio.gov/ddagw/SCCGW/geothermal.html

Oklahoma
Oklahoma Geological Survey
830 Van Vleet Oval
Room 163
Norman, OK 73019
405/325-3031

> Oklahoma Ground Water Association
  http://www.ogwa.biz
> Oklahoma Water Resources Board
  http://www.owrb.state.ok.us

Oregon
Oregon Department of Geology & Mineral Industries
910 State Office Building
1400 SW Fifth Avenue
Portland, OR 97201
503/229-5580

> Oregon Ground Water Association
  http://www.ogwa.org
> Oregon Department of Environmental Quality
  http://www.deq.state.or.us/wq/groundwa/wqgw.htm

Pennsylvania
Pennsylvania Bureau of Topographic & Geologic Survey
Department of Environmental Resources
Box 2357
Harrisburg, PA 17120
717/787-2169

> Pennsylvania Ground Water Association
  http://www.pgwa.org
> Pennsylvania Department of Environmental Protection
  http://www.dep.state.pa.us/dep/deputate/watermgt/wc/default.htm

Puerto Rico
Puerto Rico Department of Natural Resources
Geological Survey Division
Box 5887
Puerta de Tierra, San Juan, PR 00906
809/723-2716

Rhode Island
Rhode Island Statewide Planning Program
Department of Geology
University of Rhode Island
Kingston, RI 02881
401/792-2265

➤ Rhode Island Water Resources Board
  http://www.wrb.state.ri.us/index.html

South Carolina
South Carolina Geological Survey
Harbison Forest Road
Columbia, SC 29210
803/737-9440

➤ South Carolina Groundwater Data
  http://watercenter.environ.sc.edu/water%20quality.htm
➤ South Carolina Bureau of Water
  http://www.scdhec.net/water

South Dakota
South Dakota Geological Survey
Science Center
University of South Dakota
Vermillion, SD 57069
605/677-5227

➤ South Dakota Department of Environment & Natural Resources
  http://www.state.sd.us/denr/des/waterrights/wr_permit.htm

Tennessee
Tennessee Division of Geology
701 Broadway
Nashville, TN 37203
615/742-6689

➤ Tennessee Department of Environment and Conservation
http://www.state.tn.us/environment/permits/welldrill.php

Texas
Texas Bureau of Economic Geology
University of Texas
Box X, University Station
Austin, TX 78713
512/471-1534

➤ Texas Ground Water Association
http://www.tgwa.org
➤ Texas Department of Licensing and Regulation
http://www.license.state.tx.us/wwd/wwd.htm

Utah
Utah Geological and Mineral Survey
606 Black Hawk Way
Salt Lake City, UT 84108
801/581-6831

➤ Utah Division of Water Rights
http://waterrights.utah.gov/wellinfo

Vermont
Vermont Geological Survey
Agency of Environmental Conservation
103 South Main Street
Waterbury, VT 05676
802/244-5164

➤ Vermont Department of Environmental Conservation
http://www.vermontdrinkingwater.org

Virginia
Virginia Division of Mineral Resources
Box 3667
Charlottesville, VA 22903
804/293-5121

➤ Virginia Department of Environmental Quality
http://www.deq.state.va.us/gwpsc/

Washington
Washington Division of Geology & Earth Resources
Department of Natural Resources
Olympia, WA 98504
206/459-6372

➤ Washington State Ground Water Association
http://www.wsgwa.org
➤ Washington Department of Ecology
http://www.ecy.wa.gov/programs/wr/wells/wellhome.html

West Virginia
West Virginia Geological & Economic Survey
Box 879
Morgantown, WV 26507
304/594-2331

➤ West Virginia Department of Health & Human Services
http://www.wvdhhr.org/oehs/eed/swap/groundwater.asp

Wisconsin
Wisconsin Geological & Natural History Survey
3817 Mineral Point Road
Madison, WI 53705
608/262-1705

- Wisconsin Water Well Association
  http://www.wisconsinwaterwell.com
- Wisconsin Department of Natural Resources
  http://www.dnr.state.wi.us/org/water/dwg/yywell.htm

Wyoming

Wyoming Geological Survey
Box 3008, University Station
University of Wyoming
Laramie, WY 82071
307/742-2054

- Wyoming Water Well Association
  http://www.wywaterwell.org
- Wyoming State Engineer's Office
  http://seo.state.wy.us/well_regs.aspx

CANADA

Canadian Ground Water Association
http://www.cgwa.org

Alberta

Alberta Geological Survey
Alberta Research Council
Box 8330, Station F
Edmonton, AB T6H 5X2

- Alberta Well Drilling Association
  http://www.awwda.com

British Columbia

Geological Survey Branch
Mineral Resources Division
Ministry of Energy, Mines & Petroleum Resources
Parliament Buildings
Victoria, BC V8V 1X4

➤ British Columbia Ground Water Association
http://www.bcgwa.org/index.htm

Manitoba
Geological Services Branch
Manitoba Energy & Mines
535-330 Graham Avenue
Winnipeg, MB R3C 4E3

New Brunswick
Geological Surveys Branch
Department of Natural Resources
Box 6000
Fredericton, NB E3B 5H1

Newfoundland
Mineral Development Division
Department of Mines & Energy
Box 4750
St. Johns, NL A1C 517

Northwest Territories
Geology Division
Northern Affairs Program
Box 1500
Yellowknife, NT X1A 2R3

Nova Scotia
Nova Scotia Department of Mines & Energy
Box 1087
Halifax, NS B3J 2X1

Ontario
Ontario Geological Survey
Mines & Minerals Division
Ministry of Northern Development & Mines
112177 Grenville Street
Toronto, ON M7A 1W4

➤ Ontario Ground Water Association
   http://www.ogwa.ca

Prince Edward Island
Department of Energy & Forestry
Box 2000
Charlottetown, PE CIA 7N8

Quebec
Direction Générale, Exploration Géologique et Minérale (Mines)
Ministère de l'Energie et des Ressources
Gouvernement du Québec
1620 Boulevard de l'Entente
Québec, QC G1S 4N6

Saskatchewan
Geological Survey
Saskatchewan Energy & Mines
Toronto Dominion Bank Building
1914 Hamilton Street
Regina, SK S4P 4V4

Yukon
Department of Indian Affairs & Northern Development
Exploration & Geological Services Division
200 Range Road
Whitehorse, YT Y1A 3V1

ABOUT THE AUTHOR

JEFF PERSONS, CM, the president of Geo Source One Inc., holds a Master's degree in geology and is a groundwater hydrogeologist with over 35 years of experience in the geothermal heat pump and hydronic industry. Jeff began his involvement with geothermal systems in the mid-1970s as a way to encourage energy conservation and reduce U.S. dependence on foreign oil. In 1986, after a decade of promoting geothermal technology through seminars, manuals, and product design assistance, Jeff founded a geothermal services company that has evolved into Geo Source One Inc. Based in Columbus, Ohio, the company specializes in the design and installation of custom geothermal and radiant heating systems. In addition, Jeff provides design and field assistance to a multitude of architects, engineers, and contractors. Jeff is an IGSHPA/NATE (International Ground Source Heat Pump Association) Accredited Geothermal Trainer and Installer and an Adjunct Professor for Geothermal Renewable Energy Systems at the Hocking College Energy Institute. Among Jeff's numerous professional affiliations are **ASHRAE, ACCA, RSES, NGWA** (National Ground Water Association) and **RPA** (Radiant Professionals Alliance), where he is a Certified Designer and Installer of radiant heating systems.

1911 Rohlwing Road, Suite A   Rolling Meadows, IL 60008-1397   800-297-5660   www.rses.org